An Introduction to Sociology

THIRD EDITION

vwvwvwvwvwvwvwvwvwvwvwvwvwvwvwvwvwvwvwvwvwvwvwvwvwvwvwvwvwvwvwvwvwvwvwvwvwvwvwvwvwvwvwvwvwvwvwwvw

J. E. GOLDTHORPE

Honorary Lecturer in Sociology
University of Leeds

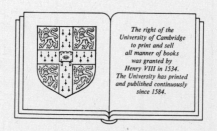

*The right of the
University of Cambridge
to print and sell
all manner of books
was granted by
Henry VIII in 1534.
The University has printed
and published continuously
since 1584.*

CAMBRIDGE UNIVERSITY PRESS

CAMBRIDGE

LONDON   NEW YORK   NEW ROCHELLE
MELBOURNE   SYDNEY

Published by the Syndics of the Cambridge University Press
The Pitt Building, Trumpington Street, Cambridge CB2 1RP
Bentley House, 200 Euston Road, London NW1 2DB
32 East 57th Street, New York, NY 10022, USA
296 Beaconsfield Parade, Middle Park, Melbourne 3206, Australia

© Cambridge University Press 1968, 1974, 1985

First published 1968
Reprinted 1969 1971
Second edition 1974
Reprinted 1975 1976
Third edition 1985

Printed in Great Britain at
the University Press, Cambridge

Library of Congress Catalogue Card Number: 81–18048

British Library Cataloguing in Publication Data

Goldthorpe, J. E.
An introduction to sociology.—3rd ed.
1. Sociology
I. Title
301   HM51

ISBNs: Third edition 0 521 24545 1 hard covers
0 521 28779 0 paperback
(Second edition 0 521 20338 4 hard covers   0 521 09826 2 paperback;
First edition 0 521 07110 0 hard covers   0 521 09547 6 paperback)

Contents

NOTE

Superior numerals in the text refer
to the notes on pp. 216–25

Foreword

by AUDREY I. RICHARDS

What exactly is sociology? This is the question our friends so often ask us and which we find so difficult to answer precisely. 'The study of society'? Yes, but we are part of society. We live and work and think and play in the context of a society, so that when it comes to the point, there are very few subjects in a university curriculum that cannot be said to have a social bearing. Economics gives us the principles which govern our consumer or producer choices, but it is ultimately our social values which determine how hard we are prepared to work. Economic history asks, and tries to answer, questions that are mainly sociological ones. Social psychology tells us how people behave as members of groups, that is to say, of society. We talk of the sociology of medicine, of education, of communications, and even of advertisement. Is sociology a separate subject at all, or is it merely a perspective or a point of view?

It is certainly a term that people sometimes find useful just because it is not too precise! Administrators tend to speak of 'sociological factors' when they mean aspects of a problem which are felt to be important, and even disturbing, but for which a ministry has no expert advisers, and with which there is no department ready to deal. A project for human betterment has been conceived. Technicians have overcome the practical difficulties. Economists have counted the costs. But yet the scheme does not get off the ground, so to speak. This is the time when people begin to talk gravely of 'sociological factors', meaning, I think, a great variety of human factors such as traditional values and habits of work; the desire to live with a particular group or category of people; conflicts between the different social roles a man or a set of men have to play; or perhaps institutions that provide the wrong kind of leadership or learning processes. Used in this way sociology seems to mean a mixed bag of different factors – a rag-bag if you like!

Yet in spite of the difficulties of definition, sociologists themselves have developed their own spheres of work during the course of the last century and a half, and this book tells us what these fields of interest are. Sociology at a university is still a very broad subject. It includes disciplines as various as social philosophy, criminology and demography. Dr Goldthorpe gives us a glimpse of a number of the problems with which modern sociologists deal. They include the family, marriage and kinship; mechanisms for enforcing law and morals; the organization of magic and religious beliefs; urban studies; and the processes of social change. Some of the most interesting pages for the beginner are those in which he describes quite concretely what the sociologist or the social anthropologist actually does when engaged on research. We can imagine ourselves choosing a sample for an urban survey, sitting in a tent in a Polynesian village, observing ceremonies or agricultural work; or conducting a Gallup poll. Dr Goldthorpe shows us, in fact, that sociology has not only defined its spheres of interest, but has also developed its own techniques of research.

There remains another important question. What kind of society are we going to study? Students naturally want to learn about their own societies in special detail and this book was actually written for the benefit of African students who have had to rely for so long on textbooks describing the structure and institutions of Western societies, chiefly those of the United Kingdom and America. Dr Goldthorpe was able to write in this way because he has had the advantage of teaching for some years in an East African university attended by students from all over this region. But he takes his examples not only from Ethiopia, Nigeria, Uganda and Zambia, but also from America, China, England and Ireland. Sociologists have found in practice that the study of a quite unfamiliar society stimulates a person to examine his own more fruitfully. I believe therefore that students from England and America will find they get new lights thrown on their own problems, if they accept as a starting point Dr Goldthorpe's own interests in Africa and its present-day achievements and difficulties.

Author's Preface to the Third Edition

I was honoured and delighted when in 1964 the Syndics of the Cambridge University Press asked me to write a textbook of sociology specially for students in the universities of Africa. Although there is no lack of introductions to sociology, most are written for students living in Europe and America and unfamiliar with the societies of the developing countries. The Syndics' far-sighted perception at that time of the need for a book written, so to speak, the other way round – beginning with the perspectives of an emergent Africa and leading on to a wider reality, including that of the affluent industrial societies – has been abundantly justified, to such an extent that there is now a need for a third edition.

In it, the text has been extensively revised to take account of the changing relations between men and women. The argument about social change has been strengthened by reference to the work of Norbert Elias. The passages on the care of children and on the household have been re-written in the light of the researches and debates of the 1970s. The treatment of social class and social mobility in industrial societies has been revised in view of recent research, especially the findings of the Oxford social mobility survey and the work of the author's namesake John H. Goldthorpe; while the succeeding passages on socialism have been reconsidered and, I hope, clarified, in no small part as a result of discussions with colleagues at the University of Leeds. Recent research has also been incorporated in other sections including those on hunting and food-gathering societies; on peasants; on individual modernization; and on redistribution with economic growth in contemporary developing countries.

I am grateful, as always, for the friendly help of the staff of the Cambridge University Press at all stages.

October 1981

J.E.G.

Part 1

ⱽⱲ

SOCIOLOGY

What is sociology?

Sociology is an organized endeavour to increase human self-knowledge and self-understanding through the systematic study of our social life. For many sociologists, it represents an attempt to apply to the study of human society the same scientific method and approach that have been so dramatically successful in yielding an understanding of the physical world. Using scientific method, we have gained an understanding of the stars, the sun, the planets; of this planet in particular; of the forms of life that inhabit it; of man as an animal, and of the social behaviour of animals of species other than our own. The quest is far from finished, and the search for more knowledge and understanding goes on more ardently than ever in the modern world; but the achievements of science have been very great, and we now understand many things that were hidden from our ancestors.

Why not, then, apply the same methods to understanding ourselves? For the last 150 years or so some have done just that: they have tried to turn our scientific eye upon ourselves as social beings and study human social behaviour and social organization in the same spirit as others have studied physical or chemical phenomena, or the social behaviour and social organization of other animals. And though the findings may be modest and tentative compared with those of physics – and we certainly cannot claim anything as spectacular as space research – nevertheless the enterprise has yielded solid results, as the reader will be able to judge for himself from part 2 of this book.

Two names have been given to different aspects of this particular enterprise: sociology and social anthropology. Tracing their history in chapter 2, I conclude that they are in principle one subject and in practice tending more and more to merge, even though in the past they have been somewhat separated. Anticipating this discussion accordingly, let me say now that when the word 'sociology' is used in what follows, I hope the reader will add in his mind 'and social anthropology'.

SOCIOLOGY AS A SCIENCE – AND MORE

The assertion contained in the opening passage is, in fact, a somewhat controversial one. Not everybody would agree that sociologists should emulate natural scientists and claim that their subject is scientific. Let us look at a study of social behaviour in another animal species – a study whose scientific status is beyond question – to see the similarities and differences between it and the study of human social behaviour.[1]

When Dr Jane Goodall began her remarkable studies of the social behaviour of wild chimpanzees in the Gombe Stream Reserve (now the Gombe National Park) in Tanzania, she encountered in an exaggerated form many of the same difficulties as those often experienced by sociologists and social anthropologists in their studies of human groups. At first they avoided her completely, and she had the greatest difficulty in getting near enough even to watch their behaviour at a distance. After many months of patient and persistent observations they began to lose their fear of her and allowed her to come closer. By this time she knew enough of their behaviour patterns to adopt some of them herself and act in a way that she knew they would perceive as conciliatory and submissive. In the next phase, so far from fleeing when she approached, the chimpanzees made her the object of aggressive displays; and when she persisted in her submissive behaviour, but stood her ground, it became possible at last for her to interact directly with them and become a part of their society. After the aggressive phase, and when the chimpanzees had lost all fear of her and her human companions, there followed a long period when their behaviour took an extremely demanding form. They invaded her camp, stole food, and ripped out tent-pegs causing her tents to collapse. She provided a supply of bananas to attract them to her camp where she could observe their behaviour, but this caused further difficulties as the chimpanzees quarrelled and fought over this food to a greater extent than they did over the wild fruit which they normally lived on. To solve the problems of observation and achieve a satisfactory relation between the chimpanzees and herself – or as we should say in human sociology to define for herself a role and establish herself in it – took much time and ingenuity.

Once she had entered into social relations with the chimpanzees, Dr Goodall was able to make many important observations. She established for instance that, contrary to what had previously been thought, they occasionally ate meat as well as vegetable foods, and for that purpose hunted other animals such as monkeys. Even more important, they made and used tools – a form of behaviour that had previously been regarded as distinctively human. Another area of their social behaviour which she was able to study was that of mating, reproduction, and family life. This was in some ways remarkably like that of humans, in others totally unlike. Thus the relations between mothers and children closely resembled those in man, and young chimpanzees showed the same need for a warm, continuous, and secure relation with their mothers as human infants do, as an indispensable condition for normal growth and development. On the other hand, however, male and female chimpanzees did not form pair-bonds. When females were on heat they were mated by all adult males in the group, so that any male might have been the genitor of the resulting infant. In chimpanzee society accordingly there is no 'father' – physical paternity cannot be established, and even if it could there is no social bond or role relationship between a male and 'his' children.

Dr Goodall came to know individual chimpanzees extremely well, recognizing individual differences in both appearance and behaviour. Instead of coldly allotting them numbers or letters for the purpose of recording observations, she knew them by names such as Flo, Goliath, and Mike. But of course the chimpanzees did not know themselves or each other by those names! And at this point we identify precisely the diagnostic difference between man and other animals: language. As Dr Goodall showed, even toolmaking is not distinctively human, but speech is. And with speech and language come the ability to perform operations on symbols like those involved in constructing a sentence. This ability to manipulate verbal symbols leads in turn to the capacity to elaborate concepts and develop ideas which influence human behaviour in ways that have no parallel in other animals. Thus although, as I have mentioned, Dr Goodall was able to observe the mating and reproductive behaviour of chimpanzees and show in what ways it resembles and differs from that of humans, one type of question she did not have to concern herself with – or ask them – was whether they were Roman Catholics and what were their views on the ethics of family limitation. Yet it is precisely with such questions that a sociologist must be concerned in order to give a complete and realistic account of mating and reproductive behaviour in humans, and account for such phenomena as the decline in the birth-rate in some industrializing countries like England, Sweden, and Japan[2] while at the same time some French-Canadian families have very large numbers of children.[3]

Human behaviour, in other words, has an added dimension over and above the social behaviour of all other animals – the dimension of ideas. A truly comprehensive and scientific study cannot fail to recognize the importance of ideas in influencing human social behaviour. Alone among animals, human beings try to explain their own behaviour, to justify it, to relate it to general principles and norms which can be articulated, asserted, denied, and argued about. Sociology is in fact to a large extent the study of the ideas that move people to action – almost to the point at which the other aspects of action seem in danger of being overlooked, and we have to remind ourselves that physical activities like those of men working, young couples courting, women nursing their babies, etc., are also among the phenomena which it is our task to observe and analyse.

There is much debate about whether sociology is a science or can ever become one, and whether sociologists should persist with the attempt or abandon it. Many of these arguments are sterile because the question is put in a misleading form, or misunderstood to mean 'Is sociology a science *or not*?' To be scientific means that we try to make statements about the world that are true and can be checked by others, and do not just represent our own feelings, responses, or private inner experience. We try, that is, to make statements that can be verified (if they are true – or, of course, falsified if they are wrong) by other observers, assuming that those observers are capable of making the observations and equally devoted to finding out the truth. If we abandon the attempt to do this, we abandon the possibility of communicating anything interesting or important to our fellow human beings, and sociology ceases to have any distinctive contribution to make to human knowledge. Yet at the same time, in order to take proper account of the dimension of ideas in human behaviour, sociologists cannot avoid a critical examination of those ideas themselves; and this demands an approach that may on occasions be more like that of the humanistic disciplines such as history, philosophy, theology, or literature than it is like that of the natural sciences such as physics, chemistry, or biology. But it is not a matter of choosing one approach to the exclusion of the other. On the contrary, the greatest challenge of sociology is that it entails adopting both. To give a comprehensive and realistic account of human social behaviour we have to be both scientific and humanistic. As the fellow human beings of the human animals whose social behaviour we are concerned to observe and analyse, we have a privileged insight into their thoughts and feelings, an intuitive understanding of their mental processes and the inner springs of their behaviour. We know what they feel like because we know what it is like to be human. The central challenge of sociological method, indeed, is to combine that insight with the objectivity of the natural scientist.

SOCIOLOGY AND THE OTHER SOCIAL SCIENCES

Perhaps the best-known social sciences, apart from sociology and social anthropology, are economics and political science; others, relevant to our purpose, are social psychology and demography. We must also consider subjects like criminology, which can be thought of as specialist studies by sociologists.

Political scientists, ever since Plato's *Republic* was written, have been systematically studying man engaged in the activities of government. About two hundred years ago economists like Adam Smith systematically began to study man engaged in the activities of getting a living and deciding on the allocation of scarce resources among different uses. For about three hundred years there have been studies of population statistics and population trends – such as birth-rates, death-rates, the expectation of life and the statistics of death from different diseases – and these studies are nowadays called demography. Psychologists are concerned with the study of such aspects of human behaviour as perception, memory and learning; social psychologists are those who are interested in these aspects of behaviour as they occur in a social setting.

Clearly all these studies are related both to one another and to sociology; any distinctions we may choose to make among them are like farmers' fences: we can put them up where we choose, and move them or remove them if they hinder us; they are not given facts of nature. But sociology is wider than any of them. It must be, because there are many important areas of social life which the more specialized social sciences leave out altogether. None of them, for example, has ever told us much about the family, marriage, and kinship in human society. To take a second example, although political scientists can tell us much about how laws are made in different societies, and those who study comparative law can tell us much about the formal organization of courts, etc., through which laws are enforced, if it were not for sociologists we should know next to nothing about the nature and causes of crime, or the effects or efficiency of different methods of treating offenders. Or to take a third example, although modern studies of comparative religion and theology have enormously widened our knowledge of different religious faiths, and also told us something about the organization of different religious bodies, there are many aspects of religion as a human activity that have been left to sociologists to study, such as the way in which new faiths arise in times of social stress, and the relation between religious adherence and social class.

Sociology, however, is much more than a mere gap-filler. If that were all, sociologists would be like depressed farmers – latecomers on the scene, having to cultivate poor scrub land between the more favoured holdings of established cultivators. Emphatically we are not like that. Sociology has arisen in part from a conviction that social life needs to be viewed as a whole if it is to be properly understood. The whole is more than the sum of its parts. Sociologists have not hesitated to trespass boldly on the ground of their fellow social scientists in insisting that the political and the economic, the psychological and the demographic aspects of any particular social group or social situation have to be seen in relation to one another. One example already mentioned is the fall in the birth-rate in Victorian England, which has been paralleled in other industrializing societies such as Sweden and Japan at comparable periods in their development. Such changes would remain completely puzzling if they had been studied in demographic terms alone. When social scientists like Banks, Myrdal, and Taeuber[4] studied this phenomenon, their explanations involved a study of the way in which economic changes had altered the circumstances in which husbands and wives made decisions about how many children they should have, movements of public opinion on 'the population question', political events and circumstances like controversies over proposed new laws, and legal events such as notable trials.

Sociology and social anthropology, therefore, are best seen as one generalizing and synthesizing discipline, including within its scope the more specialized social sciences and concerned to see the relations among all aspects of social life.

TERMS AND CONCEPTS

Like other sciences, sociology has its vocabulary of technical terms. Some of these are invented words; many of them, however, are ordinary familiar words which sociologists use in a special technical sense. In this practice sociologists are no different from other scientists. Even so familiar a word as *gas* was invented by a seventeenth-century scientist, while physicists have refined common words like *force, weight, mass, gravity,* and even *time* to the point at which they have very special meanings a long way removed from those of everyday speech.[5] In exactly the same way, sociologists sometimes use invented words like *uxorilocal,* and quite often use terms like *class, culture, organization,* and *institution* in a special sense, more precise than that of ordinary speech. Just as in other sciences, too, a mere vocabulary is not enough, and to understand fully the meanings of the words we have to explain them in relation to a system of concepts.

We may start with *action.* An action is the fundamental unit which we as sociologists observe, and it is usually defined as any unit of behaviour that has social meaning. For example, a movement of the hand is an action, or unit act, which may be a signal to another person to be taken as a friendly greeting, a tender farewell, a summons, or in various other ways. Most of the things we do in the company of other human beings – working, eating, playing, talking – are obviously social actions. It might be thought that the things we do when we are alone are not social actions accordingly because they cannot serve as signals to others; but that would be a mistake. When a person withdraws from the company of others that in itself is a social action, and the circumstances in which he withdraws and his motives for doing so are certainly of sociological interest. Thus he may withdraw in order to work better at some task that requires peace and quiet, and that someone else expects him to perform. Or withdrawal may be a sign of anger following a quarrel. Or it may have a religious meaning, if for example someone withdraws temporarily to pray, or for a longer time to be a hermit and give himself over to meditation. Or the withdrawal may be forcible and represent the punishment of solitary confinement.

Equally, it might be thought that the physiological processes which go on in the human body without attracting attention or acting as signals do not constitute action in the sociological sense, and a great deal of the time this may be so. However, even the most intimate physiological processes may come to have social meaning at times and on occasions. Thus the beating of the heart may have very great social significance if it is the heart of a person who is thought to be on the point of death, or that of a man who is undergoing a medical examination for the exacting and well-paid profession of an air-line pilot. Digestion acquires social significance when it is believed that a digestive disorder like gastric ulcers can result from social conditions like anxiety, over-work, and hasty meals in restless surroundings. Or to take another example, some interesting studies have been done on eye movements, which may function as signals between people, even though they are scarcely aware of them. For instance 'At the end of each speech A is likely to Look at B. This is taken as a signal that A has finished and B may speak.'[6] There are indeed few movements or processes of which human bodies are capable that do not sometimes become invested with social meaning, and come accordingly within the sociologist's field of attention.

Beginning with the unit act, and following Parsons, we regard action as taking place in a *situation* which has a number of components or aspects.* It includes the actor (that is, the person on whose actions we are for the moment focussing our attention) and one or more other actors. It includes the physical environment of

---

*The works of Talcott Parsons contain several different expositions of his analysis. Possibly the fullest and most definitive is in his *The Social System* (1952); a more condensed version is in T. Parsons and E. Shils (eds.), *Towards a General Theory of Action*, part 2 (1951).

the action, for example trees, houses, doors, tables, chairs. It also includes, very importantly, the *expectations* of the actor himself, and other actors. Even if other actors are not physically present, their expectations may play a decisive part in the meaning of the action which we observe. Let us take the homely example of a woman cooking. Her situation includes the cooking pots, the fire or stove, the supply of food – the material environment and apparatus, that is – but it also importantly includes the expectations of her husband and children, not home yet, that they will return to find the meal ready; and it includes in turn her own expectations of their expectations, and of their reactions when they do come home (such as 'I'm hungry! When will supper be ready?').

When actors in a situation are acting according to well-defined expectations in this way, it becomes possible to say they are assuming *roles*. A role, indeed, can be regarded as a bundle of expectations; the role of a wife/mother consists of all the things she is expected to do for her husband and children. In the case of a diffuse role like that of wife/mother, we need to separate different *role sectors*; in that role, indeed, what the husband expects his wife to do and to be may compete or conflict with what her sons and her daughters may expect of her. There may thus be *intra-role conflict* when the same person occupying the same role is subject to conflicting expectations in the different role sectors.* In addition, we may also get conflict between the expectations upon the same person in different roles which he or she may occupy. Thus the duty to cook for her husband and children in her role as wife may conflict with the same woman's duty in her role as daughter to go and look after her sick father; or a man's kinship obligations may conflict with his duties as a teacher or government officer.

An important point about the role concept is that an individual can occupy many roles. Indeed it is almost impossible to avoid occupying several roles in the sphere of kinship alone, where the same person is (as we have seen) wife, mother, daughter, and also daughter-in-law, possibly cousin or clan-sister (according to the particular system of kinship in her society) and so on. In the modern world, as we shall see in chapter 5, there is a tendency for people to occupy more and more different roles in other spheres of

*Modern role analysis and earlier views are well summarized in N. Gross *et al.* *Explorations in Role Analysis* (1958), part 1.

life than kinship. Thus besides being a son, grandson, husband, brother, father, etc., a man may also be a bank clerk, a trade union branch secretary, the citizen of a state, member of a political party, churchwarden and youth club helper. From time to time he may further occupy the role of bus passenger – a rather transient role in contrast to the more permanent ones we have just been considering. Similarly, from time to time he occupies the role of customer (in a shop, in relation to shopkeeper or shop assistant), patient (in relation to a doctor), taxpayer (in relation to a chief or tax inspector), and so on. Some sociologists use the term *role-set* for the whole collection of roles occupied by any one individual.

Every role forms part of a social system or social structure. A role cannot, indeed, be conceived in isolation; it exists solely and completely in its relation to counter-roles. Thus the counter-role of wife is husband; the counter-roles of mother are sons and daughters; the counter-roles of bus conductors are passenger, driver, manager, supervisor. In principle, any social structure can be drawn in diagram form. The kinship diagrams which form part of chapter 4 are examples of social systems or social structures; so are the formal 'organization charts' sometimes to be seen on the wall of a government office or large business. In the same way, informal groups, such as those of students in the same class or hall of residence, can be charted according to their friendship and avoidances. Such charts are sometimes called 'sociograms'. In all such diagrams, whether of formal or informal structures, the lines joining the symbols stand for particular relations. In the kinship diagrams, double lines like this = represent the relation of marriage; single lines vertically represent descent; single lines horizontally represent the relation between siblings (brothers or sisters). In a sociogram, the lines represent some such relation as that between students who would choose to share a room.

Social systems may be large or small. They range from the small groups we have been considering, such as a family or a group of student friends, through middling-sized systems like that of a clan, a university, a government department or a business firm, to large structures like a whole tribe or a nation-state. Any such structure can be thought of as a system or network of roles.

We now turn to the concept of *culture*, which is of the utmost importance for sociology. Culture in man consists essentially of a system of tools linked with a system of symbols. As we have seen, it is now recognized that man is not the only tool-making animal, and this is not quite the distinctively human accomplishment it was once thought to be. Nevertheless, the tools and other artefacts of man far surpass those of other animals. There is a world of difference between even the simplest human tool like a stone axe or a dug-out canoe and the sort of tool which Goodall describes chimpanzees as making and using – a twig stripped of its leaves to poke into a termite's nest, or a handful of leaves to soak up water out of a hole. When we come to the higher levels of material culture in human evolution, through agriculture and the wheel to the internal combustion engine, electricity generation and space rockets, the difference is obviously far greater again. The difference between human artefacts and those of other animals is only partly to be thought of in terms of the greater amounts of material embodied and the longer time and greater labour involved. The most important point is that it is inconceivable that men could ever have developed their more complex tools without their ability to manipulate symbols and communicate with one another in symbolic languages. To make such tools involves design – a symbolic process including the consideration and rejection of a number of possibilities ('on paper', as we say in the higher material cultures) before a decision is reached about how to make the artefact itself. This process involves men in communicating with one another, discussing possible designs and ways of making the object, some men giving instructions to others about the tasks they are to perform, some men learning from others how to make such objects, and above all the symbolic communication of an understanding of the scientific and technical principles involved. Symbolic communication in language is indeed indispensable to the making of all but the simplest human artefacts. It is for this reason that we regard the tools and the symbols as inextricably interwoven in the complex whole of human culture, which distinguishes man from his closest biological kin among the great apes, and which has enabled man to become, from the biological point of view, an extraordinarily successful animal, growing very rapidly in numbers and dominating the natural environment to a greater extent than any species past or present.

Moreover, the whole system is learned. It follows that human cultures and the adaptive behaviour associated with them can change rather rapidly over time – very much more rapidly than if they were genetically inherited and had to be subject to the slow pressures of natural selection. It also follows that human cultures differ from one another far more profoundly than the systems of behaviour and response by which other animals communicate with one another, even though we now know that there is a good deal of learning and even a kind of oral tradition in some other species too. But all dogs, for example, submit by lying down and exposing the neck, and greet by jumping up and licking noses. There is nothing in the rest of the animal kingdom to compare with the profound differences among human languages like, for instance, Swahili, French, and English. Where communication is symbolic, the attachment of a particular meaning to a particular word is essentially arbitrary. We might as well say *nyumba* or *maison* as *house*.

Sociologists and social anthropologists, then, have come to think of human cultures as systems of tools linked with systems of learned symbols, and to include within this concept the following components.

(1) Material culture – the tools. It is in this sense of the word that archaeologists speak of, for instance, Sangoan culture. All that now remains of the culture of the men who used to live at Sango Bay in Uganda are a few of their chipped pebbles – part of their material culture. Their language, kinship system, political organization, and so on have vanished for ever. Sociologists and social anthropologists use a somewhat wider term, technology, to include the culturally-transmitted knowledge of how to make the tools and how to use them.

(2) Language. As we have seen, language and tools are inseparable in human cultures, and it is through language that technology is transmitted and developed. Language, however, has wider uses. For example, as we see in chapter 7, it enables man to settle disputes in quite a different way from other animals – by debate and discussion, involving the statement of abstract general principles of right and wrong – in other words, through appeal to law, custom, or morality. Equally, it is the basis for all other distinctively human achievement including art, science, sport, and religion.

(3) Over and above language and technology, therefore, culture includes symbolic values of all kinds – ideas of right and wrong, beliefs, rules and norms, the cultural definitions of the behaviour appropriate to roles, moral and artistic values.

Another way of looking at culture is summed up in the phrase 'the social heritage'. Culture is what we inherit through being members of a particular society or group. First and foremost we think, then, of the cultures of national or tribal groups – Kikuyu, Ibo, Nyakyusa – each embodied in a language and in a material technology. However, although this is a good first approximation, it is a little too simple. If a man becomes a Muslim he becomes the heir to Islamic culture even though he may also be a Muganda (and heir to Ganda culture). We really have to think of every social system and sub-system as having its own culture or sub-culture. Even so small a group as a single household may develop distinctively different ways of doing things, likes and dislikes; there may be a few words which perhaps have a rather special meaning for the members of that particular family, for example, a specially treasured photograph, or a peculiar taste in breakfast food. It would be accurate to speak of the sub-culture of that particular household, viewed as a sub-system of a larger system, and remembering also that although the sub-culture may be different in a few particulars, in many respects it draws its culture ready-made, as it were, from the surrounding society. The concepts of culture and of social system are thus integrally related.

Perhaps we can illustrate this by considering the simplest possible group, consisting of two people. Such a group may grow up when two students meet at college and, after a while, a relation develops in which one becomes, let us say, the steady studious type while the other is gay and sociable, one habitually lends the other books, lecture notes, etc. This is a brand-new social system, growing up literally out of nothing, in which each develops a stable system of expectations of the other's actions – that is, each assumes a role. Equally we may say that the system has its own sub-culture. At the same time most of the culture of this tiny group is drawn from the wider society that surrounds the two friends. They communicate in some language such as English even though they may make free with it, and jokingly use some particular words as a kind of private code. Their material culture is largely 'given', consisting as it does of rooms in a college fitted with desks, tables, beds, etc. Moreover their behaviour to one another will be affected by whatever expectations have been defined in their culture in the very word *friend* itself (or its equivalent, such as mate, buddy, oppo, chum). It will, after all, make a difference if they are of the same sex or of opposite sex. If the latter, strongly culturally defined expectations of the roles respectively of boy- and girl-friend will, most likely, affect their relation – conventions concerning courtship, rules about the admissibility of women into men's halls or residence and vice versa, moral values concerning faithfulness, the exchange of gifts, leading up perhaps to the conventions of engagement and the laws of marriage. These *cultural* aspects come into the situation of the young couple because they influence the expectations upon them of 'significant others' – the individuals who occupy roles in their *social system*, as for example father, mother, father's brother, warden of hall of residence, tutor, or fellow-student.

Finally, we should always remember that all we are concerned with in sociology are processes in time. As Norbert Elias* has well reminded us, every act is a process in time; and although much action is patterned and predictable, and so can be thought of in terms of role and social structure, no action is ever repeated exactly. Even in the most patterned of relationships, the interactions between people change, often subtly and imperceptibly. To distinguish between social structure and culture on the one hand, and social change on the other (as was done in some older textbooks) is quite false and misleading. For example, no relationship might appear more constant than that between mother and child. Yet ideas about child care have changed over time, and with them the ways in which mothers interact with their children. In such a case we are concerned with change in the content of the relation between two roles which, however, continue to have the same positional relation in the social system. Not all changes are like this. Some are purely structural changes, that is, changes in the social system itself. These may occur when completely new roles are created. For example, the roles of 'foreman' or 'bank clerk' simply did not exist in the traditional social systems of Africa, though they are now commonly enough accepted. In the modern development of African states new social systems like those of the bank, the factory, the mine, the political party, or the university are set up, and people who already occupy a set of traditional roles add others in the new systems to their role-sets. Moreover each of these new social systems has its own culture or sub-culture – its

*Especially in his *The civilizing process*, British edition (1978), appendix 1 (Introduction to the 1968 edition), pp. 230–1.

own material technology, its own language (in the technical terms used in mines, banks, political parties, and so on). Thus, as Gluckman[7] has put it, if we insist on using so misleading a term as 'detribalized', we have to think of a man as being 'detribalized' when he rides on a lorry from his homeland to the Copperbelt, 're-tribalized' when he returns, 're-de-tribalized' when he goes a second time and so on. It is more sensible and more accurate to think of him as moving from one social system in which his roles are those of son, chief's subject, etc., to another in which his role is that of mine-worker in relation to a foreman, manager, wages clerk, each system having its own culture. The kinship and tribal roles which he still occupies during his absence become (as Parsons says), latent, but they may still affect his actions, for example, in sending money home. As we shall see in chapter 5, this kind of change is particularly characteristic of societies undergoing growth of scale, like those of modern Africa. The social system becomes more complex quite simply through the addition of many new sub-systems.

Very often, of course, this sort of social change occurs as the result of innovation, whether by way of invention or discovery. For example, the invention of the motor-car within the last hundred years has very obviously led to the growth of new social systems in the form of the great motor manufacturing corporations. The discovery of copper, gold, and other minerals in parts of Africa has led to the setting up of new social systems, in the form of the mining companies. Technical changes, however, do not stop there. The invention of the motor-car has led to a concomitant need for motor roads, and with it the setting up of new social systems in the form of Public Works Departments, highways authorities, and so on, with new roles like foreman and ganger. It has also led to the creation of other new roles like lorry-owner and taxi-driver in many an African village. The possibility of making a living by means of a lorry or taxi brings about changes in the economy of the local community, with the development of a new and possibly upstart group of men with money, rivalling more traditional authority; and so we find taxi-drivers playing a not unimportant part in the recent political history of Uganda, emphasizing the importance of this new role.

Some other factors that bring about social changes are demographic, that is, changes in the size and composition of the population. Even as simple a change as growth in sheer numbers does not necessarily, or even usually, mean just 'more of the same'. It tends to bring about changes in the social system and the culture as well. A particularly good example is afforded by the effects of population growth among the Nyakyusa. The old system of age-villages, which depended on there being plenty of land, has now largely been superseded as land has become scarce and therefore valuable. Instead, the lineage has become more important because of the tendency for men to lay claim to valuable land by inheritance, where traditionally they got it as members of an age-set.[8] In the same way, there is an example in chapter 4 of the way in which the greater length of life in modern western countries has affected family structure, as old people lead independent lives in their own households, and can play more actively the role of grandparent.

But that is not the end of the story. Social systems and sub-systems should not be thought of as necessarily fitting harmoniously together; and social changes do not necessarily, or even usually, occur as a process of smooth adjustment, with change in one sub-system being followed by corresponding changes in others until the whole system reaches a new state of balance or integration. More usually, change occurs through *conflict*, or to the accompaniment of conflict. Conflict is an aspect of change. There are many possible modes of conflict; it is a term which sociologists use rather widely, to mean everything from fighting to debate, including competition and even bargaining. In chapter 7 modes of conflict and the central problem for society of limiting conflict to its non-violent modes – 'the conference table rather than the battlefield', as the current phrase has it – are dealt with in some detail. Further, just as conflict has many modes, so it may take place between many different pairs of people, groups, interests, or sub-systems. One form of conflict that has received much attention in European and American sociology is that between employers and workers, which Karl Marx regarded as the main if not the only form of conflict in an industrial society. This view, however, is regarded by some modern sociologists as too simple. Conflicts between workers and employers do indeed occur. They are widespread and commonplace; but so, for example, are conflicts between local and central governments, between farmers and cattle ranchers in some states in America, between taxi-drivers and bus companies, between road transport (including both taxi-drivers and bus companies) on the one hand and rail transport on the other, between farmers who want to keep their land and municipal authorities who need it for housing schemes, between Christian missions and traditional authorities, as for example over the question of female circumcision in Kenya in the 1920s; and so on without end. Even in traditional societies in Africa there were, it would appear, conflicts between clans over land, between clan heads on the one hand and priests on the other for power, and so on. Occasions for conflict have probably greatly increased with the growing complexity of society in modern conditions, and accordingly conflict appears both as an effect and a cause of change.

Not that it is possible simply to equate the two. Conflict has many different possible outcomes. Military conflict, war, generally leads to the victory of one side over the other, and the changes that then occur are the result of whatever terms the victor imposes. The outcome of a more peaceful conflict, such as a lawsuit over land, may be the vindication of one party's claim over the other's. But sometimes conflict may lead to innovation – for example when an industrial dispute is ended, not so much in a victory for one side, which makes the other worse off, as in a productivity agreement in which both sides become better off. Equally, however, a conflict can continue in deadlock, or stalemate, in which tensions are unresolved, hostility continues and no change occurs.

PROBLEMS OF METHOD

At the beginning of this chapter I suggested that both scientific method and an approach like that of the humanistic disciplines were necessary for a comprehensive study of human society. The fuller implications of this view will perhaps now have become clearer, especially in the last few paragraphs, as we see that in studying such areas of human life as culture, conflict, and change, sociologists are dealing with the same kind of subject-matter as that which is also dealt with by the arts and humanities, such as history, literature, and even journalism. There is no reason to regret this. On the contrary, precisely one of the ways in which sociology is valuable is in bridging the gap between two areas of study, the arts and the sciences, which in many schools and universities are kept altogether too separate. But this attempt to bridge the gap between arts and science raises two important questions. What do sociologists do that is different from literature, history or journalism? And what are the special problems of applying scientific method to the study of human society? We discuss these questions more fully in chapter 3, but it will be well to introduce them now.

Historians, journalists, and creative writers are concerned, in their different ways, to tell a story. Creative writers tell about imaginary people who nevertheless resemble real people in their problems and their social situations. Historians tell a balanced, well-considered story about the past actions of people in society, while journalists try to communicate quickly what has happened to people in the recent past. Sociologists can often use their accounts but in a different way and for a different purpose: to compare, to analyse, to test out whether sociological ideas on how things work are correct, to make, if possible, general statements in the form 'if . . . then . . . '. To some extent the sociologist's attitude to social happenings is like that of the geologist to specimens of rock. They are examples, instances, evidence to be analysed, classified, related to one another in some way that makes sense.

But, of course, the 'bug on a pin' attitude (as two American sociologists called it) will not do.[9] We are concerned, not with inanimate objects that can be thrown away at the end of the experiment, but with human beings with feelings and rights. The sociologist too has feelings, rights, and moral and social duties like the people he or she studies. He or she acts in the same social situation, even if it is one entered only for the purpose of observation. The observing sociologist is a social being, acting in relation to others even when observing them.

This poses some special problems, and the first is objectivity. It is particularly hard for a sociologist – harder than for other scientists – to be objective about his or her subject-matter. Personal likes and dislikes can hardly be avoided; and even if they could, too detached an attitude on the sociologist's part would blunt an instrument that is required for the sensitive observation of other people's gestures, feelings, even (so far as they can be surmised) their unspoken thoughts.

Moreover, sociologists may experience conflict between their sense of obligation to the people they study and their duty as scientists to render full and accurate accounts of their discoveries to their fellow-scientists. Sociologists often learn facts discreditable to their subjects. What are they then to do? To publish such facts may lead to accusations, including self-accusations, of betraying the trust of those who have welcomed and helped the inquisitive stranger, and for whose hospitality a debt of gratitude is due. At a somewhat lower ethical level, too, a sociologist may not wish to incur unpopularity in the community in case further field-work is undertaken, if not by the same investigator, then perhaps by a colleague or pupil. But to suppress or distort the facts, to fail to render a full and fair account to fellow-scientists, would be the worst betrayal a scientist can commit, namely the betrayal of truth.

The second problem for the sociologist is complexity. Humans are highly complex animals, and their social behaviour and social organization are among the most subtle and complex of all the phenomena that scientists have tried to observe and analyse. Even in the simplest everyday activities of human life – those of a group of people working together, or children playing, for example – so many things are going on at once and the complexities and subtleties of the action are so great as to make it virtually impossible for one person to record in full what is happening. Observation and recordings are possible only if a great deal is left out and taken for granted. This means that we can observe only by abstracting what is judged to be important for the particular scientific purpose for which the observations are being made; and this in turn implies a prior decision about the purpose of the study. Are we, for example, concentrating on the relation between speech and gesture, or are we studying social status in the group and the nature of leadership, or are we investigating the relation of the informal social structure to patterns of work in the group under study? I deal with the problems of this nature more fully in discussing experimental observations on small groups in chapter 3.

A third problem for sociology arises from the fact that, as I said at the beginning of this chapter, ideas inspire action and have to be included accordingly among the objects that sociologists must observe and analyse.

In the natural sciences, a clear distinction can usually be made between the phenomena being studied on the one hand, and the human organism, the scientist, who is doing the studying on the other. Thus the natural phenomena of (for example) the movements of the planets or of glaciers, the laying down and wearing away of rocks, the behaviour of ants or monkeys, can be thought of as going on 'out there', independently of the observer. The scientist gathers information about these phenomena through his senses – sight, hearing, etc. – aided and extended by suitable instruments like telescopes, microscopes, thermometers, etc. This information is then analysed through logical processes – classification, comparison, etc. – and brought into relation with a system of ideas – hypotheses, theories – about how the various phenomena being observed are connected to one another and how the world, or the particular aspect of it being investigated, 'works'. Hypotheses which are tested by fresh observations, and verified, are for the time being regarded as known facts, though nothing is ever known for certain and established ideas are always subject to review in the light of new observations or new theories. Science represents accordingly a closer and closer correspondence between the phenomena of the world 'out there' and the knowledge which is 'in here' – inside the head of the scientist – and which is then communicated to fellow-scientists.

The processes by which the social scientist comes to know about the phenomena of human social behaviour are not basically different from those of the natural scientist, but there is a complication. For the phenomena in which the sociologist is interested include ideas, yet the hypotheses and theories which constitute the mental apparatus of the social scientist (like any other scientist) also consist of ideas. Ideas thus appear, as it were, on both sides of the boundary between the observing scientist and the world 'out there' of the phenomena in which he is interested. It becomes rather difficult to think in terms of a boundary or distinction between what is known on the one hand and the act or process of knowing on the other, and the effect is disconcerting, rather as if an amoeba were to be found jumping rapidly from the objective end of a microscope to the eyepiece and back again in an attempt to observe itself.

Theories about society are ideas, which like other ideas can themselves be the subject of sociological study and analysis. For this reason we can have a sociology of sociology, for sociology can be studied as a human social activity just like any other. Sociological theories are also social facts. Moreover, some theories about society have importantly influenced human actions in the past and continue to do so in the present. Such theories have to be considered in two ways: as theory and as fact.[10] As theories they may be true or false, and stand or fall by the test of truth; whether true or false, however, they exist as social facts influencing people's actions, and as subject-matter for the sociologist accordingly. A particularly apt example is that of Marxism. On the one hand, the writings of Karl Marx and his successors contain a number of ideas which some sociologists have taken seriously in formulating their own researches into aspects of modern society. Examples which I give below are those of 'embourgeoisement' and of class conflict. On the other hand, the same body of thought has also been enormously influential in shaping major events and processes in the modern world, especially since the coming to power of communist parties in some major countries. Clearly Marxism is a massive social fact.

But though there are problems of method which sociology and social anthropology to some extent share with the other social sciences, it would be wrong to give the impression that these are insuperable, or that they have effectively prevented sociologists from making useful observations and advancing our understanding of the world in which we live. On the contrary, many important sociological studies have now been done which have had scientific value in the sense that they have significantly added to human self-knowledge. Some such studies have proved to have value also in providing a better basis for social action than the ignorance, misinformation, or prejudice that prevailed before they were done. Many have proved in addition to have moral and educational value.

THE RELEVANCE OF SOCIOLOGY

It would be possible to cite a long list of studies to demonstrate the relevance of sociology and social anthropology to a changing Africa, and a few examples must suffice.

Although the prosperity of Ghana was based for sixty years or more on cocoa it was not until 1963 that the first full-length study was published of the migrant cocoa-farmers of southern Ghana. Previously it had not even been fully appreciated that the cocoa-farmers *were* migrants, and there had been what Polly Hill, the author of the study, calls 'the myth of the small peasant farmer as the backbone of the industry'.[11]

Another African migration was that of labourers from Rwanda and Burundi into Buganda, together with some from other parts of Uganda. Before studies were carried out by the East African Institute of Social Research in the 1950s it was not known why the migrants left home, what made Buganda so attractive as an area for employment, how the immigrants were employed when they got there, how long they stayed, or how far they were incorporated into Buganda society.[12]

Scores if not hundreds of studies have been carried out by social anthropologists of the traditional cultures and social organization of societies in Africa and elsewhere, but their studies have not been confined to the traditional. They have also studied such societies in transition, as in the example already cited of the studies by Monica Wilson and P. H. Gulliver of changes in land tenure and social organization among the Nyakyusa.[13] Many studies have been carried out of African towns and urban social life, and I list some of these at the end of chapter 5. Studies have been made of educated African elites, for example in Ghana by Busia and Jahoda,[14] in Nigeria by the Smythes,[15] in South Africa by Leo Kuper,[16] in East Africa by myself and later by van den Berghe,[17] in the Ivory Coast by Clignet and Foster.[18] Another study of a group who subsequently became the centre of world attention was that of Indians in Uganda by H. S. Morris.[19] And an issue of modern African politics which has not been neglected by sociologists and social anthropologists is that surrounding words like tribe and tribalism.[20]

Relevant though sociology may be to an understanding of the world, however, it should not be thought that the results of sociological research can always be applied in any direct or simple way to improve the lot of the people studied. Sociologists must often be on their guard against raising people's hopes. Although a sociological study may sometimes reveal bad conditions which can be, and are, promptly remedied, quite often no immediate reforms follow. Sociologists sometimes have to be pessimistic. For example, they may find that tensions between two groups, or between (say) a central and local government, have their roots in social situations that are not likely to be changed very easily or very rapidly. And even if remedies for bad conditions can be suggested it usually takes more than a sociologist's report to prod unwilling authority into action, and overcome prejudice, inertia, or vested interest. Sociological study does not guarantee that social action will follow at all, or that if it does it will be beneficent or effective. But we can be quite sure of one thing: where there is sociological study there is at least a possibility that social action will be based on facts and reason, whereas without it there can only be misinformation and prejudice.

Some sociologists have said that all social research should be therapeutic in aim – that is, sociologists should go into the field only at the invitation of the people they study, and with the aim of helping them to overcome their problems – rather as if they were medical men, called in to help sick people and gaining knowledge of health and disease in the process.[21] Most of us, however, would think that this was going too far. For the reasons suggested above, sociologists may well find that little or nothing can be done to improve the situation in the fields they study. If sociologists always had to show useful improvements as a result of their studies, their possible choice of research topic would be narrowed to an extent that would seriously restrict the development of the science. We do not study any science solely for the sake of its useful applications; all science has a value, intellectual, moral and educational, as a human activity pursued for its own sake. Let us take these values in turn.

First the *intellectual* value of sociology is basically that of understanding human society, how social systems work, how people's behaviour is modified by their circumstances. There is value in the comparative study of human societies, which brings with it an understanding of what institutions are universal and fixed, because they correspond to the universal needs of man's nature and what, on the other hand, is the range of variation, the widely differing ways in which different societies meet human needs. Thus, for example, every society must have a system of kinship, marriage, and family relations, to regulate mating and birth and the care of infants; but the details of different kinship systems differ very widely, as some societies trace descent through the father, others through the mother, some permit a man to have only one wife at a time, others allow polygamy, and so on. In the same way people in different societies have many different solutions to the universal human problems of making a living, settling disputes, and curing diseases.

But the collecting and classifying of the different ways of behaving in different societies has more than an intellectual value. It has a *moral* value also. In doing it we come to understand that other people's ways, however strange they may seem at first sight, may nevertheless meet their needs, or may be reasonably intelligent responses to their particular situation. If we find that other people's actions are at least intelligible to us we look at them as our fellow human beings more easily. We are made more tolerant, we experience a widening of horizons that might otherwise have been limited by our immediate experiences to a view only of our own society.

This leads us to the *educational* value of sociology. Learning how other people arrange their societies may lead us to a healthy scepticism, a tendency to ask intelligent questions, about our own. It has been well said that the hallmark of a university-trained mind is intelligent and unprejudiced scepticism.[22] Further, the study of sociology must make us aware of the sources of bias and prejudice in ourselves – and, as we have seen, a person who is not aware in this way has not been successfully trained as a sociologist. Thus students of sociology are led to ask many searching questions about their society and themselves. Many sociology students find this process disconcerting and unsettling. Being led to question everything, they may, for a time, experience bewilderment and even serious insecurity.

Most sociologists come through this 'uprooted' phase as they appreciate the relation between facts and values more clearly. Intelligent and unprejudiced scepticism does not preclude us from holding to values and acting on them. What it does do is ensure that the values to which we are committed are not based on ignorance or prejudice, but rationally defensible, and related either to values that are more or less universal in all human societies (like the prohibition of incest) or necessary pre-conditions for social life itself (like respect for the life and property of other persons).

THE RELATION BETWEEN FACTS AND VALUES

This problem arises because every society is the source of its members' values, while it is also the object which the sociologist studies. Other people's values are facts about those people, which it is the sociologist's task to observe and analyse as objectively as possible. Yet the sociologist too is a social being, acting according to values. In his or her professional work, the sociologist's prime value-commitment is to truth, and the endeavour is to make statements about the society being studied which (it is hoped) will be true, and can be verified by any other competent observer. In other roles, the sociologist will undoubtedly be motivated by other values too, including love, family sentiment, patriotism, and political conviction. These attachments are all perfectly proper, and indeed unavoidable, since we can act only in the light of values. It is of the utmost importance, though, to separate the factual analysis of the events and processes that the sociologist observes from his or her evaluations or recommendations about the society or situation concerned.

Let us take two examples to illustrate this relation. The first concerns infant mortality. In some countries, such as Sweden and Australia, fewer than twenty babies out of every thousand die in the first year after birth; at the other end of the scale, in some other countries, notably Africa and Asian countries such as Burma, the rate is more like 150 to 200 deaths out of every thousand.

On the question of fact there might be room for argument about the accuracy of these statistics. Could the difference be accounted for by the way in which births and deaths are registered in the countries in question, whether people frequently neglect to report births or infant deaths, whether they understand how long a year is, and so on? In such a case, however, we might well conclude that if anything infant deaths were under-registered in developing countries like Burma, so that the true rate would be even higher and the contrast with Sweden even starker.

On the question of values, most sociologists would probably make it clear (explicitly or by implication) that they do not approve of the early deaths of children. They regard a low infant mortality rate as a desirable state of affairs and a high rate as deplorable; and, still at the level of values, they might add some recommendations about improving methods of child care in Burma. This case is a fairly easy one, for presumably nobody seriously suggests that it is good that many babies should die, and we are concerned with values that are universal in all societies.

For our second example let us take two imaginary societies, A and B. In society A there is a strongly centralized traditional system of social control, so that though people are in awe of the paramount and his officers they are relatively secure against attacks on their persons and on their cattle and granaries. Society B lacks a tradition of central government, and disputes are settled by feuds between clans, so that fighting between clans is common, and with it murderous attacks and attempts to drive off cattle.

Here it is not so easy to say which political system is preferable. Some might say that the advantages of peace and security over a wide area in society A was worth the extortion and corruption to which most strongly centralized political systems are prone. Others might find the arrogance of the privileged and the servility of the peasants in such a system distasteful and find good words to say of the manly virtues of courage, alertness, and brotherly comradeship of society B, where all men look each other in the eye as equals and all are equally insecure.

In such a case, the sociologist's first task clearly is the objective, dispassionate description and analysis of the two political systems, showing clearly how each works as a functional system and the way in which each part is related to other parts. Particular care must be taken to distinguish this, the factual part of the analysis, from the value interpretation. There is no harm in the latter so long as it is clearly distinguishable from the factual analysis; so long, that is, as the sociologist makes it clear when a value-judgement is being introduced. One of the most important benefits of a sociological education is to make us aware of the possible sources of bias in ourselves. As sociologists we have the best reason to know that our upbringing in a particular society is a potent source of values. Equally, though, we are alerted to the issues on which we rebel against, or reject, the values to which we were brought up, and are the better able to correct our own biases accordingly.

In addressing students who have been brought up in Africa I am greatly helped by knowing that they have already learned one important lesson in sociology: they know already that different people have different ways. The diverse tribes of traditional Africa, each with its own language, kinship system, way of government, and outlook on the universe are paralleled in Africa in transition by the differences among African peoples and the non-African immigrant communities, between life in modern towns and in the traditionally minded countryside and between the small-scale world of local communities and that of modern states, business firms, bureaucracy, and political parties. Though this rich experience of diversity does not always go with the tolerance it should teach, at least those brought up in Africa can take it for granted and go straight on to ask why and how, to organize their experience in their minds and try to make it make sense. This puts them one step ahead of many of their fellow-students in western countries.

The task of sociology is first to understand the difference between societies and cultures. Secondly, we are concerned to understand the processes of social change. In modern Africa the very rapid process, which can be called the modernization of traditional societies, is going on. The isolation of groups like traditional African tribes is breaking down and they are being drawn into the institutional system of the one world of the twentieth century – that one world which I shall call modern urban industrial society. African students may have more to learn about this than they realize. It is not just that that towns of Africa are small, so that those who know only Accra or Nairobi may find it hard to imagine what life is like in a city or conurbation with a population of millions, like London or New York, the West Yorkshire conurbation or the Ruhr basin. It is also a matter of understanding a society in which (for historical reasons rather than of necessity) monogamy prevails and families are small; where nearly everybody earns a living by working for money and hardly anyone lives on the land; where nearly all children go to school and nearly everybody can read and write; where everyone is heavily exposed to the mass media of radio, television and newspapers; where large-scale systems of social welfare have supplemented the family as a support in sickness, old age and other crises of life and where, accordingly, much of people's lives is given over to large-scale organizations such as the state and large business corporations. Many African students have not experienced living in such a society though they will have seen it reflected in the life of some African towns and in the cultural products – films, novels, etc. – of the west. This is the kind of society that is now growing and spreading its influence everywhere in the world, particularly in Africa. As modern African leaders fly to New York, London, or Moscow to negotiate with their counterparts there, raise loans from Swiss banks, call in Israeli technicians or Swedish teachers, they vividly illustrate the growth of the links between African societies and this one world of modern urban industrial society. It is, therefore, most important for students everywhere to make a particularly thorough study of the institutions of that one world, and know the nature of the advancing giant better.

Finally we do not know nearly enough about Africa. Students of sociology in western countries find much that they need to know already prepared for them, the research done, the textbooks written. We know far less about African societies and much of what we do know is in the form of research reports rather than textbooks prepared for students' use. Most of it, so far, is also the work of non-Africans. I must list, as my third task, that of stimulating some of the readers of this book to be the sociologists of the new Africa. There could hardly be a more exciting challenge.

SUGGESTIONS FOR FURTHER READING

A. Inkeles, *What is sociology?* (Englewood Cliffs, Prentice-Hall, 1964). A good, short introduction.

Peter L. Berger, *Invitation to sociology: a humanistic perspective* (New York, Doubleday, 1963; London, Penguin, 1966). As its title implies, this book inclines to the humanistic rather than the scientific view. It especially well conveys the sceptical, irreverent temper of sociology.

R. W. Firth, *Human types* (London, Nelson, 1938). A classic introduction to social anthropology. A somewhat fuller work is the same author's *Elements of social organization* (London, Watts, 1951, and Tavistock, 1971).

Salvador Giner, *Sociology* (London, Martin Robertson, 1972). A full and concise presentation of the subject.

CHAPTER 2

Sociology and social anthropology

In the previous chapter, I passed quickly over the relation between sociology and social anthropology. We must now go into more detail.

Sociological studies of the early nineteenth century had a strongly evolutionary orientation. Early sociologists took it for granted that, just as evolution had occurred among living organisms from simple and lowly forms of life to more complex and more highly specialized plants and animals, so human societies had evolved from small to large, from simple to complex, and from those with little control over their environment to those that could adapt themselves to changed circumstances effectively. Auguste Comte (1798–1857), who is generally regarded as the founding father of our science, set out its aims thus:

the study of social phenomena considered in the same spirit as astronomical, physical, chemical or physiological phenomena, that is, subject to natural invariable laws, the discovery of which is the special object of investigation . . . to discover through what fixed series of successive transformations the human race, starting from a state not superior to that of the societies of the great apes, gradually led us to the point at which civilized Europe finds itself today.[1]

A remarkable passage to have been published in 1822, twenty-seven years before *The Origin of Species*!

Another early sociologist, Herbert Spencer (1820–1903) – regarded as fellow founding father with Comte – also took a strongly evolutionary point of view. It was indeed, in his own phrase, 'stamped on his mind'. Just as progress in the evolution of animals and plants consisted of the increasing inter-dependence of specialized organs, so in the evolution of human society.*

---

*The evolutionary approach so completely permeates Spencer's whole work that it is difficult to select a single short quotation. The reader will find a moderately concise summary of his view in *The study of sociology* (1878), ch. XIV.

31

If it was taken for granted that social evolution had occurred, and if it was further assumed that the most highly developed societies were those of European countries in the nineteenth century, where were the less developed or 'primitive' societies to be found? Two answers suggested themselves. One, in the history – and even more the pre-history – of 'our own' (i.e. European) societies, and, two, among those peoples who had not undergone the industrial revolution and who were accordingly viewed as contemporary primitives, surviving from an earlier stage of human evolution.

Evidence about early man was not lacking from the archaeological discoveries of the nineteenth century. Digging up the skulls and other bones of primitive men and the remains of their handiwork – fireplaces, pots, cave paintings, graves, chipped stone implements – gave at least some idea of their physical appearance and the way they made a living. But many features of society leave no fossils. Elaborate burial mounds might attest the existence of chiefs or kings, men of more importance than commoners, and might give some idea of funeral rites and hence even of supernatural beliefs, but for evidence of early social organization, nineteenth-century scientists looked mainly towards the social life of then existing primitive peoples, such as those of Africa, Australia, and the Polynesian and Melanesian islands. Just as their material technology – the use of implements made of stone, bone and other simple materials – could be shown to resemble that of early man, so it was presumed that their social organization could be characterized as 'stone age'. Hence the titles of some books of the period, including for example an early and in many ways valuable study of the Kikuyu of Kenya – *With a prehistoric people*.[2]

The pioneer of social anthropology was Lewis H. Morgan (1818–81). As a young man he became interested in the indigenous people of his home state of New York – the Ho-de-no-sau-nee, known to white Americans as the Iroquois – and he studied their social organization and that of other North American Indian peoples at intervals during a lifetime primarily devoted to the law.[3] Most of the early observations in social anthropology were indeed the work of people who, like Morgan, were not trained full-time social scientists, and they notably included missionaries and colonial administrators whose work took them to far-away places (from a European point of view) like Africa or the Pacific. Some of their studies reached a high level of detail and accuracy. For example there are the accounts of the Melanesians by Bishop Codrington,[4] of the Baganda by the Rev. John Roscoe,[5] and of various Australian tribes by Sir Baldwin Spencer (a professor of zoology) and Mr F. J. Gillen (a Government official).[6] It was not until the 1880s that the first full-time study of a 'primitive' people by a trained observer was carried out by the American Franz Boas among the Eskimo.[7] The first British anthropological expedition, that of A. C. Haddon, C. G. Seligman and their companions to the Torres Straits in 1898–9, also collected data on the social organization as well as the physical characteristics (such as skull shapes) and the technology of the peoples they visited.*

The search for human origins among the so-called 'primitive' peoples during the nineteenth century took place at the same time as the first fact-finding studies among European peasants and the working class in towns. As early as the 1840s a Belgian mining engineer named Frederic le Play (1806–82) was studying the life, and especially the family life, of the peasants among whom he had first lived as a lodger on his travels. Later, with support from the French government, he was able to give himself full-time to such studies.[8] In England, earlier and rather impressionistic studies of the life of the London poor were followed in the 1880s by the minutely thorough work of Charles Booth (1840–1916), a wealthy Liverpool shipowner who was also a distinguished statistician, and his assistants. Though the search for origins was lacking in these cases the underlying motive for such studies was closely similar to the pioneer studies in anthropology: to investigate and report upon areas of human social life which, though not in the strict sense unknown – and Booth in particular said explicitly that 'every fact I needed was known to some one and that the information had simply to be collected and put together' – were unknown, or not well enough known, to science.[9]

The sociological theorists of the late nineteenth and early twentieth century, therefore, had a wide range of comparative data about the social life of non-European peoples available to them, as well as knowing a good deal about their own societies. Of the four major theorists of the period 1890–1920, two – Max Weber and

*The results of the Torres Straits expedition were published in numerous papers extending almost to Haddon's death in 1940.

Pareto – made little use of this information, but it figured promi-
nently in the work of Emile Durkheim and L. T. Hobhouse.
Indeed, Durkheim's fourth and possibly greatest work, *Elementary
forms of the religious life*, consists essentially of an analysis of the field
material of Spencer and Gillen on the magico-religious beliefs and
practices of the Australian peoples they had studied. This aimed at
discovering the essential social function of religion in its simplest
form; that is, in a society with a simple social organization, and in
which religion is uncomplicated by the existence of a separate
special institution, a specialized priesthood, a body of scripture
leading to doctrinal complications, and above all a historical tradition of change and development in religious ideas and organization. Durkheim also made use of anthropologists' findings in his
earlier work, investigating the differences between societies with a
complex system of division of labour and simpler societies in
which most men perform the same tasks.[10] Somewhat similarly,
Hobhouse's use of anthropological material was as examples of the
way in which important human institutions – marriage, morals,
social class – worked in societies at a lower or simpler level of
evolution.[11] Hobhouse, in collaboration with Wheeler and Ginsberg, carried out an exhaustive statistical analysis of the then
known information on the social institutions of 'the simpler
societies' (as they called them), correlating, for example, the
prevalence of slavery with the level of technological control of the
environment[12] (see chapter 5). Until about the time of the First
World War the approach remained strongly evolutionary.

   The evolutionary approach in sociology, however, did not last
long once full-time field-work, in the modern sense, was developed. Here the important pioneers were A. R. Radcliffe-Brown
(1881–1955), whose first field studies were among the Andaman
Islanders in 1906–8,[13] and Bronislaw Malinowski (1884–1942),
whose major field studies were carried out in Kiriwina (on the
Melanesian islands known to Europeans as the Trobriands) in
1914–18.[14] In particular, Malinowski expressed his opinion of the
inadequacy of the evolutionary view as a guide to field-work in
forceful terms. He regarded in a similar way the so-called diffusionist view, which was concerned with the way in which particular 'culture traits' – tools, ways of doing things, designs, or even
customs – had been copied, or learned, and so had diffused or
spread from one people to another. The evolutionary view invited

him to regard a tool, such as a digging-stick, or a custom, such as matrilocal marriage, merely as a quaint survival of a stone-age type of existence, a living fossil of an earlier state of society. The diffusionist invited him to inquire from whom the people he was studying had learned or copied the way of digging with a stick, or the custom of matrilocal marriage. Yet for a field-worker living among and making friends with Melanesians, both points of view seemed inadequate. It seemed far more interesting and sensible to study their way of life as a vital, viable response to the problems of living faced by all men everywhere. The digging-stick was for them clearly not a quaint survival but the essential implement in their way of raising crops and living from one crop to the next. As for matrilocal marriage, when a man and a woman marry they must live somewhere; roughly speaking with his family, with hers, or in a new household on their own. What, in Kiriwina society, prompted the choice of the second of the three possibilities? Questions like these seemed more relevant than references to a presumed matriarchal stage of the evolution of marriage of which matrilocality was to be regarded as a survival. Upon investigation along these lines, according to Malinowski, it would frequently turn out that the explanation for one institution would be found in its relation to another. Digging-stick agriculture would be related to a land tenure system that could not be viewed in isolation from a system of chieftainship, which was in turn related to a kinship system including matrilocal marriage. In other words, the social life and the technology of a primitive people – or for that matter any people – would best be understood as a system of interrelated institutions, functioning together in such a way that minimum human needs were met – such as the needs for food, shelter, the care of the young, the maintenance of health, and the allaying of anxieties about things beyond human control.

The functionalist view, as it came to be called, represented a great break-through for social anthropology and had its effects also in sociology. A number of the pupils of Radcliffe-Brown and Malinowski, who taught at various British and American universities in the period 1920–40, proceeded to carry out field studies of a standard never since surpassed; and the functionalist view, which prompted them to look for the relations between different customs and institutions, and to search for connections if they were not immediately apparent, undoubtedly played a great part in developing so high a standard of field-work. Moreover, it had other consequences. The view of non-European peoples as 'primitive' receded. Many of the investigators of this period stressed the way in which the cultures they were studying were adapted to meeting human needs and were internally consistent and well adjusted. But though non-Europeans were not now seen as primitive, they were still seen as different. Indeed, the whole interest and value of their cultures, for the anthropologists, lay in their difference from that of their own western European and North American societies. As Margaret Mead wrote:

If a long line of devoted biologists had been breeding guinea-pigs or fruit-flies for a hundred years and recording the results, and some careless vandal burnt the painstaking record and killed the survivors, we would cry out in anger at the loss to science. Yet, when history, without any such set purpose has presented us with the results of not a hundred years' experiment on guinea-pigs, but a thousand years' experiment on human beings we permit the records to be extinguished without a protest. Although most of these fragile cultures which owed their perpetuation not to written records but to the memories of a few hundred human beings are lost to us, a few remain. Isolated on small Pacific islands, in dense African jungles or Asiatic wastes, it is still possible to find untouched societies which have chosen solutions of life's problems different from our own which can give us precious evidence on the malleability of human nature.

Such an untouched people are the brown sea-dwelling Manus of the Admiralty Islands north of New Guinea.[15]

For anthropologists in the 1920s and 1930s the search was for 'untouched societies' in which they aimed to be, if not the first European visitors, at least among the first, before administrators, missionaries, traders and labour recruiters had upset the balance and set in train changes that were bound to have unforeseen repercussions right round the whole of native societies and cultures.

This point of view, too, was in general accord with that of many sympathetic, liberal-minded European colonial administrators, and with the policy, put into practice in various parts of the European colonial empires, of indirect rule. Functionalist anthropologists were not always or entirely against change, and their personal knowledge, friendship and respect for members of the tribes they studied were enough to safeguard them against the apartheid ideology as it later emerged. Many of them were quick to expose the hypocrisy of policies and attitudes embodied in phrases like 'separate development'. Yet a feeling that it was right to temper change, to safeguard native peoples against its more disruptive effects, accorded well with the indirect rule idea, which Malinowski and several of his pupils publicly endorsed.[16] Anthropology had to change its own ideas again (as we shall see later) before it could study social changes as rapid and fundamental as those taking place in Africa since the Second World War.

The golden age of social anthropology had, further, important effects upon the development of sociology. On the side of empirical research, the impressive achievements of social anthropologists during the 1920s and 1930s led to its being commonly said that 'we' knew more about the cultures and ways of life of people in remote Pacific islands or African forests than we did of 'our own' (western European and American) culture. Some American and European sociologists accordingly set out to emulate those achievements by doing studies, along the lines of anthropological field studies, of western urban societies. One of the earliest such studies was that by Robert and Helen Lynd in 1924–5 of the American town to which they give the fictitious name of 'Middletown'. In his foreword the anthropologist Clark Wissler calls it 'a pioneer attempt to deal with a sample American community after the manner of social anthropology'.[17] Another American, W. Lloyd Warner, was trained as an anthropologist under Radcliffe-Brown and in 1926–9 carried out a field study of an Australian aboriginal tribe in purposeful preparation for the study of American urban society, to which he proceeded in the 1930s.[18] In Britain, too, the success and prestige of social anthropology provided part of the impetus for the founding in the 1930s of the organization named Mass Observation, one of whose founders, Tom Harrisson, had had field experience in the Pacific.[19]

A second effect upon sociology was the adoption of functionalism as a theoretical approach. This took place somewhat later, in the late 1940s and early 1950s, and led to intense controversy. At that time, indeed, the great debate in sociology was that between the functionalist approach, in which society was seen as a system of interrelated parts kept together by consensus, and an opposed view which laid more stress on conflict and saw society as held together in the last resort by coercion. This controversy is referred to several times later in this book; it is dealt with directly in chapter 7, while it also affects the two possible ways of looking at social class, as we see in chapter 6.

A third consequence was the exploration of the borderline between sociology and social anthropology through the study, by methods like those of social anthropologists in the field, of western peasant societies. Robert Redfield (1897–1958) was a pioneer of this type of study. He found a continuity which he named the 'folk–urban continuum' between the life of primitive people and modern western society, a continuum along which an important intermediate point was represented by peasant societies, like those which he studied in rural Mexico.[20] (I take up this idea more fully in chapter 5.) Similar studies were done, by Arensberg and Kimball, among Irish peasants in County Clare,[21] and by Redfield's pupil Horace Miner in the French-Canadian village of St Denis and also in rural communities in the United States and modern West Africa.[22] Miner also attempted to settle whether it is urbanism itself, or western cultural influence, that makes town life in developing countries the centre of the characteristic social changes with which we are familiar. Thus the study of western peasant communities could be complemented by the study of non-western towns, and the problem for research was to find a town that was free from distinctively western cultural influence. Of a very short list of possible towns, Miner chose Timbuctoo, which, though under nominal French rule at the time, had hardly been affected by either colonial administration or Christian missionary influence.[23]

Meanwhile, however, anthropology had not been standing still. The great wave of field-workers, pupils of Radcliffe-Brown and Malinowski, who set off in the 1920s and 1930s in search of 'untouched societies', included some, like Raymond Firth, who succeeded in their quest, and were able to carry out functionalist analyses of societies in which change was not yet a seriously disruptive force.[24] Others, however, and especially some of those who came to Africa, had a different experience. For example, Audrey Richards, whose field-work among the Bemba of Zambia (or Northern Rhodesia, as it was then called) began in 1930, was already, by the late thirties, studying the changed form of marriage as practised among the Bemba miners on the Copperbelt.[25] By the late 1930s, the Rhodes-Livingstone Institute (now the Institute for Social Research, University of Zambia) was in the van of a new approach in anthropology, associated with the names of Max

Gluckman,[26] J. Clyde Mitchell,[27] and above all Godfrey and Monica Wilson, whose little book on social change was an extremely important pointer, far ahead of its time, to developments in sociological and anthropological thought that took place in the 1950s and 1960s.[28]

What, in essence, was the nature of this new approach? Functionalism had been a great step forward in its time because it rejected the view that customs and culture-traits were of interest as survivals of an earlier stage of development. Its concentration on the here and now – on what, in technical terms, was called a *synchronous* analysis, an analysis at one moment in time – was well suited to the study of small scale, geographically isolated, and non-literate societies; for, as we have seen, it led to the search for the principles of integration, the ways in which things worked together to meet basic human needs. Since non-literate societies had no written records they had, in the strict sense, no history; and since conjecture about origins was rightly seen as a waste of time, and things could be assumed not to change very much during the two years or so of a conventional field trip, a synchronous 'this is how it works here and now' analysis was quite appropriate.

In areas like Zambia, or Buganda (where Lucy Mair, another of Malinowski's pupils, made a field study early in the 1930s),[29] however, the fact of change was too pervasive to be ignored. In such areas, to ignore a time dimension was not only silly, it was also unnecessary, for these were precisely the areas in which a certain amount of written history existed – true, not over a very long time-span, but at least since the first European colonial officials and missionaries kept records and diaries, and since the first Africans learned to write, and court records, diaries, and a vernacular press became available. At the same time, some anthropologists began to study oral history; and later, in the 1950s, anthropologists began to enter a new kind of partnership with historians, and became interested, not in pseudo-history in the old evolutionary tradition, but real history. Their studies, in a word, became *diachronic*.

An excellent example of the new approach is afforded by the various studies which have been done over the years in the Kingdom of Buganda. As we noted above, the Baganda were the subject of one of the classic studies of early missionary anthropology, that of Roscoe. In the 1930s they were again studied, this

time by one of the new wave, schooled in the functionalist
approach, yet well aware of the fact of change, which permeates
the whole of Mair's book. The team of social anthropologists who,
in the 1950s and early 1960s, turned their attention to the Kingdom from the East African Institute of Social Research at Kampala,
were accordingly able to give their study a truly historical depth
from the beginning. In addition to the books of Roscoe and Mair,
there were the writings in Luganda of Sir Apolo Kagwa on the
clans, the customs and the kings of the Baganda[30] and a wide range
of other documentary material, including the official records of the
British government of the Uganda Protectorate, the memoirs of
various important government officials and missionaries, official
and missionary papers, letters, diaries, and the private papers of a
number of leading Baganda, past and present. In the face of such
rich documentation a synchronous functionalist analysis of
Buganda in the 1950s would clearly have been ludicrously inadequate. In addition to seeing things as they were and how they
fitted together it was clearly both possible and important to see
how they had got the way they were and how the past had shaped
the institutions of the present during a century of change. Social
anthropologists, historians, political scientists, geographers, economists and psychologists accordingly collaborated in a series of
books and published papers. The effects of economic change – the
success of cotton and coffee as peasant cash crops, and the associated labour migrations of other tribes into Buganda – were analysed by economic historians, anthropologists, and a geographer.[31]
A historian and a political scientist collaborated in a study of what
they termed British overrule, a textbook instance of the indirect
rule policy, and its consequences.[32] Another political scientist put
Buganda into a wider setting and related its politics to those of
Uganda as a whole.[33] And finally, anthropologists, a psychologist
and an economic historian drew together the associated social
changes in kinship, land tenure, and the system of rank and
leadership, bringing the story up to the eve of independence in
1962.[34]

There could hardly be a clearer demonstration of how far social
anthropology has moved from the crudely evolutionary ideas with
which it began in the last century. The word 'primitive' has been
dropped altogether. Richards, Fallers, and their fellow-workers
were, quite clearly, interested in the social system of the Baganda,

and in the changes that have taken place in their society as an interesting subject of study in its own right.

Yet if social anthropology cannot now be defined as the study of primitive society, what is its distinctive subject-matter? What now separates it from sociology, the study of society without a qualifying adjective? What – if not an outright merger – is the new relation between the two subjects?

At the present time, it does not seem possible to give a short or simple answer to this question. Different sociologists and anthropologists would answer it differently. Although no formal line can now be drawn and although, as we have seen, there is a well-developed tradition of work at the shadowy margin between the two subjects, there remain differences in approach, in tradition, and in method. To some extent social anthropologists prefer to study a society as a whole, whereas most sociologists work on particular problems or institutions. Thus an anthropologist will still study (say) the Luguru of Tanzania, whereas a sociologist will more typically be at work on recruitment to the theological colleges in England. Secondly, the literature and traditions of the two subjects, though they overlap, are appreciably different. Durkheim seems to be common to both but university students of social anthropology may be required to read the works of Morgan, Robertson Smith, and Rivers, which would not be included in most sociology reading lists, while sociologists are called on to study the works of Parsons and Weber, which are not usually required of anthropologists. Thirdly, and perhaps most important, is the distinctive field method of social anthropology, which will be described in more detail in the next chapter. All who have undergone it agree that there is no substitute for the experience of camping in some remote spot, learning a language with little or no written grammar, coming to terms with the members of a small, isolated local community and learning their ways and their social structure by direct observation and partially participating in their life. Although a few sociologists, too, have adopted a rather similar method, the field experience of most sociologists is different. In many cases it consists of knocking on doors, interview schedule in hand, in some city suburb, and there are sociologists who manage without field-work altogether. There is, accordingly, a type of society to which the field methods developed by social anthropologists in the golden age of the 1920s and 1930s are uniquely applicable. We now see that it is incorrect to use the word 'primitive' of such societies; more accurately, they are small-scale societies in which a single-handed investigator, in one or two years, can get to know everybody and virtually everything that matters. From this point of view, a French-Canadian village is no less small scale than a remote village in the Cameroons or a Pacific island. This new view of the scope and the value of social anthropology is well summed up in two phrases of John Beattie: small-scale societies, and other cultures.[35]

This view has the further great advantage of finally removing any suggestion that social anthropology is the study of 'colonial peoples' – or, even more bluntly, the study of dark-skinned peoples by scientists of European descent.

It is true that there may be some value in the study of culture by strangers. From this point of view, an Englishman may not be the best person to study some aspects of English society, because he takes too much for granted. Just as the onlooker may see the game more clearly than any of the players, so it may take a stranger to perceive the meaning, the inter-connections, even the peculiarity, of ways of doing things that a native Englishman takes for granted about his own particular society. It was for this reason that the definitive and monumental study of the position of Afro-Americans in American society was carried out neither by an Afro-American nor a white American, but by a Swedish economist.[36] From this point of view, studies I have already cited – that of the English-speaking American Horace Miner in a French-Canadian village, and by the Americans Arensberg and Kimball in a parish in Ireland – were done as much by strangers as Malinowski's field work on the Trobriand Islands or Beattie's in the kingdom of Bunyoro. In the same way, recent studies by Indian anthropologists, mostly of a cosmopolitan Hindu background, have been done of tribal communities in India.[37] Chinese anthropologists have carried out studies of Chinese villages and small towns, while a social anthropologist of West Indian descent has studied immigrant communities in Britain, including Arabs and Chinese.[38] In Africa, I have already mentioned the work of Professor K. A. Busia, and there seems no reason to doubt that future generations of social scientists will enlarge their understanding of 'other cultures' by means of field study both within their own continent and beyond its shores. The process has already begun. A study of Black Muslims in the United States by a Nigerian social scientist affords an apt example of the African academic counter-offensive.[39]

SUGGESTIONS FOR FURTHER READING

N. S. Timasheff, *Sociological theory, its nature and growth* (New York, Random House, 1955). A standard work on the development of sociology, especially in the nineteenth century, and the ideas of the early sociologists.

H. E. Barnes, *An introduction to the history of sociology* (University of Chicago Press, 1965). An encyclopaedic work of reference on the great sociologists of the past.

B. Malinowski, *A scientific theory of culture* (Chapel Hill, N. C., University of North Carolina Press, 1944). The most explicit and comprehensive statement of Malinowski's functionalist view.

A. R. Radcliffe-Brown, *Structure and function in primitive society* (London, Cohen and West, 1952).

J. H. M. Beattie, *Other cultures* (London, Cohen and West, 1964). The thoughtful statement by a modern social anthropologist of the position and value of his science in an age in which the word 'primitive' has ceased to be acceptable.

CHAPTER 3

What sociologists do

It will already have become clear to the reader that sociology is a very wide subject. The things that different sociologists do are very different, so much so that it is not always easy to see how they are related. To take two extreme cases, sociologist A spends almost all his time reading the books and articles written by other sociologists, and from time to time writes books himself on subjects like 'How far were Max Weber's ideas influenced by those of Karl Marx?', or 'Is a classless society possible?' Sociologist B, on the other hand, has little time for reading; he spends his days in the headquarters office of a business firm, designing questionnaires and organizing interviewers to find out whether people have heard that Solso soap washes whiter, or how they intend to vote at the next election. Yet both would call themselves sociologists, and would be acceptable as members of a learned body such as the British or American Sociological Association.

In this chapter I will try to list, with examples, the range of activities carried on under the name of sociology and to see the common thread that runs through them all. As before I use the word sociology as short for sociology-and-social-anthropology.

I will begin by dividing the activities of sociologists into fact-finding and theory. As we shall see this distinction is nowadays less important than it was in the past and will have to be blurred somewhat later. Though some sociologists may specialize in one or the other, many carry out both fact-finding and theoretical work at different times and may switch from one to the other in the course of a single piece of work.

FACT-FINDING

1. *Three types of social survey*

A great deal of the work of sociologists consists of finding out facts by asking people. I have already quoted the famous remark of Charles Booth that 'Every fact I needed was known to someone'[1] and following on the method which he originated of the survey of urban social conditions the art of the social survey has become very highly developed. Booth and his immediate successor Rowntree, in York, carried out their surveys by collecting information about every household in the area under study. The next great development was when Sir Arthur Bowley, in surveys of some other English towns in 1912–13, realized that equally great statistical precision at far less cost in time and effort could be gained by sampling. By taking about one household in twenty, with great care to avoid a biased choice and ensure that the sample was random and representative, he was able to estimate the proportion of households in poverty and other facts at little more than one-twentieth of the cost of visiting every house.[2]

In a much more haphazard way, and for a different purpose, sampling surveys were also being developed in the United States at about this period. Here the interest was in forecasting the results of elections – at which, in the American system, large numbers of state and municipal workers might lose their jobs as a result of a change from a Democratic to a Republican majority, or vice versa, in the local legislature. The first rough-and-ready 'straw polls' go back as early as 1824. In the early 1900s the *Literary Digest* magazine attempted to make election forecasting more reliable by sending out large numbers of ballot cards through the mail to people listed, for example, in telephone directories or the registers of car owners, asking the recipients to fill in how they intended to vote, and mail back the card at the magazine's expense. Such samples, of course, were unrepresentative, since car owners and telephone subscribers tended to be among the wealthiest people, and the results of some polls in the 1920s and 1930s were badly wrong for that reason.[3] By adopting sounder methods of sampling, however, some American firms like the Gallup and Crossley organizations were making reasonably reliable forecasts of election results as early as the 1930s and today only a very closely contested election or a totally unexpected last-minute swing of opinion seriously upsets the forecasts of the polls.

The modern social survey arises from the coming together of the British urban social survey, with its primary interest in poverty and social problems, and the American public opinion poll. As I have hinted, many modern social survey organizations are business firms. From time to time, and especially in the weeks before an election in multi-party democratic countries like America, Britain, and western European states, they survey public opinion on political issues and recoup their costs by selling the results to newspapers and broadcasting organizations, for which they have 'news value'. At other times, they make money by means of market research – a rather wide term which means assessing for manufacturers and other business firms the market for their products and the effectiveness of their advertising. By arranging a steady flow of work, it is possible to maintain a more or less permanent organization carrying out a survey or two every week. A typical organization of this sort might have several hundred or even up to a thousand part-time interviewers, mostly young married women, of whom perhaps 250 to 300 would be employed on any one survey. With each interviewing some ten to fifteen people, the size of the sample would be around 2,500 to 3,000, which, provided there is no bias in the selection, should give results that can be reasonably relied upon within a possible margin of error of about two per cent.[4] A small headquarters staff to design the questionnaires and a statistical department to analyse the results are kept in reasonably steady employment if the firm gets enough commissions from manufacturers, retailers and so on. Not all such organizations, however, are business firms operating for profit. Some governments, such as that in Britain, maintain social survey departments and there are also organizations with the special function of assessing the size and reaction of audiences to the mass media or radio and television for the guidance of the broadcasting authorities.

Such social survey organizations may, from time to time, contribute to sociological research in a more fundamental sense by being employed by university research workers as an alternative to 'do-it-yourself' surveys, with student interviewers, carried out by the staffs of sociology departments in their spare time. A notable example was the study of Professor David Glass and his fellow-workers on the subject of social mobility in Britain, the field-work for which was carried out by the Government Social Survey, the cost being defrayed by a grant from the Nuffield Foundation.[5] I shall discuss the results of this survey in chapter 6.

Since the time of Booth, Rowntree and Bowley, the term 'social survey' has also come to be used in two other senses: a general descriptive study of the life of a local community, usually a town; and an investigation into the extent, nature and causes of a particular social problem.

The urban social survey owes much to American, as well as British, pioneers. 'Middletown', which I mentioned in the last chapter, still represents a model of its kind, while the detailed studies of Chicago life by the famous school of sociology there in the period 1915–40 were also influential.[6] Many hundreds of urban surveys must now have been conducted, including a considerable number in Africa. I mention some examples at the the end of chapter 6.

In addition to their intrinsic interest such studies are often sought after by administrators for the information they yield on social problems in the town – poverty, bad housing, insanitary living conditions, crime and prostitution. They are also vital to town planners for the essential information they give on the various functions of the different parts of the town and for guidance on how conditions can be improved without stifling the life of the place. For the same reason some public authorities, concerned with rehousing or redeveloping urban areas, include sociologists among their staffs to advise on social development and avoid the kind of mistake that is made when (for example) shops are sited inconveniently far from houses, or destructive behaviour by children results from lack of a space where they can play legitimately.

A third type of social survey is concerned with a particular social problem, and the investigator is usually trying to assess its size or prevalence, analyse its causes and make suggestions for public action for its remedy or alleviation. Sometimes the methods of sampling and interviewing may be appropriate; for example, Professor Townsend for his study of family life, poverty, and dependence upon state aid among old people in London drew a quasi-random sample from doctors' lists and interviewed his subjects.[7] An African example of a social problem survey was that carried out in 1961 on juvenile prostitutes in Nairobi. The main field-work, in this case, was done in their spare time by a group of social workers, the survey being directed and the report prepared by Julius Carlebach of the Child Welfare Society of Kenya. Sampling was not practicable and the field-workers drew upon the case files of the girl prostitutes who were already known to them, while further information was obtained by questioning British soldiers attending a V.D. clinic about the girls who might have infected them. In this it was possible to amass a great deal of information about the characteristics of young prostitutes – their age, educational standard, dress, ability to speak English, cleanliness and physical development – while a detailed description could also be written of their social circumstances and the way in which they practised. The recommendations lay stress on the need for training facilities in more suitable occupations; 'we are dealing', it states, 'not so much with depraved as with deprived youngsters' whose chief need is for the security, affection, and training which they have hitherto been denied.[8]

2. *Field-work in social anthropology*

In contrast to the brief and somewhat superficial relationship between the interviewer and subject, which characterizes social survey methods, the standard method of field-work in social anthropology aims to immerse the field-worker almost totally in the society being studied, so that he or she gets to know a small number of people well and has the opportunity to observe their actions over an appreciable span of time – waking up in the morning, going to work, cooking, cultivating, engaging in festivals or the settlement of cases, or just joining in village talk. As we have seen this method was perfected in the 1920s and 1930s by the generation of anthropologists who were the pupils of Malinowski and Radcliffe-Brown. It has been followed since without much modification, except that field-workers of the new generation try to validate their conclusions statistically, and may even, while in the field, carry out studies of the survey type. But the basic aims and methods remain the same.

Assuming that he or she is a stranger to the area, the field-worker generally has two immediate problems on arrival: to set up house, and to learn the language. In order to save themselves the time of doing domestic chores most field-workers employ one or two local people as domestic staff, who may also act as advisers on some aspects of relations with the local people, for example on the etiquette of giving and receiving presents and visits. A household is set up, sometimes in a tent, more often in a local government rest camp, mission school, or some such building. Some field-workers have had houses built for themselves in the local style, remunerating the builders appropriately in cash or kind. The next task is to learn the language. This will be comparatively easy if it is one which has already been committed to writing and in which there is a published grammar and dictionary, and field-workers in areas where (for example) Swahili is spoken can come already prepared by a few months' study in their home countries, for example in Britain at the School of Oriental and African Studies in London. In some cases, however, the field-workers may have to practise the difficult art of learning the language by ear. Proficiency is vital. It is obviously important that field-workers should understand properly all that is addressed to them. Less obviously, perhaps, they may find 'overheards', remarks not intended for their ears, more revealing still of some aspects of social relations. For the first few months, then, the social anthropologist must arrange language tuition. A local person such as a teacher or government clerk may be engaged as interpreter, and may also help in the early stages with introductions to people and with the first outlines of the local social structure. It is very important, though, to get over this stage as soon as possible. Helpful as local assistants can be, they can also be an embarrassment and a source of bias. Inevitably, as members of the local society themselves, they will present a one-sided view of certain aspects of it: the Christian view, perhaps, of the magico-religious life, or one clan's view of a disputed case. As soon as possible the field-worker should become self-reliant, though many have found that assistants can make a most valuable contribution later in the research, when the anthropologist knows what information is needed and can double or treble the rate at which it is collected by employing a local assistant or two.

Having begun to learn the language, the field-worker will then generally begin to collect basic information about the people in the locality. A common practice is to do a kind of small-scale census, finding out everybody's name and clan, who is related to whom, who lives in whose household, what land they cultivate, and so on. This information will form the basis for the chapters about the kinship system in the book which will eventually be written. Meanwhile it will point to questions for further inquiry. For example, it will quickly become apparent whether people trace descent through the father or the mother, and whether wives join their husbands' households at marriage or vice versa. This will prompt questions about, for instance, how far a woman becomes a member of her husband's clan, in what circumstances she can leave him and return home, what property she can own, and her rights of inheritance. The answers to these questions may be obtained a little later, when the field-worker's fluency in the language is sufficient for intelligent conversation with people who have had such experiences. He or she may have to wait till disputed cases come before a court to see on what principle they are decided.

From kinship and the everyday routine of life – cultivating, cooking, bringing up children – the field-worker may move on to study the system of law and authority. At this point, and possibly during the second year in the field, he or she may decide to move from the ordinary village or community where work began to the court or capital of a chief or council. Generally it is a mistake to begin there, for people usually speak less freely to a person closely associated with authority. Once the anthropologist has established his or her independence, however, it is often a good place to go. At this stage, too, modern anthropologists often find written records of great value, including, for example, court records during and since the colonial period, the archives of the colonial administration relating to the district, mission records and the vernacular press. It is at this later stage that modern field-workers often try to put their data into statistical form and carry out surveys to establish, for example, what proportion of men have more than one wife, how many of the households occupy plots of land of different acreages, what is the incidence of divorce, how long have men and women been to school, and similar information.

Two years is regarded as about the right length of time for a field study. Some anthropologists have done good studies in one year but this is generally possible only if they already know the language. Firth, for example, spent one year on the island of Tikopia on his classic first field visit, but he already knew Maori, a closely similar language, and was thoroughly conversant with other Polynesian cultures.[9] A visit of one year, too, involves the risk that the year chosen may be for some reason quite exceptional because of drought or floods, or some unusual political disturbance.

At the end of a year or two the field-worker goes home to his or her university with (as Beattie describes) 'a suitcase full of files containing . . . enough material in the shape of notes, texts, and figures to occupy me for years'.[10] The process of digesting, analysing, and preparing the data for publication then follows. Most field-work is done by young graduates on a post-graduate research grant from their parent university or a research foundation. Some such grants provide for a few months' writing-up time after field-work, though the process in fact takes years rather than months; some grant-awarding bodies make no such provision, and the preparation of the material has to be done in the field-worker's spare time from a university teaching post. Many field-workers prepare their material initially as a thesis for a higher degree, M.A. or Ph.D., and this takes a year or two. Eventually it finds its way to the public, including the people among whom the field-work was done, in the form of either a book or of articles in learned journals. The delays are usually long. Seldom less than five years, sometimes twenty or more, may elapse between the end of a field visit and the publication of the results.[11]

With what motives do social anthropologists do field-work? The answer 'To get a Ph.D.', though true enough in many cases, is not really adequate. We still have to explain why bright young scholars should choose social anthropology rather than some other academic subject as an outlet for their talents. Field studies by the standard method may be undertaken to fill in gaps in the ethnographic maps. For example, during the 1950s, field-workers associated with the East African Institute of Social Research carried out studies among all the important tribes of Uganda and most of those of Kenya. During the 1960s, accordingly, it seemed sensible to devote the major attention to Tanzania, where modern (or indeed any) accounts existed of only a few of the 130 or so recognized tribes. However, merely to go on adding another tribe to the list – after the Luguru, the Pokomo, after the Pokomo, the Gogo, and so on, almost for ever – can become a little uninspiring, and this is not the only motive for field-work. Another, more important in some cases than others, is a sense that it is urgent to record quickly a culture and way of life that is about to change radically in the foreseen future. Thus, when the Kariba scheme was planned, it was immediately clear that the way of life of the valley Tonga would be drastically changed within a few years, as the people were physically moved out of the areas to be flooded and taught a new way of life based on fishing in the lake behind the Kariba dam. A series of studies of these people was carried out as a matter of urgency by the Rhodes-Livingstone Institute (since re-named the University of Zambia Institute for Social Research).[12] Similar studies of 'disappearing cultures' have been carried out, or urgently called for, in many other parts of the world, and an issue of the *International Social Science Bulletin* in 1957 was devoted to this.[13] Thirdly, many anthropologists are concerned both to amass information (a vital part of any scientific activity) and to test out new ideas, theories, and points of view. In studying one particular chosen society, a field-worker may wish to consider whether any light is shed on it by an idea such as segmentary structure, which influenced many anthropologists following Evans-Pritchard's study of the Nuer.* Having learned the language and the basic social structure of one society, a social anthropologist may well be able to take part in organized schemes in which a number of field-workers collected data in a standardized way, so that valid comparisons are possible. A number of social anthropologists in East Africa in the 1950s, for example, collected information about the positions and career histories of chiefs, enabling a comparative study to be published.[14]

In the foregoing account the field method of social anthropology has been described in the form in which it has developed over the last forty years or so. During this period literally hundreds of field studies have been done, broadly along the lines I have here outlined, as the reader may see by looking at the social anthropology section of his university library. As I explained in the last chapter, most field-work, hitherto, had been done by scientists of European or American descent among peoples in Asia, Africa and the Pacific. The method that has been developed bears some marks of its origins in a social and political situation which is now disappear-

*A segmentary structure is one in which larger groups (e.g. clans) are divided into smaller sub-groups (e.g. lineages). Men of different lineages might dispute, but the clan would unite against another clan. See the section on descent groups in the next chapter; see also E. E. Evans-Pritchard, *The Nuer* (1941).

ing. Whether the end of the colonial era means the end of field studies of this type, however, is doubtful. Small-scale societies, for which this is the appropriate method of study, still exist in great profusion while, at the same time, there is no lack of social scientists eager to carry out such studies. In such a situation skin colour is completely irrelevant. If American, British and European anthropologists and sociologists study African societies there is no reason why African social scientists should not do so too – or indeed return the compliment by studying groups in America, for example – I mentioned that at least one Nigerian social scientist has already done so. In so far as this occurs it seems fairly safe to suggest that the experience and the methods of study developed in the past will still be found valuable.

3. *Studies of past societies*

Field-work and social surveys alike are done among people who are alive. What happens if a sociologist wants to study a past society? We cannot interview people who are dead. Instead we must study their lives through whatever documentary evidence they may have left. (As we have seen, this limitation really precludes the study of non-literate societies of the past.) Naturally, this method has serious limitations. The documentary evidence is seldom complete and it may break off at just the most tantalizing point. However, sociologists have managed to piece together useful evidence on, for example, the social mobility of mandarins in traditional Chinese society,[15] Anglo-Saxon kinship,[16] and the changes that have occurred in the size and composition of English households over the last two or three hundred years.[17]

I have already mentioned, in chapter 1, a good example of historical sociology: the study by Banks of the social factors that led to a fall in the birth-rate in England after the 1870s.[18] In the 1950s, when Banks was working on this problem it was obviously too late to interview and question English parents of seventy or eighty years before. Statistical studies had already shown that the fall in the birth-rate began among the middle classes – not those at the very top of the social scale, but those in the ranks next below the top, professional men, civil servants, teachers, clerks and the like – and spread down the social scale, reaching the skilled and unskilled manual workers by the 1920s, though miners and

agricultural workers still tended to have larger families throughout. Banks' sources of information included the newspapers of the
time, both local and national, books on household management
and magazines read by the middle classes, which he scanned for
evidence of the incomes and expenditures of middle-class families
and the censuses and other official statistics of the period, such as
income tax returns. Banks also includes a detailed study of the
nineteenth-century English novelist Anthony Trollope, both in
terms of Trollope's own life as a civil servant who became a
successful novelist, and also of the middle-class attitudes to family
life which pervade his novels. A particularly dramatic event of the
time was the trial in 1876–7 of Charles Bradlaugh and Annie
Besant on charges arising from their publication of a book on birth
control methods, which made the middle classes generally aware
for the first time that such methods existed. It was not, however,
the first time that family limitation had been publicly discussed in
Britain. Earlier in the century, stimulated by the *Essay on population*
by the Rev. Thomas Malthus, the middle classes had concluded
that it was unwise to marry before a man could support a family
but, after marriage, as many children as God cared to send were
acceptable. The rapidly rising standard of life of the middle classes
from 1830 to 1870 made this a reasonable policy – hence the
proverbially large Victorian families of the period. After 1870,
however, a number of changes occurred. The so-called Great
Depression, unimportant though it was by the standard of the
slumps of the 1920s and 1930s, was enough of a check upon the
growth of middle-class incomes to call in question the wisdom of
having large families that could threaten the standard of living to
which they had become accustomed. A number of other changes
also made middle-class children more expensive to their parents.
The introduction of competitive examinations for entry to the civil
service and some other professions, the custom of sending all the
boys, and even some of the girls, to boarding schools, instead of
educating them at home, new habits like summer holidays by the
sea and the growing difficulty and expense of employing domestic
servants (consequent upon the enormous growth in numbers of the
middle class itself: with two or three servants to each middle-class
family in the late nineteenth century there were nearly two million
domestic servants in England, and they were the biggest single
occupational group[19]) all coincided to make Victorian middle-class

parents think again about the question of family limitation. Just at that moment the Bradlaugh-Besant trial showed them how.

In such a study, the distinction between historical sociology and social history is a fine one and perhaps not of the first importance. For our purpose the point is that to investigate so interesting and relevant a question as that which Banks studied, a sociologist must, so to speak, half turn himself into a historian, spend his time in libraries and archives and collect his data according to the methods and disciplines of a historian, while retaining a sociologist's interest in the proof or refutation of hypotheses about how social facts are related to one another.

4. *Experiment*

In a recently reported experiment, pregnant females gave birth in a laboratory. They were then, with their babies, randomly divided into two groups, one group receiving a normal diet while the other received a low-protein diet, and after weaning the young continued to be given the same diet for the duration of the experiment. Each of the two groups was then again divided into subgroups which were subjected to different environmental conditions. Some were isolated in conditions in which there was as little sensory stimulation as possible: 'The chambers produced a light-proof, sound-attenuated environment. Blowers provided air circulation and a continuous masking noise.' Others were kept in pairs with daily contact with their keepers, and were allowed to spend an hour a day with five playmates in a large play-space containing many toys. Careful records were taken both of their physical development and of their social behaviour, including such activities as touching each other, fighting, playing follow-my-leader, and the adventurous exploration of unfamiliar surroundings.

The experimenters concluded that

In all responses observed except the fighting response, whatever effect early malnutrition produced, its effect was always exaggerated by environmental isolation and depressed by environmental stimulation . . . Decreases in exploratory behaviour were also observed to result from early malnutrition. The fighting response, however, appears in contradiction. During the one-hour 'play' period of stimulation . . . the malnourished were observed to engage in considerably more fighting behaviour than their well-nourished controls.[20]

At this point the horrified reader may be reassured – these experiments were carried out, not on humans, but on rats. Such an example brings home to us the great difficulties of experimenting in so drastic a way with factors affecting social behaviour in humans. The most obvious considerations are ethical, and normal people in normal circumstances simply would not want to impose such conditions on their fellow human beings as to deprive them of normal food, isolate them in unnatural surroundings, or deprive children of the playthings and the opportunities for play that they need for their normal development. On the rare occasions when comparable experiments have been done on captive human subjects – as in some cases in the Nazi concentration camps in the 1940s – they have rightly been regarded as abominable crimes.

Even when this particular consideration does not apply, however, and when experiments can be devised that are not cruel, unjust, or otherwise objectionable, there still remains the difficulty that the people concerned will almost certainly know that they are being experimented on and may alter their behaviour in response to that knowledge. This difficulty became very clear in some classic early experiments on fatigue among industrial workers carried out by Elton Mayo in a factory near Chicago in the 1920s.[21] In one famous experiment, a small group of five girls assembling telephone components were separated from their fellow-workers in a small room in which, over a long period, their working conditions were experimentally changed – lighting was made bright and dim, rest-breaks were allowed or not, meal times were altered, and so on. No matter what changes were made, however, the girls' output improved. Even when their conditions were restored to exactly what they had been at the beginning of the experiment the improvement continued and the investigators were forced to conclude that the girls' reaction to being the centre of interest was so great that it exceeded and masked the effects of all other changes. Not that this experiment was regarded as a failure on that account. On the contrary, the result was important, both negatively in disposing of some earlier hypotheses about fatigue in industry, and positively in pointing the way to further research in industrial relations. But it illustrates well a real difficulty in doing a sociological experiment.

Nevertheless, there are two main ways in which sociologists

have sought to gain the benefits of experimental methods. Some genuine experiments have been done in laboratory conditions on the ways in which small groups interact and, with proper controls, it has sometimes been possible to isolate the effects of a particular social change upon the people subject to it.

The most notable series of laboratory experiments on small groups were those of Professor R. F. Bales of Harvard in the period 1946–9.[22] The arrangement adopted was of two adjoining rooms – one rather like a seminar room in a university building, in which the experimental groups met, the other rather like an adjoining tutor's room, where the observers were stationed. One-way glass separated the two rooms so that though the experimental groups in nearly every case knew that they were being observed their actions were undistracted by the observers' activities. Sound was transmitted by microphone and amplifier, with arrangements for recording if wanted. A fairly wide variety of groups was observed. These included self-consciously experimental groups, in which, for example, volunteers met to solve chess problems through group discussion and also real-life groups, such as those of ex-soldiers suffering from neurotic disorders, meeting weekly with their group therapist, students meeting their tutorial adviser, an academic seminar discussing an M.A. thesis and married couples jointly filling in a questionnaire about how they brought up their children, ran the home, etc. (The last-named was one of the few tests in which the subjects were observed unawares, their permission for the use of the record of their conversation being sought afterwards.)

The most difficult part of the research was to devise a system of categories into which the actions of members of the experimental groups could be classified by the observers at the necessary speed – actions in this case, as always, including verbal actions. Once this had been done, and observers trained, it was possible to analyse, for example, the work of the academic seminar, which, like other groups, showed a rather well-marked sequence. First, addressing the task in hand, the group tended to build up tensions among the members, which had to be resolved and relieved as time went on by more and more 'expressive' actions in an atmosphere of laughter and back-slapping solidarity. The method is, of course, limited to the kind of group activity that takes place in a room and usually by people sitting on chairs around a table. It would need considerable adaptation for studying, for instance, the activities of a group of miners underground or of soldiers on manoeuvres. Moreover the situation and the type of problems imposed by the limitations of the method do, it must be admitted, give the experimental situation a certain artificiality.

Nevertheless, with all its limitations, the method has achieved its modest successes, among them a very considerable refinement of the concept of leadership. Bales tended to assume, in his early experiments, that the leader could be identified as the person who initiated most action. Later, however, he began to relate the action-profile of members of his experimental groups with their popularity, as assessed by the others' responses to questions such as 'Who had the best ideas?' and 'Whom did you like best?' It began to emerge that the most active participant with the best ideas was not necessarily the best liked member of the group. People who were active and contributed ideas for solving the group's problem and yet remained popular were rather rare. Bales points out that theirs are the attributes of what in politics and history we call a 'great man'. More usually, in the absence of so gifted a person, there tend to be two leaders: the 'task specialist', or instrumental leader, who gets the job done at the cost of some unpopularity, and the 'social specialist', or expressive leader, who repairs the damage to group solidarity by being warm, responsive, and conciliatory. This analysis had the merit of being immediately applicable to the study of one particular small group, namely the nuclear family, for (as we see in the next chapter) in western society the husband/father conventionally assumes the role of instrumental leader and the wife/mother the expressive role.

Sometimes sociologists may take advantage of a particular change or innovation in society and study its effects, even though they do not control them, and thus carry out what may be termed a quasi-experiment. A good example of this was the study by Professor Himmelweit and her fellow-workers of the effects of the introduction of television in an English city, Norwich, in 1955–6, as part of a wider study of the effects of television upon children.[23] In such studies it is, of course, important to try to isolate the effects of the particular change being studied from other changes which may happen to occur at the same time. In the Norwich television study, all the children in two age-groups in Norwich schools (10–11 and 13–14) were asked a series of questions at school about their activities, tastes, ambitions and general knowledge. A year later, when the B.B.C. had completed a television transmitter in the area, the same children (that is, those who had not left school in the meantime) were retested. Some of the children now had television at home while others had not. Each child who now saw television regularly was matched with a non-viewing child of the same age, same sex, same social class (on a simple manual and non-manual division according to their fathers' occupations) and same intelligence as revealed by school I.Q. tests. In this way it was possible to remove any bias that might have arisen from the probability that, for example, the better-off non-manual families would have been the first to be able to afford television, and to compare the activities and attributes of two matched samples. Any other social changes affecting the population as a whole would presumably have shown up in both the samples, while the difference that television viewing made would show up among the viewers alone. In this way it was possible to isolate the effects of television from other coincidental social changes almost as rigorously as if the investigators had been able to control the whole situation, allowing some children to see television but keeping it from others.

A somewhat similar method has enabled sociologists to contribute to the discussion of another important issue of public policy, namely the question of whether the death penalty deters people from committing murder. At one time this seemed destined to be a matter of eternal controversy. Comparisons could be made between countries which imposed the death penalty and those which did not, for example between England and Switzerland in the 1920s; but these might fail to take into account significant national differences between the two countries. For example, it might be asserted, with very little hope of either proof or refutation, that the Swiss were less violent than the English, or that because towns in Switzerland are smaller the activities of criminal gangs are less serious there. If, on the other hand, studies were made of a single country before and after the abolition of the death penalty, such as Britain before and after 1965, these might be held to be falsified by other changes which happened to take place at the same time. For example, the abolition of the death penalty might occur at the same time as advances in surgery which preserve the lives of victims of murderous assaults, thus tending to reduce the murder rate without any real lowering in the level of violence or of murderous intention. However, while such studies were not conclusive, their general effect has been to cast serious doubt on the deterrent effect of the death penalty. But the most convincing evidence comes from the United States, where some states – including Rhode Island, Michigan, Wisconsin, and Minnesota – abolished the death penalty while others retained it. Comparisons could accordingly be made within a single nation between the trends in the murder rate in each of the abolitionist states and those in contiguous states which retained the death penalty. Thus Michigan's experience could be compared with those of Ohio and Indiana over a period of more than forty years, Rhode Island with Massachusetts and Connecticut, and similarly with the other abolitionist states. The result of these studies was to show that the murder rate in abolitionist states was just about the same as that in contiguous retentionist states. Moreover, the trends over time in the murder rate were also virtually identical in states with or without the death penalty. In the face of such findings it becomes hard to maintain that the death penalty makes any difference. Similar studies were also done of particular types of killing, such as those of police and prison officers. Here again, the results were the same; there was no significant difference in the rates between states with or without the death penalty, which can accordingly not be said to afford any protection to those officers. Such studies point to the same conclusion: that the death penalty has no deterrent effect.[24]

THEORY

It is the commonly accepted view of most sociologists that the collection of facts by itself is a rather pointless activity. To be most useful and significant the selection of the facts to be observed and their interpretation should be guided by a theory that is explicit and valid – a system of ideas, that is, about what facts are relevant and what are not and a set of hypotheses, or provisional ideas, to be proved or invalidated, about how the facts are related to one another. A good deal of the teaching young sociologists get in their undergraduate courses aims to equip them with just such a system of ideas, which, it is hoped, they will apply in their later studies and researches. At the same time the discovery of new facts, which goes on all the time, continually makes the revision of theoretical ideas necessary – the dropping of hypotheses that have proved wrong, the abandonment of concepts that have proved inappropriate or unhelpful in observing and understanding the real world of social phenomena and the trying out of new ideas. It follows that most sociologists are theorists for part of their time – they try to work out the system of ideas they need to do their research and revise them in the light of the facts they discover. Some sociologists spend most of their time on the side of theory and make their most notable contributions there.

From the beginnings of sociology until very recently it could broadly be said that there was a great gulf between theory on the one hand and observation and empirical research on the other. The early sociologists' theories were attempts to reach general laws or conclusions about the development of societies and the ways they worked. In attempting to be comprehensive they were so vague as to be incapable of being tested by observation or experiment and virtually useless as a guide to empirical research. We have already traced in some detail one such case, that of evolutionary theory, in the previous chapter. The proposition that societies evolve, or have evolved, is not one that can be tested by reference to observable facts; while, as we have seen, the evolutionary interpretation of the customs of non-western people proved of little value to the anthropological field-worker in guiding his observations or subsequently interpreting them. At the same time, empirical researches, like those of the English poverty studies or the American polls, went on unrelated to the systematic if grandiose ideas of Comte and Spencer on evolution, or Marx on class and class conflict.

Since about 1945, especially in the United States, serious attempts have been made to end this division and bring theory and research into a closer relation to one another. In part this movement has taken the form of a reconsideration of the older theories, with the aim of seeing if their grand concepts could be broken down into more manageable ideas suitable for empirical testing. The American sociologist Robert K. Merton, for example, has carried out a kind of syntactical analysis of the various uses of the word 'function' in social science – that derived from mathematics, for example, when we say that one thing is a function of another, or $y = f(x)$; that derived from physiology when we say that the function of an institution is to fulfill one or more specified needs; and so on – and has gone on to coin the word dysfunction, to mean the negative effects of an institution, the way in which it thwarts or counteracts another, or has a disruptive effect on the society as a whole. In another essay, Merton has tried to see if Durkheim's concept of *anomie* can be put to use in classifying different types of deviant or delinquent behaviour.[25]

As a third example, we may take the attempt by two English sociologists, David Lockwood and J. H. Goldthorpe, to refine and put to use a concept taken from the works of Karl Marx.[26] Marxist theory refers to a process known as embourgeoisement. That is, it is contended that when manual workers become well-off they tend to lose their working-class identity and militancy and become more middle-class. Lockwood and Goldthorpe have pointed out that the question, 'Is the worker going middle-class in an affluent society?' can be regarded as compounded of three separate questions, each of which calls for its own answer.

(1) How far do affluent workers assume a style of life and patterns of economic consumption like those of the middle class?

(2) How far do they change their working-class outlook – their support, for example, for trade unions, and their militant attitude against 'the boss class' – and come to share middle-class attitudes, for example in desiring to own their own houses, in making individual provision by saving for the future, in valuing thrift and industry?

(3) How far are affluent workers accepted in informal social relations by middle-class people – and how far do they want to be?

In studies of affluent workers in England – car workers at Luton – Lockwood and Goldthorpe have found that these questions can be tested in actual surveys; suitably designed questions, for example, can elicit people's attitudes towards home owner-ship and trade union membership.[27] The vague concept of embourgeoisement can, as it is put, be made operational.

The operationalization of concepts (as it is rather regrettably termed) is, then, one of the ways in which modern sociologists have tried to close the gap between theory and research. In more general terms we can think of the theoretical activities of modern sociologists under four main heads.

1. *Methodology*

Many sociologists are, unfortunately, prone to use the word methodology when they mean method. There remains, however, a proper and legitimate use of this term for the analytical study of the methods used by sociologists. The procedures by which hypotheses are derived from theories, and tested against observation and the validity of the methods used to test them are involved. For example, careful thought needs to be given to the design of before-and-after studies like that of the effect of television in Norwich, which was described earlier, and this is a proper task for methodology.

As a second example of a methodological problem, we may take the difficulty that frequently arises in sociology because many of the things that we want to investigate cannot, in the usual sense, be measured. For example, as we will see in chapter 6, it is a fairly simple matter to arrange a list of occupations in order of prestige, saying, for example, that medical practitioners have higher prestige than primary teachers, who in turn have higher prestige than building labourers. What we cannot do is to put numerical values on prestige and say that doctors have a prestige of 10, teachers of 6, labourers of 2. In other words, occupational prestige scales are ordinal, not interval scales. In the same way it is fairly straightforward to ascertain people's political attitudes by means of a suitably designed questionnaire or interview schedule. Again, we can possibly arrange such attitudes along a scale from radical to conservative, or modern to traditional but, without putting numerical values on their attitudes in a quite arbitrary way, we cannot *measure* political attitudes. To want to find a relation between occupational prestige and political attitudes is a very natural thing for a sociologist. In a western country it would be expected that people of lower occupational prestige would be more radical in their politics, but to correlate the two variables in the ordinary sense is impossible since we can measure neither of them.

The problem for methodology, therefore, is to find some way of correlating ordinal scales in the way that the correlation coefficient enables us to correlate interval scales. The solution in this case proves to be the application of a branch of mathematics known as information theory. The sort of mathematics which most of us learned at school, being concerned with measurement and number, turns out to be largely inappropriate for sociology and some new developments in sociological methodology may be expected from the application to sociology of other, less well known, branches of mathematics, such as information theory and set theory.

2. *Analytical theory*

This branch of theory may be regarded as the establishment of a set of interrelated concepts which can be applied to the analysis of all social action. It is associated especially with the name of Talcott Parsons, some of whose ideas I have already used in the introduction to terms and concepts in chapter 1. It was Parsons who, in his first book, *The structure of social action*,[28] concluded that action is the basic unit that sociologists observe and consider. In his later works he elaborated the concept of action in relation to the situation, the personality of the actors and others in his situation, the system of roles that they are acting, the culture of the system or sub-system, the desired goals of action, and the values that affect the actors' choices of one action rather than all possible others.

In Parsons' analysis an actor is seen as 'cognizing' the situation – that is, perceiving it in his senses, and forming an understanding of it; 'cathecting' towards it – that is, reacting to it in an emotional way and arriving at the feeling of what he *wants* from it; and 'evaluating' it – that is, considering it in the light of a system of values including his ideas of what he *ought* to do. Parsons and his fellow-workers have greatly elaborated the different types, or modes, of action that are possible, which are called the pattern variables. The analysis is carried on at three levels – the personality, cultural and social system levels – and no situation or action can be complete unless all are taken into account. How a person acts in a particular situation will depend on what sort of person he is and personality attributes such as intelligence, impulsiveness or perserverance are obviously relevant. But the culture, that is the system of expectations and evaluations which he shares with others, is also highly relevant. At the same time the situation may, and in real life often does, limit the possible choices of alternative actions pretty narrowly. Thus, to take an example, a prisoner who (in terms of personality) is prone to violence may very badly want (cathexis) to hit a warder. If he does so, he knows (at the level of cognition) that the consequences for him will be serious. The situation (including walls, locks, rules and prison officers) may be such as to make escape from them impossible; he must be presumed, in Parsonian theory, to decide, consciously or unconsciously, whether the satisfaction of hitting the warder and making a scene is worth the punishment that will follow, and 'optimize his gratification' – that is, reach the best level of satisfaction that is open to him in the situation, even though it may be a low one.

Parsons' attempt, therefore, has been to construct a theory of sociology rather like the supply-and-demand sort of economic theory – a set of concepts which are at one and the same time logically consistent, and suitable for classifying the data which sociologists might collect. It is a set of categories rather than a set of propositions.[29] Its typical sentences take a weak form such as 'we are concerned with . . .' or 'it is expedient to consider . . .' – both frequently employed by Parsons – rather than strong statements of the form 'If A then B', of which a theory, in the full sense, consists. Nevertheless the greatness of Parsons' contribution is best shown by the way in which, however incomplete and unsatisfying modern sociologists may find his ideas, nearly all use his system of analysis whether they recognize it or not. It is impossible now to think of what sociology was like before Parsons. His other achievement has been to resolve the age-old difficulty about free will and social causation. Parsons' system is strictly voluntarist – that is, according to his ideas every actor is free at every moment to decide how to act. Yet the possible actions open to him may be very limited and the choice may be a heavily loaded one. In this way the free will of the actors is seen as quite compatible with the possibility of making, in a perfectly ordinary everyday way, reliable forecasts of social actions, for example that an English queue will remain orderly, or that the three o'clock train will leave tomorrow at three o'clock.

One weakness of Parsons' theory, on the other hand, is that it too strongly emphasizes consensus, that is the extent to which people in a social system think alike, and makes too little of conflict and coercion. Parsons, indeed, seems to imply that a social system exists only in so far as there is consensus about role-expectations – that is, only in so far as people understand what is expected of them and in so far as their understanding of their roles is the same. This has led to criticism of Parsons for what has been called 'an

over-socialized conception of man'.[30] Some European sociologists
such as Dahrendorf[31] and Lockwood[32] have urged that alongside
the 'consensus model', whose usefulness they do not deny, we
should always put the alternative 'conflict model' in the explanation of any actual social behaviour. Equally, in the United States,
sociologists such as Gross and his colleagues, while fully acknow-
ledging their debt to Parsons in the development of role theory,
have found in their investigations of real-life roles, that there is a
great deal of conflict. Teachers, for example, expected school
superintendents to be quite different kinds of people and do quite
different things from what members of school boards expected
them to be and do.[33] Instead of role consensus being a postulate,
they say, it must be treated as an empirical variable. That is,
although we may find that people agree about the behaviour to be
expected of a role, we cannot assume that they will automatically
or necessarily agree. It is our business to go and find out. Even
more fundamentally, Goffman has suggested that it is simply
untrue that people are socialized or develop into conformity with
roles. To quite a large extent exactly the opposite happens and
people's personalities develop in opposition to, or against, the roles
assigned to them. A trivial example is the contents of schoolboys'
pockets; a more serious, but analogous, example of a need for
privacy and individuality concerns the activities of the inmates of
an asylum in evading, cheating and subverting the official expectations of the role of mental patient.[34]

3. *Theories of the middle range*

This term is applied to concepts and propositions which sociologists may devise to meet the needs of their particular research
work, even though they may not be linked with any systematic
body of grand or analytical theory. As an example we may take the
terms assimilation, pluralistic integration and accommodation as
applied to immigrant groups in Britain by Professor Little and his
colleagues at the University of Edinburgh. Briefly, assimilation
means complete absorption in the host community. The immigrants completely accept and adapt themselves to the culture of the
receiving society, which in turn completely accepts them, even to
the extent where their origins are ignored or forgotten. Pluralistic
integration implies acceptance as equals, especially in economic

and civil life, of a group which nevertheless retains some of its own ways (in religion, for example, or the continued use of a mother-tongue as a second language) and is regarded therefore by the host community as separate and different though equal and accepted. Accommodation is a relation in which the receiving society is not openly hostile, but not particularly friendly either. It implies acceptance on terms, co-existence in which there may be less than equality of treatment in economic and civic rights, and in which 'residential proximity, private social intercourse, and intermar-riage' may be denied.[35]

With these distinctions in mind, the Edinburgh workers have been able to analyse the factors and processes that make respect-ively for assimilation, pluralistic integration, and accommoda-tion. According to Collins' account, Muslim seamen and their families on Tyneside seek no more than accommodation, since the strength of their attachments to the Islamic religion and Arabic culture is such as to make the culture of English society of little attraction for them. This particular group, accordingly, did not seek to become English and acquiesced in the local authority's policy of segregating them in a separate housing area. West Indians, on the other hand, wanted more than an accommodation in British society. Since they were English-speaking, lacked a strong attachment to a non-English religion or culture, admired English society and wished to share in it they sought a position nearer to a pluralistic integration. The colour prejudice of many people in Britain, however, made it difficult for them to attain this relation, and frustration and tensions between immigrant and host societies were generated.[36]

Theories of the middle range, then, arise to meet particular needs in interpreting the data of particular researches. They are not necessarily connected with any wider body of theory. Their great strength is that being grounded in observed social facts they are concrete and realistic. Their weakness is that they are not necessarily applicable to other research problems or to other societies. The generalizations that the Edinburgh theories make possible about race relations in Britain, for example, may not be particularly helpful in understanding the situations in the United States or South Africa.

4. *Dynamic theory*

The great sociologists of the nineteenth century – men of the calibre of Comte, Spencer, Durkheim, Weber and Hobhouse – attempted, as we have seen, to devise theories that would interpret society and social change on the grand scale. Few sociologists are nowadays so ambitious; but the discussion of grand theory is not extinct, and some recent books have attempted to continue the great tradition. We will briefly consider one example.

Karl Wittfogel's book *Oriental despotism* is concerned to analyse a type of society – he regards it as being a type in the fullest sense of the word – that arises when the economy is based upon irrigated agriculture.[37] His examples embrace Asiatic and Near Eastern societies, both in the remote and recent past, and include an African case: the traditional society of the Chagga. Where men's livelihood depends on the maintenance of canals and other large-scale public works they have to be willing to be organized in a large-scale way, to submit to periods of tribute or corvée labour both regularly and at short notice when an emergency threatens; and there has to be a strong central management or administration to maintain the waterworks and organize the large bodies of corvée labour when they are called out. Such a society will not, therefore, be segmentary. Nor will it be feudal, since feudal administration is too decentralized and the essence of the irrigated society ('hydraulic society', to use Wittfogel's term) is a strong central administration which can permit no rivals. Equally it cannot be bourgeois, since a middle class of traders or professionals, though it may exist, cannot be permitted to be strong or independent and it can hardly be democratic. Once organized in this way, by the use of terror where necessary, a hydraulic society can use its mass labour force for other purposes – the building of pyramids or magnificent temples for the priest-king, the building and maintenance of roads (efficient communications being vital to the system) and the supply of the small but highly professional army which the régime needs to keep control internally and guard its wealth, food supply and vulnerable irrigation works from the attacks of prowling nomads on the outskirts. Wittfogel, then, wants to do two things: to establish this as a type of society, one of four or five broad types into which all human societies past and present may be classified, and to analyse how its features are related to one another and grounded upon its basic economy.

Now that I have tried to give some account of the different kinds of things which modern sociologists do, it remains only to add a brief note about who pays them to do it – that is, about sociology as a profession. It is a very small profession in terms of numbers. The greatest concentration of sociologists is to be found in the United States, where in the mid-1960s there were an estimated 3,000 holders of doctor's degrees in sociology, some 2,700 sociologists were professionally registered, and active members and fellows of the American Sociological Association numbered some 3,600.[38] The great majority of these were teachers of the subject in universities and colleges. In Britain, it was estimated in 1973 that on a somewhat less strict definition there were about 2,000 teachers of sociology, 1,200 of them in the higher education sector; and there were in addition about 900 employed full-time in research. Of the latter, many were in university research institutes. Some worked in local government organizations, some in various departments of central government; and there were relatively few in industry and commerce, including market research.[39] Compared with, say, the medical profession, with its 348,000 registered practitioners in the United States and 65,000 in Britain in the mid-1970s, such numbers are not large.[40] In other countries they are even smaller; and in African countries, too, the number of full-time posts available for qualified sociologists to practise their profession is likely to remain very limited and to be confined mainly to the teaching of the subject in universities, colleges of education, and the like. Perhaps we should argue from this that while sociology may be a subject which many people should know something about, it is one from which few people can hope to make a living. So that while universities should make it available as a subsidiary, optional, or combined subject to as many students as possible, they should build up only rather small, select honours schools of students studying sociology alone.

SUGGESTIONS FOR FURTHER READING

Margaret Stacey, *Methods of Social research* (Oxford, Pergamon, 1969).
J. H. M. Beattie, *Understanding an African kingdom: Bunyoro* (Holt, Rinehart

and Winston, 1965). The best short account known to me of a social
anthropologist's field methods and experience.

J. H. Madge, *The origins of scientific sociology* (London, Tavistock Publica-
tions, 1963). Summarizes an impressive range of the classics of sociological method.

Part 2

vwvwvwvwvwvwvwvwvwvwvwvwvwvwvwvwvwvwvwvwvwvwvwvwvwvwvwvwvwvwvwvw

SOCIAL INSTITUTIONS

CHAPTER 4

Kinship, marriage and the family

In this and the remaining chapters, we turn from what sociology is and what sociologists do to consider in general terms what they can tell us about the major institutions, or institutional clusters, in human societies. We consider these under the five heads of institutions concerned respectively with: kinship, marriage and the family; getting a living; inequality and social class; social control; and ritual. The needs that they meet are universal, grounded deep in our biological and psychological nature, yet the ways in which our basic needs are met differ widely in different societies. (It will be apparent from this way of putting it that our standpoint is broadly a functionalist one, though not one unaware either of conflict or of change.)

In every society there are institutions that take account of the difference between men and women, by regulating the terms upon which they mate and reproduce, the choice of a marriage partner and the division of labour between them. Broadly, we call these institutions marriage. A related set of institutions exists to deal with the biological fact that, in the human species, the young are extremely dependent and go on being so for a long time. The period of immaturity in humans, about a quarter of a normal lifetime, is far longer than in most other animal species. At the other end of life, too, ageing humans need care and help. The cluster of institutions around the need to care for children and old people we call the family. Kinship is an even wider term. It connotes the whole network of relationships based on birth and descent – between parents and children, between siblings (brothers and sisters, children of the same parents), and between individuals and their wider kin such as parents' siblings, grandparents, and so on.

Like most words in ordinary speech, the English word 'family' is loose and ambiguous. Sociologically it is important to distinguish between the family as household and the family as kin. By 'household' we mean the group of people, usually but not necessarily related by descent or marriage, who live together and share food. A person's kin are, as already indicated, all those people with whom a relationship based on descent is recognized. They are naturally a much larger set of people than the co-resident kin who form a household. The term 'nuclear family' is applied to the group consisting of a married couple and their children, who in many societies constitute both a household and the kernel or nucleus of the whole kinship system.

MATERNAL CARE

Many studies of the development of young children have emphasized their need for continuously affectionate care, without which their physical and mental development are liable to be seriously impaired. Most of the evidence, it is true, is from industrial countries; there seems little reason, however, to think this is anything but a universal human need. Much of it was assembled in a famous and influential report in 1951 by John Bowlby, and can be summed up in his words:

It is believed to be essential for mental health that the infant and young child should experience a warm, intimate, and continuous relationship with his mother (or permanent mother-substitute – one person who steadily 'mothers' him) in which both find satisfaction and enjoyment.[1]

Much of Bowlby's evidence was negative, taking the form of clinical descriptions of what happened to children who for one reason or another were deprived of normal maternal care, whether temporarily (as when child or mother had to go into hospital) or permanently (as in some orphanages or children's homes run like hospitals, with nurses working in shifts, so that children could not attach themselves to one mother-substitute). Bowlby concluded that maternal deprivation could do serious and irreparable harm, retarding general development, especially speech, impairing intelligence, and above all handicapping the child's ability to accept and return affection and so form relationships with others.

As a direct result of Bowlby's report, institutions caring for destitute children were largely reorganized into smaller units with 'houseparents' to give them something more like a normal family life, while arrangements for their foster-care in other families were also favoured. Such changes have been judged almost wholly beneficial. More controversial has been the greater reluctance it inspired to part children from their natural mothers, which has sometimes had disastrous consequences.

Bowlby's work has stimulated much further research and debate; his ideas have been refined and to some extent qualified by later authorities.[2] In these debates, Bowlby's central thesis remains unchallenged: that children need care and affection, and can suffer untold distress for lack of them. It has been disputed, though, whether the damage done by maternal deprivation is really so irreparable as Bowlby maintained. Cases have been reported in which dedicated care by substitute parents has restored children who have suffered appalling neglect and ill-treatment to normal levels of physical and mental development. It is also disputed whether Bowlby was right to suggest that 'one person' should care for a child, or whether a child can actually benefit from interacting with two, three, or even more adults in turn, as in traditional African family life. And, though Bowlby is often misunderstood on this point, he himself made it clear that the person on whom a young child can securely rely for affectionate response need not be the woman who bore him. Nor need that person necessarily be female, though his use of the feminine word 'mother' as both noun and verb might seem to imply as much. Fathers too can take an active part. In the light of such considerations, perhaps we should speak simply of the care of children rather than their 'maternal care', and substitute for 'mothering' some other word such as 'parenting'.

Nevertheless, in most hitherto existing societies the person who has been responsible for caring for a child has been the child's mother. During pregnancy and while breast-feeding there are natural limitations on what a woman can do. After weaning, too, most women in most societies have assumed a continuing responsibility for the care and upbringing of their young children. The limitations imposed by these responsibilities have traditionally formed the basis of the division of labour between the sexes as recognized in marriage and practised in the organization of the household. Thus in many African societies women stayed at home cultivating the gardens, looking after domestic livestock such as poultry, and cooking, while the men ranged further afield herding cattle, hunting, and going to war.

THE HOUSEHOLD

As usually defined, a household may consist of a person living alone, or a group of people, not necessarily related by marriage or descent, who live in one place – a single dwelling or a cluster of dwellings – and share catering arrangements and the preparation of food. Households differ widely in size and composition, both within a society and among societies. While many households may consist only of a married couple and their children, some may be larger. Thus among the Bemba, according to Richards' account, a large household might comprise a man and his wives, his married daughters and their husbands and children, and his unmarried sons, living in a group of houses forming part of a village. The men worked on the land under his direction, the women did the housework under that of the senior wife.[3] But though polygyny was admired there, as in many traditional African societies, a man had only one wife at first, and not all men later added even a second. Many households therefore were small. In traditional India, the so-called joint family consisted of a man and his wife, his sons and their wives and children. The brothers were supposed to be economic partners, and the women did the housework under the mother's direction. But though joint family life was admired and many people aspired to it, only a minority of households were joint.

In western Europe in the past, some households included unrelated lodgers, while some wealthy households were much larger than the rest, with unrelated servants (agricultural workers in the country, craftsmen in town, as well as domestic servants) living under the same roof as the master and his family. The households of the poorer classes were correspondingly smaller, being depleted of young unmarried men and women who were 'in service' and lived in the households of the rich. There were always a substantial number of single-person and two-person households: about one in every five in England, according to Laslett.[4] In modern times, personal service of that nature has well-nigh disappeared, and households of all social classes approximate to the same patterns. While these notably include the conventional nuclear family, there are also increasing numbers of smaller households. These include elderly couples, single-person households, and 'mothers alone' with a child or children.

DESCENT GROUPS

In most if not all societies, social relations are recognized with a wider range of kinsfolk than the immediate family of co-resident kin who form a household. In many societies, including those of traditional Africa, people related by common descent belong to groups known as lineages and clans. Lineages are groups who are related by common descent from a known ancestor, every step in the line of descent being known. Clans on the other hand are groups of people who regard one another as kinsmen and act towards one another as if they were of common descent, even though common ancestry may not be traced with certainty. Indeed, clans often have mythical common ancestors and maintain their identity by totemic rules like not eating the meat of some animal. It follows that there can be – and usually are – lineages (groups of known common descent) within clans (wider groups where common ancestry is presumed rather than traced). Equally, there may be lineages of different depths, and here anthropologists who describe (in English) the kinship institutions of the peoples they study have to adapt the terms they use to what they find. Usually, a minimal lineage means the smallest descent group, outside the nuclear family, to which people think of themselves as belonging. Quite typically it is one of three generations' depth, that is it comprises the sons and grandsons of one man, for example. In a particular society there may also be a maximal lineage; that is, the largest lineage to which people think of themselves as belonging. Not uncommonly again, the limitations of the human memory being what they are, such a lineage is of seven or eight generations' depth. And in a particular society there may be lineages in between, for which terms like major lineage or minor lineage would be used by an anthropologist writing in English.

As an example we may take the Ganda system, as outlined in Fallers' *The king's men*.[5] There were about thirty-seven clans. Each was regarded as being descended from a founding ancestor and each had a clan head who might also hold an associated political or ritual office. For example, the head of the Lungfish clan was

Gabunga or grand admiral of the kingdom. The bigger clans held lands which were widely scattered all over the kingdom. A major lineage, however, might possess a compact block of land, an estate, within which the minor lineages would hold contiguous estates, subdivided again among the minimal lineages. In this case, since descent was not traced right back to the founding ancestor of the clan, the clans were totemic – the Lungfish clan, for example, would not eat the fish of their totem – and this acted as a kind of test or mnemonic. If you met a girl who also refused lungfish you knew she was a clan sister!

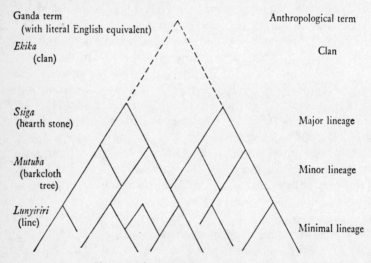

Fig. 1. (After Fallers, *The king's men*.)

Descent may be traced through either father or mother. Descent through the father used to be known as patrilineal; nowadays the term agnatic is used more often. Descent through the mother – matrilineal or uterine descent – is possibly less common and less well known, though it prevails in the traditional kinship systems of a wide area of Africa – the so-called 'matrilineal belt', covering roughly from southern Tanzania and Zambia westwards – and also in some other areas for which good anthropological accounts exist. In a matrilineal system a man is of different clan and lineage from his father, and the same clan and lineage as his mother and his mother's brother. The Bemba of Zambia are an example.

Figures 2 to 4 will illustrate patrilineal and matrilineal descent

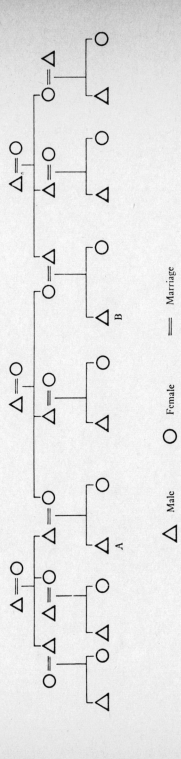

△ Male   ◯ Female   = Marriage

Fig. 2. Here are two men A and B, and their relatives.

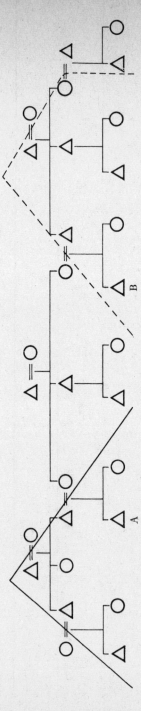

Fig. 3. *Patrilineal*. In a patrilineal system, A and B are members of two different groups.

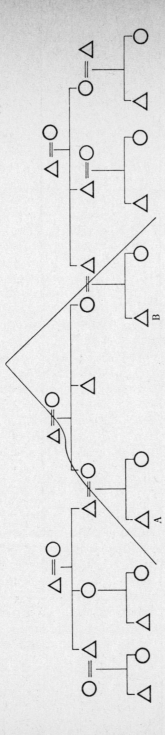

Fig. 4. *Matrilineal.* In a matrilineal system, A and B are members of the same descent group.

and we shall return to them and to figure 5 in discussing the bilateral descent system of western European and North American peoples. For the moment let us note that descent affords a principle, widely used in non-western societies, for arranging people into groups. A descent group is unique and unambiguous; the question of whether you are or not descended from a certain named ancestor is something that you and everybody else knows and there can be no doubt about it. Membership of a lineage or clan, therefore, is a definite and permanent thing about a man or woman. Such groups can, accordingly, meet when necessary to decide matters of common concern – the marriage of one of their members, for example, the inheritance of a dead member's property, or the use of land possessed by the group. They can be (though they are not always) corporate groups possessing and making decisions about assets such as land. Many of the readers of this book will presumably belong to some such group and may well have personal experience of the way it works.

Matrilineal and patrilineal descent are not the only possibilities. Some peoples, for example in West Africa, have systems of double descent in which there are both matrilineal and patrilineal groups operating for different purposes. For examples, among the Yako as described by Forde, patriclans and corporate patrilineages on the one hand and matrilineages on the other had different but equally important functions from an individual's point of view.[6] The inheritance of immovable property such as house sites, farm plots, oil-palm clusters and planted trees, for example, was a matter for the patrilineage. Matrilineal kinship, however, took precedence in the inheritance of transferable wealth, especially livestock and money, which a man might accumulate in his lifetime. Both matriclans and patriclans, too, had ritual functions, and both had originally been exogamous, though at the time of Forde's field-work exogamy was strictly enforced only within the matrilineage.

Finally, there is the fourth possibility that descent may be reckoned equally on both sides, or bilaterally. Bilateral descent characterizes – and for a very long time has characterized – the people of north-western Europe including the English, and also societies of English or north-western European origin such as those of the United States, Canada, Australia, etc. When an Englishman speaks of his family, he usually has in mind primarily the nuclear family of which he is a member: as a child, his parents

A's kindred

B's kindred

Fig. 5. *Bilateral*. In a bilateral system, A and B are kinsmen, and some of A's kin are also B's kin, but some are not.

and siblings; as an adult, his wife and their children. Secondarily he thinks of his family as including his grandparents, his parents' siblings (whom he calls uncles and aunts), and his parents' siblings' children, to all of whom he applies the term cousin. Outside this circle, while more distant 'relations' (=kinsfolk) may be known and recognized, the ties of kinship are of hardly more effect than those of friendship or neighbourhood. Most English people know little or nothing about their great-grandparents, and if they know their second cousins (kin with a common great-grandparent) it is more by accident than anything else.

Figure 5 will show that where kinship is reckoned bilaterally in this way descent groups are impossible. Although siblings have the same circle of kin as one another, the circles of cousins and more distant kin partly overlap and partly diverge from one another. In the diagram, A and B count one another as cousins since their mothers are sisters and they have a common grandfather and grandmother. A's 'relations' on his father's side, however are not regarded by B as 'relations'; conversely, B's relations on his father's side are not thought of as being related to A.

In a bilateral system, therefore, the circles of kinship shift according to who is speaking. The terms clan and lineage clearly do not apply here, and the term kindred is recommended. Each person has a kindred, but – save for siblings – no one's kindred is the same as anyone else's. The outer circle around A, for example, might roughly delineate those who would come to his wedding, while the outer circle round B would correspond to those who might feel under an obligation to attend B's – along with friends and neighbours. Neither, however, could possibly make decisions about the division of property between A and B; not being unique groups, they could not have any corporate existence or powers, for example, to hold land or other property.

It follows that the English, and societies derived from them, could not possibly have a clan or lineage system and in fact they do not. (The Scots traditionally had clans, which still exist, though now mainly as picturesque survivals. In this as in many other ways Scottish society has become very Anglicized over the last two or three hundred years.)

KINSHIP TERMINOLOGIES

The descent system, along with other features of the kinship system, of any society is reflected in the system of kinship terms used in that society. Broadly speaking, a person applies the same term to those kin who are regarded as belonging to the same category, and who, from the point of view of the person speaking, occupy similar kinship roles.

As an illustration, we may take the contrast between the Gurage, a tribe of Ethiopia (Fig. 6 – as described by Shack),[7] and the English system (Fig. 7) – that is, the terms commonly used by English-speaking people. Anthropologists writing in English have had to devise a less ambiguous system for scientific usage among themselves. In setting out a kinship terminology, it is conventional to denote the person who is speaking by the name ego, which is Latin for I (the first person singular pronoun). In neither of the two cases given is the terminology complete; in fact it is very difficult to get a complete terminology onto one piece of paper!

Gurage kinship is strongly patrilineal. It is organized in clans which are divided into maximal lineages and subdivided into major and minor lineages. Each descent group is associated with a geographical area in which it is dominant. Thus a maximal lineage is associated with a district while a minor lineage forms a cluster of related patrilineal homesteads which Shack calls 'the core of a village'. A man's relations with his patrilineal kin are of the greatest importance in his life and· this strongly patrilineal emphasis is reflected in the kinship terminology. Though the term *aba*, father, is used only for the one real father, the term *ebeya* has a wide extension; it includes father's brother, father's brother's son and brother's son and is extended to all males of the father's clan. *Ebeya*, patrilineal kinsman, is, however, distinguished very clearly from *mwena*, the term for matrilineal kinsman – mother's brother, mother's brother's son, and even mother's brother's daughter. From the Gurage point of view a different term is required because these people stand in a quite different relation to a man. 'The kin of the mother are not obliged to defend a man, to perform mortuary rites for him, or to support his heirs, and if they perform any of these it is not as a consequence of institutional norms of kinship behaviour.'[8] In the same way, the term *anatcwat*, which includes father's sister, father's brother's daughter, and brother's daughter,

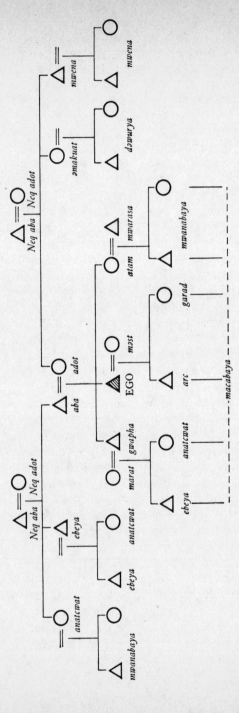

Fig. 6. Gurage kinship terminology (after William A. Shack).

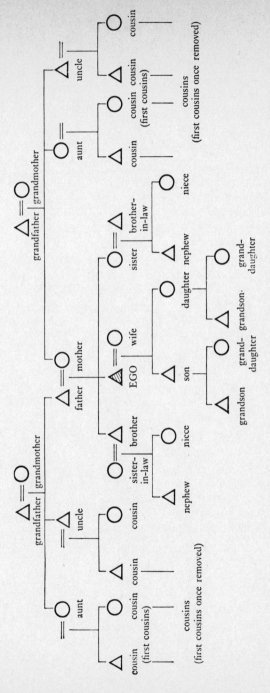

Fig. 7. English kinship terminology.

is quite distinct from the terms *əmakuat* (mother's sister) and *dəwurya* (mother's sister's children) which are applied on the mother's side.

By contrast, the bilateral nature of English kinship is faithfully reflected in the use of a term like uncle, which is applied to both father's brother and mother's brother. An uncle in an English child's life is a person who is rather kindly and indulgent, and gives presents at Christmas and on the child's birthday; both maternal and paternal uncles do so equally. Similarly the term aunt is applied to both father's sister and mother's sister, while, as we have seen, the term cousin (or, to be strictly accurate, first cousin) is applied bilaterally to any parent's sibling's child, or to put it in another way any person with a common grandparent. There actually exists in the English language a set of terms for distinguishing more distant cousins: thus a second cousin is a person with a common great-grandparent; a first cousin once removed is a child of a first cousin (or, reciprocally, a parent's first cousin), the 'removal' being by a generation.[9] But the great majority of English people do not understand these terms and seldom, if ever, have occasion to use them.

It is clear that great difficulties and misunderstandings may arise when translating kinship terms from one language to another. Thus from the point of view of most Africans, an English word like uncle may seem hopelessly vague, when the difference in one's relation with mother's brother and father's brother may be very great. Similarly, in the context of an African society, one needs to distinguish relatives of the same generation and the same clan from those of the same generation, but a different clan, who in English are both cousins. Equally, from an English point of view, a term like the Gurage *ebeya* is confusing, since there is no way of telling whether it means uncle, cousin, or nephew.

MARRIAGE

In all societies arrangements exist for the social recognition of who may legitimately mate with whom, which we call marriage. While the social recognition of mating itself may be of some importance, its importance is probably outweighed in most societies by that of legitimating the children that may result – that is, giving them social recognition, an identity, a name, membership of a socially recognized group and some indication of who must assume the obligation to support them and their mother. Marriage is probably best regarded as an anticipatory provision for those needs.

While all societies have a system of marriage (and make a social distinction between legitimate and illegitimate children) there are wide variations in different marriage systems. The more important variables concern the number of mates each marriage partner may have; the locality of the marriage; the arrangements that exist for the transfer of wealth at the marriage; and the terms, if any, on which a marriage may be dissolved.

(1) How many mates? In existing human societies there are three possibilities. Most societies recognize *polygyny*, that is, the right of man to take more than one wife. In a few societies (not in Africa) there is *polyandry*, in which a woman is simultaneously married to two or more men. One form is fraternal polyandry, in which the wife comes to live with a group of brothers in their house. This is practised among some peoples of the Himalayan region. In the other type, matriarchal polyandry, the wife stays at home and her husbands, who are not necessarily related to one another, come to live with her in turn.[10] And thirdly, especially in Europe and societies of European origin, there is *monogamy*, the rule which limits one man to one wife and vice versa. A fourth possibility is termed group marriage. In it a group of men would share marital relations with a group of women. It does not exist in any known human society, and its only interest is that some nineteenth-century sociologists, without any evidence, postulated it as having existed at an earlier stage of human evolution.

(2) Where does a young couple set up home? Here there seem to be three possibilities: at his home, at hers, or somewhere else. The old term for the arrangement when a wife moves to her husband's family's household is *patrilocal* marriage; a more modern term is *virilocal*. The opposite, when it is the man who moves, is termed *matrilocal* or *uxorilocal* marriage. The third possibility, that they set up a new household somewhere else, is termed *neolocal* marriage.

(3) As to the transfer of wealth there again seem to be three possibilities. Wealth may be transferred by the husband, or his kin, to the bride's family to seal the marriage, as a recognition of their 'upfostering' her and as a pledge against the dissolution of the marriage. This, of course, is the system familiar in Africa, correctly

termed *bridewealth*, always remembering that the bridewealth may take the form of the husband's labour services to his father-in-law rather than cattle, hoes, or money. In some other societies – traditional European societies, for example, and still in the Irish countryside – the opposite system prevails and a wife brings with her a portion or *dowry* in the form of money, or other wealth such as land, to endow the marriage and match the husband's contribution in the form of his labour and his obligation to maintain the wife and her children. (It is, of course, a common error to confuse dowry with bridewealth.) The third possibility, associated with neolocal marriage, is for the transfer of wealth to take the form of gifts to help the young couple to set up the new household. In England these are called *wedding presents*. The near kin of both bride and groom contribute and so do friends, neighbours and workmates. The presents customarily take the form of useful household goods such as saucepans, tea sets, or blankets. In the United States the word 'shower' is used, the bride being, as it were, showered with gifts.

CHOICE OF MARRIAGE PARTNER

1. *Negative – exogamy and the prohibition of incest*

In no society does a man or woman have a completely open choice of marriage partner. There are always some restrictions on the marriage and mating of near kin, while, on the other hand, there are, in many societies, positive rules or recommendations, principles on which people are supposed to act in making a choice of marriage partner.

To deal first with the negative principles, the restrictions or prohibitions, it is important to distinguish between exogamy on the one hand and the prohibition of incest on the other. *Exogamy*, literally 'marrying out', refers to the rules which exist in every society about the categories of kin whom a person may not marry. *Incest*, however, means the offence of sexual relations between near kin. Clearly these two prohibitions are related, for if a man and a woman are such close kin that sex relations between them would be regarded as incestuous, then they could hardly be allowed to marry. But the converse is not true. Sex relations outside marriage do, after all, occur to some extent in all societies.

In some societies it would be perfectly possible for a man and a woman to be too closely related for marriage, yet not so closely related that an act of sexual intercourse between them would be regarded as incest. A good example illustrating this distinction is afforded by the laws of England. Here incest is (briefly) sexual intercourse between a woman and her grandfather, father, brother, half-brother or son. The 'prohibited degrees of kindred and affinity', however, list twenty-three categories of kin whom a woman may not marry, and reciprocally twenty-three whom a man may not marry.[11] These include, for instance, her mother's brother, her brother's son, and her mother's second husband. Under English law none of these men could marry her, but if any of them were to have sex relations with her neither he nor she would be committing the crime of incest. In sociological terms we should say that in England the rules of exogamy delineate a wider circle of kin than the rules about incest. In Scotland the position is quite different. There incest is much more widely defined as intercourse between parties within the degrees of relationship specified in the 18th chapter of the Book of Leviticus. In former times (to be exact from 1567 to 1907), the law about the prohibited degrees was based on the same Biblical authority, though in the twentieth century Scots law has been somewhat amended by legislation applying to both England and Scotland.[12] It may happen, therefore, that in some societies the two sets of rules coincide, so that as Robin Fox puts it 'those who are forbidden in marriage are forbidden as sexual partners also. But it cannot be assumed that they do; this has to be demonstrated.'[13] Failure to make this distinction has resulted in confusion in much writing on this subject.[14]

Incest in the strict sense of sexual relations between near kin is not only prohibited in all human societies, it is regarded in all with such extreme horror that many people think its avoidance is instinctive – an inborn or hereditary pattern of behaviour. It would be odd if this were so, for man, as far as we know, is the only animal with this particular aversion. In man the instincts are of less importance, and intelligence and learned behaviour of more importance, than in other animals, so this consideration alone should make us wary of accepting the instinct view. There are a few – a very few – exceptions. One frequently quoted is that of the divine kings of ancient Egypt, who are known to have made a practice of marrying their sisters in order to preserve the ritual purity of the line, but this is the kind of exception that, in the strict sense, proves the rule, for its exceptional nature proves that the rule exists for the majority of people. It seems more likely that far from being an instinctive aversion the strength of the feelings that incest arouses points to its prohibition being a learned reaction to something that would otherwise be very much desired. A number of theories have been put forward to account for all the facts; none do so quite completely or satisfactorily, but that put forward by Talcott Parsons seems to come nearest to meeting the case.[15] Parsons agrees with Freud that 'what is forbidden is what is most desired' and satisfactorily links the strength of the incest taboo with Freud's view of the development of the mother–child relation and the sex drive in children. In order to prevent a boy's sexual affections from being attached to his mother, they are blocked after the period of complete dependence and directed outside the family and into those strong friendships with other boys of the same age (in Parsons' term, the one-sex peer group) which characterize the years from about 8 to 13, 'when', as he puts it, 'the individual is above all learning to perform extra-familial roles'. After some years of the boys' group, gang, or age-set, boys and unrelated girls begin to meet one another in groups *as equals*; the groups then disintegrate and boy–girl pairs form, leading to the phase of courtship, marriage, and the starting of new nuclear families, when the cycle repeats itself.

Parsons' theory is of particular interest to African sociologists because it links the incest prohibition with the phenomena of age-sets and age-grades. I would elaborate Parsons' theory a little further and say that though the one-sex peer group seems to be a universal human phenomenon the extent to which it is institutionalized and made part of the formal social structure differs widely in different societies. Some, like the Kikuyu, make it the main principle, along with a clan and lineage system, of the whole social organization. The age-mates with whom a young boy plays and herds goats become his fellow-members of an age-set (*rika*) when they are circumcised together. They form the warrior grade together. Later, when they are ousted by the next *rika*, they settle down into married life together. Later still they become the elders, settling disputes, making the laws, and acting as the priests and ambassadors of their people.[16] In one African society, the Nyakyusa of southern Tanzania, the age-set of young men used, traditionally, to settle together and stay for the rest of their lives in an age-village.[17] At the other extreme some African societies made little use of the age principle; among the Ganda, for example, power and prestige went with the king's favour, irrespective of age; young men could be chiefs. The position in western societies is towards the Ganda end of the scale. Age-sets of boys who play and go to school together remain mainly as informal groups, only formalized very slightly in a few cases when, for example, a school or college holds a class reunion.

But to return to the prohibitions and restrictions on the choice of marriage partner, in societies with descent groups it is usual to find that they are exogamous. Thus in many African societies clans are exogamous, that is, no man may marry his clan-'sister'. Kinship terminologies, indeed, usually symbolize and reinforce that prohibition by extending the term 'sister' to all female members of the clan of the same generation, or by using a term like the Gurage *anatcwat* for a wide range of female members of the same clan. However, it is not always the clan that is the exogamous group. Where there are a few large clans, such as among the Kikuyu, the exogamous group may be a smaller segment of the clan, such as a sub-clan or lineage.

Societies that reckon kinship narrowly might be expected to extend the restriction of marriage over a narrow range of kin. This applies especially to western societies. As has already been noted, these societies lack descent groups and think rather in terms of circles of kin, and the laws about the 'prohibited degrees' follow the same kind of pattern. In most western countries, indeed, marriage with as near a relative as a first cousin is permitted and not uncommon, though it is illegal in some American states. A non-western society in which the marriage of even closer kin was permitted, however, was the Pacific island of Tikopia. Here, according to Firth, there were four clans but they were not exogamous, and marriages between near kin were common. He even records two cases of marriage between half-siblings; such unions were strongly disapproved at first, but they were eventually accepted, and the children were regarded as legitimate.[18]

Although, as suggested above, the social function of the prohibition of incest remains obscure, that of exogamy is clear enough. Because exogamous groups have to enter into marriage relations with other like groups, the hostility or conflict that is possible among such groups is limited. As can easily be imagined, it would be highly inconvenient if one exogamous clan were on such bad terms with other clans that the courtship of their young people was seriously hampered, negotiations over bridewealth made more difficult, and the meeting of kinsfolk at the wedding socially awkward. Furthermore, exogamy results in some women of one group living as wives in another. If there were fighting between the two groups, a man might inadvertently kill his brother-in-law and thus make his sister a widow and her children orphans. Even a state of tension that made it difficult for a man to call and see his sister and her children, and share a meal in her house, would be likely to be regarded as a source of embarrassment to be ended as soon as possible. Exogamy, then, is an important factor in some societies in maintaining peace and limiting hostilities within a wider community.

Another class of prohibitions or restrictions on the choice of marriage partner are those of *endogamy* or 'marrying in'. In some societies, people are forbidden to marry outside their own group. For example, not so long ago in Africa there would have been strong opposition to the idea of a young person marrying outside his own tribe, unless it were to a member of a closely related tribe. In modern South Africa, the officially-designated racial groups are practically endogamous. Under the Prohibition of Mixed Marriages Act of 1949 a valid marriage cannot take place between a white and a non-white person. Marriages between Indians, Coloureds, and Bantu are not illegal, but they rarely occur in practice because of differences of religion and language and in some cases other restrictions such as those of caste. Thus we may say that the white group are endogamous by law, while the non-white groups are almost so in practice. A society in which both endogamy and exogamy impose significant customary restrictions upon a person's choice of marriage partner is that of India. Here, generally speaking, a caste is endogamous while its constituent kin groups (*gotra*) are exogamous. Generally speaking, that is, an Indian must find a partner of the same caste but of a different *gotra* within that caste. Certain qualifications must be made to that general statement, however. First, not all castes are alike in their customs. Secondly, there is an arrangement known as *hypergamy* by means of which a man may take a bride of a slightly lower caste, though this would not be allowed if the two castes were of widely different rank. Under such an arrangement the woman 'marries up' in the social scale, and her kinsfolk have the satisfaction of demonstrating that they are very nearly equal in their caste position to that of the man's group. However, the opposite arrangement (which would be termed *hypogamy* in the technical language of sociology) is not permitted according to the customs of Hindu society. Thirdly, among the most emancipated sections of modern Indian society some people are beginning to disregard caste restrictions of this kind.

2. *Positive – principles and preferences*

In some societies there are preferred marriages; that is, choices of marriage partner which a young man or woman is expected or urged to make. Preferential *cross-cousin marriage*, for example, was traditionally an institution in some African societies, cross-cousins being the children of siblings of opposite sex. Such a preference may be related to the idea of conserving cattle-passing, bride-receiving relations between two friendly clans, or alternatively, of reversing such a relation and getting back in one generation the cattle passed in the previous generation for the parents' marriage. The two possibilities are illustrated in figures 8 and 9.

Other preferred or expected marriages common in traditional African society included *sororal polygyny* – that is, when a man took as a second wife his first wife's sister, an arrangement which, like

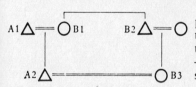

Fig. 8. In this case, assuming it is a patrilineal society, if A2 marries B3 then the A's are again passing cattle to, and receiving a bride from, the B's – a relation it may be desired to conserve.

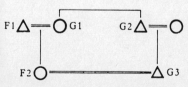

Fig. 9. In this case, again assuming patriliny, if F2 marries G3 then the F's are recovering from the G's the cattle (or their equivalent) which were passed for the marriage of F1 to G1.

the cross-cousin marriage just considered, tended to conserve good relations between two descent groups. Another such arrangement was the *levirate*, when a man took as a wife (possibly as a second wife) the widow of his deceased brother. The advantages were here that the bridewealth arrangements need not be disturbed and the widow was assured of a place and a husband to assume responsibility for her.

Marriage in traditional Africa was commonly thought of as a group matter. Not one that concerned the husband and wife alone, but one which, through arrangements such as the bridewealth and the levirate, also concerned the descent groups of the two marriage partners. This attitude is in contrast with that which has prevailed in western countries in modern times and also with the situation which modern changes have brought about in Africa, in which marriage and the choice of a partner are regarded much more as a matter of individual choice. In a modern society, the range of choice is much wider – the sheer numbers of young women whom a young man meets, and vice versa, are far greater than they were in traditional small-scale societies. In such conditions, far greater scope can be, and is, given to compatibilities of temperament and taste. Somewhere among those milling crowds in the street, the factory, the dance hall, or the students' union, there may be Mr Right. How do you recognize him when you meet him? According to the popular cult known as romantic love, rational processes are supposed not to come into it at all – you just know. More soberly, sociologists such as Winch have been led to think that there are two principles unconsciously at work affecting mate selection in western countries: *homogamy* and *heterogamy*.[19] Although there are no rules or laws about it, the majority of marriages in western countries take place between people of similar social class status (as we shall see more fully in chapter 6). This is not entirely surprising since it is with people of similar social class status that a young person mainly associates. The social classes are broadly (though again not rigidly) segregated in different residential areas, attend different schools, and spend their daily lives in different workplaces. Compatibility of taste also has a good deal to do with it. Members of a particular church or religious denomination will meet others of the same beliefs; those with a particular interest in a particular sport or recreation such as tennis or music will meet in the appropriate societies; the politically minded will find themselves canvassing at elections in one another's company; and so on. Homogamy of social class, leisure interest, and education characterize mate selection (the word homogamy being weaker than endogamy, to imply a tendency rather than a rule). Heterogamy – a weaker word than exogamy, again – refers to the tendency at the psychological level for people to find their needs being met, their weaknesses compensated, by choosing a partner of different type of personality – a dominating man, for example, being happiest with a submissive wife. The sheer numbers of potential mates whom a person meets in large-scale societies is so great that it is possible for both principles to operate.

THE CONTENT OF KINSHIP RELATIONS

It is clearly insufficient to think of kinship only in so abstract a sense as descent. While it is clearly important for every social individual to carry, as it were, the label of a group that gives him identity and individuality, kinship is concerned with much richer, subtler and more pervasive relations between people. Even in rather formal terms we have to consider *inheritance* – the principles which in any society govern the distribution of a dead person's property – and *succession* to a status or role, for example that of a chief or even that of head of a household. Inheritance and succession may be linked, as they are in many traditional African societies, where whichever son becomes his father's heir becomes also the successor to his social responsibilities. This son may, for example, inherit his father's wives, except of course his own mother, and may have to assume responsibility for the minor children of his father. Moreover, a knowledge of the situation that will exist at a man's death may powerfully affect social relations during his lifetime. For example, in Buganda, where there is no fixed rule of inheritance but a good deal of discretion as to which of a man's sons becomes his heir and successor, brothers vie with one another for his favour during his lifetime, and this is related to the very common pattern in Ganda society of rivalry and even hatred between brothers.[20]

Kinship also affects where people live. The relation between kinship and residence is not a simple one; it is rare for a residential group to be a descent group, for if there is a rule of exogamy then men and their wives must be of different descent groups. Even a household, which is the smallest residential group, is not usually made up of people of the same descent group. When we turn to larger descent groups, such as lineages or clans, the same thing applies. In many societies clans, or lineages, have land which they inhabit and which they share out for cultivation among their members, so that it is common – in many parts of traditional Africa, for example – for there to be clan lands, on which the dominant group are people of a single clan. It is not usually possible, however, for clan lands to be *exclusively* occupied by the dominant clan, if only because their wives must be of other clans – assuming, that is, that the clan is exogamous. In practice, too, we find that men of other clans also may occupy land in other clans' areas. Thus in one area clan A may be dominant and members of clans B and C may be accepted as clients or subordinates; in another area, where clan B dominates, members of clan A may live as dependants. Thus among the Nuer each clan is the dominant or aristocratic group in its own area, but takes a lower status elsewhere.[21] Among the Gurage, as we have seen, a minor lineage forms the 'core of the village' in the area in which it is dominant.

THE FAMILY IN MODERN WESTERN INDUSTRIAL SOCIETY

I have already mentioned some of the peculiar features of the kinship system of the English and similar societies. It may now be useful to summarize and extend the analysis, since this form of kinship is of special importance in the modern world. We may then be in a better position, in the final section, to ask how far it is likely to spread to Africa.

A brief and formal description of kinship in these societies would state that descent is bilateral. It might seem from the use of the surname that there is a patrilineal emphasis; children take their father's surname, and a woman takes her husband's at marriage. But the appearance of patriliny is not borne out in other aspects of descent, or of kinship generally. The kinship terminology is perfectly bilateral. There are accordingly no descent groups of the nature of clans or lineages. Marriage is monogamous, and has always been so – even in pagan Anglo-Saxon England, before

Christian influence became important. The principle of not more than one married couple per household has prevailed for a long time also, certainly for at least three hundred years. Marriage is accordingly neolocal. The typical household consists of the nuclear family: a man and his wife and their children. When the children grow up they leave their parents in a two-person household and set up a new home. Clearly we are making generalizations here, and there are many individual exceptions to this pattern; yet it is normal in both senses of the word. It applies to the majority of people, and it is also thought of as normal.

Talcott Parsons, indeed, goes so far as to speak of 'the isolation of the nuclear family' in modern industrial society and attributes this state of affairs to the rise of modern industry, which demands that men should be mobile, able to move easily when their employers transfer them elsewhere or to find other work.[22] This view, however, seems to be incorrect on two counts. First, recent research (notably by William J. Goode, and confirmed also by the historian Peter Laslett) seems to show that the size and composition of English family groups has changed hardly at all since before the industrial revolution, save only for the disappearance of the living-in servant, to which I referred earlier, while other work, notably by Lorraine Lancaster on the Anglo-Saxon family, seems to indicate that not much change has taken place even over the last fifteen hundred years.[23] It seems clear that modern industry did not create the English family. On the contrary, it may be that the compactness of the traditional family structure with its lack of widely extended kinship ties, helped to facilitate the rise of industry, and partly explains why it took place in England first. Secondly, the word 'isolated' in Parsons' phrase is certainly exaggerated. To say that the household is the nuclear family is not to say that English people lose touch with their old folks. All recent research tends to confirm that though old people live in independent households in English and American society, they mostly live near their middle-aged children and keep in close touch with them, daily visits being quite usual. Children move freely and frequently between their parents' and their grandparents' houses and most old people can rely on getting help from their children, especially their daughters, in illness or other need.[24] Willmott and Young, in a famous study of kinship in Bethnal Green (a part of London) found a particularly close relation between a young married woman and her mother.[25] In another study of a middle-class suburb of London they found that, though middle-class people lived farther away from their old folks in terms of miles, car ownership and the telephone enabled them to maintain contact and be available in emergency just as much as among the working class.[26] They and other sociologists accordingly speak of 'the three-generation family' or the 'modified extended family' in industrial societies.

The changes that have affected the family in the west over the last hundred years are not changes in the kinship structure. They have been demographic changes and changes in role relations within the family.

Profound changes have taken place as a result of the fall in the death-rate and in the birth-rate over the last century. The improvement in mortality conditions and the lengthening span of life in western countries means that there are far more old people surviving. Old people have longer to play the role of grandparents and, to the extent to which they keep their health, they are able to maintain their independence – which in nearly all cases they cherish – for far longer. The rise of the household consisting of one or two old people has been dramatic in western countries since 1900. At the same time, since the end of the nineteenth century, family limitation has been more and more widely practised, so that many if not all conceptions now take place as a result of parents' deliberate choice. Though birth-rates fluctuate, they are low compared with those in former times, and four children constitute a large family. Small families (in the sense of small numbers of children) may in turn be related to the improvement in mortality conditions, since it is now rare for a child to die; and where most children born can be relied upon to survive, there is more reason to limit the number born. At the same time the rise in the expected standards of child care and the little that parents can expect to benefit from their children's economic contribution, make children something of a costly luxury, to be indulged in only to a strictly limited extent. With fewer children and a growing tendency for old people to live in independent households instead of as dependants with their married children, households generally have become smaller and smaller.

The demographic changes that have affected the American family have been summed up by Glick in the following table, which shows the age at which various important events happened to the average American woman in 1890 and 1950.

Median age at	1890	1950
First marriage	22·0	20·1
Birth of last child	31·9	26·1
Marriage of last child	55·3	47·6
Death of husband	53·3	61·4
Own death	67·7	77·2

The average experience of an American woman in the late nineteenth century was that by the time her last child was married her husband was already dead and she had about twelve years' life left to spend as a dependant in the household of one of her married children. By 1950, slightly earlier marriage and far fewer children meant that the average American woman was finished with child-bearing at the age of 26 and when her last child married she still had thirty years' life to look forward to, fourteen of them with her husband.[27]

Such changes have truly revolutionized the life of women in industrial countries. Along with their legal and political emancipation, for the first time in human history women can look upon the bearing and rearing of their children not as a life's work in itself but as an episode. Women have entered many types of employment formerly the preserve of men, and attitudes have changed towards their going out to work. Some women always did so, but they were largely those who 'had to' because they had no man to provide for them as husband or father. Then in some western countries the view prevailed that it was proper for married women to go out to work, but not when they had young children to look after. That implied a 'three-phase model' in which on leaving school a woman spent a few years in employment, then withdrew to have her children, and later might resume paid work when her children no longer needed her full-time attention. Many women still follow that pattern, but some find it disadvantageous. To resume work as a secretary or hairdresser is one thing, but a career in the professions or business management demands an uninterrupted commitment. Equality of the sexes, it is now argued, requires that women should be no more handicapped than men by family responsibilities. Such arguments clearly have a bearing on the debates about Bowlby's 'maternal deprivation' (pp. 74–5). With 'parenting' rather than 'mothering' for the care of children, perfect equality would also entail the equal sharing of household tasks and the virtual abolition of the division of labour between the sexes. While some married couples in industrial societies have genuinely tried to achieve that aim, it seems likely that many do not even really aspire to it.[28]

THE FAMILY IN AFRICA IN TRANSITION

The modern western family, as exemplified in the novels, films and other art forms that reach modern Africa, and in the personal experience of those of the African elite who have lived abroad, is one of the cultural influences at work changing the traditional patterns of kinship. Traditional systems provide the starting-point for change. Christian missions and Islam have been among the influences at work. Colonial administrations, in introducing systems of law based on those of the European colonizing powers, accordingly had to take into account both the diverse customary systems of kinship and marriage and the fact that some Africans were pledged, through Christianity, to lifelong monogamy. They also had to administer marriage laws appropriate to the non-African minorities, whether of their own Christian or Jewish countrymen, Hindu or Sikh Indians, Arab or Pakistani Muslims, or Greek or Syrian Christians. The present laws and systems of organized behaviour concerning the family, marriage and kinship in African countries are, in consequence, extremely confused – a tangle in urgent need of reform yet one which few independent African states have begun to tackle.

Confusion arose, first, as a result of conflicts among the different traditional systems when men and women of different tribes began to meet and enter into sex relations instead of tribes being relatively isolated from one another as in the traditional way of life. For example, by the 1930s problems were arising on the Copperbelt, the Rand and similar areas, as a result of unions between people of matrilineal and patrilineal tribes. Consider the case of a Bemba man and an Ngoni woman. According to Bemba ideas, the children would be of her tribe and clan. According to her kinsfolk's way of looking at things, however, they would take their tribe and clan from their father. Recognized by neither kin group as their own such children would be, in the strict sense, detribalized.

The introduction of money also had profound influence upon African marriage. As we have seen, traditional bridewealth pay-ments took the form of such things as cattle, which were contrib-uted by the husband's descent group and distributed among the bride's. Divorce, though possible, was not easy, since agreement had to be got to reverse the process – the woman's kin had to be persuaded to return the cattle, which were then shared out again among the divorced husband's people. With money payments, which a man could earn himself by a few months' or years' work in town or in the mines, marriage became a more individual matter and both the descent groups became less involved – especially as the bridewealth often proved to have been spent if there was a divorce later. Where marriage had traditionally been by service, the absence of young men in employment outside the tribal area – for example, Bemba men on the Copperbelt – involved the sub-stitution of money payments to the father-in-law with the result that something more like a bridewealth system grew up among those peoples also. A further consequence was the intrusion of a more commercial spirit into bridewealth transactions. Tradition-ally, the marriage payments had been customarily determined in kind and amount; in modern times, a bride might come to be 'valued' in money terms, a secondary education, for example, making her worth more to her father. Bridewealth might thus become, in a more literal sense of the word, bride-price.

The attitudes of the various Christian missionary bodies were a further influence. From as early as the fifteenth century Roman Catholic missionaries found themselves in difficulties over African polygamy, anticipating as they did the final ruling of the Council of Trent (1545–63) that it is forbidden for a Christian to have more wives than one.[29] With the growth of Christian missionary in-fluence, especially in the late nineteenth and early twentieth century, more and more Africans were married in a Christian church, whether or not they also went through African customary rites. Such marriages had two important implications. In the eyes of the church any subsequent unions which the man might enter into with other women (during the lifetime of his 'ring wife') could not have the status of marriage, but constituted a sinful breach of the marriage vow. The 'ring wife' alone had the status of his wife and in consequence the sole right to inherit his property. Her children alone were legitimate and again had overriding rights of inheritance. Obviously these views conflicted with those traditional amongst most African peoples, and for many the conflict led to a good deal of hypocrisy, well exemplified by the incident related by Mair:

Backsliders are not refused admission to church services, the argument being that church attendance may lead them to repent. Whether they are refused communion I am doubtful. The attempt to apply this sanction impartially might lead to highly embarrassing situations with important personages; I saw one such personage at the Christmas Communion service at N——, who to my knowledge and to that of the entire native community, has nine wives in addition to the lady who sat at his side.[30]

Secondly, church marriage had important consequences later if the marriage should break up. On the question of monogamy the different Christian churches are united. On divorce, however, they differ among themselves. (These differences, incidentally, have important consequences for the tangled divorce laws of some European countries, especially England; a discussion of these, however, would take us too far afield here.)[31] At the risk of over-simplifying, the Roman Catholic church takes literally the sentence 'Whom God hath joined let no man put asunder' and regards marriage as indissoluble during the lifetime of the spouses – though it does recognize nullity in certain cases. The Protestant tradition, both Lutheran and Calvinistic, on the contrary, is to recognize divorce though deploring it, and in suitable cases to permit divorced persons to marry others while their first spouses are still alive; the Church of England, long torn on this issue, has now recognized the irretrievable breakdown of marriage as ground for 'putting asunder'.

Against breaches of their marriage law the churches had, first and foremost, to rely on spiritual sanctions, with the final sanction of excommunication (since a person taking the Holy Communion while in a state of sin involves himself in the gravest spiritual danger). There was also a relation, however, between the laws of church and state. Before dealing with it, however, I must begin by outlining the position and the different policies on marriage of the different colonial powers.

From the point of view of a colonial administration, to introduce and insist upon a marriage law like that of their own European states was clearly impracticable. Some powers, notably Britain, did not even particularly want it. Others, notably Portugal and Belgium, regarded its eventual introduction as part of their 'civilizing mission' and were prepared to move towards it but it was recognized that progress would be slow. Meanwhile there was no alternative to a policy of pluralism. For a long time the law would have to continue to recognize and enforce the traditional systems of customary law of the various African tribes, in marriage as in other matters – land tenure, inheritance and so on. At the same time there seemed no reason to permit (for example) Europeans living in African colonies to take several wives or get divorces by returning bridewealth. It seemed only right and proper to apply to them a law similar to that of their own home country. In the same way, recognition and effect were given to the marriage laws of other ethnic minorities – Hindus, Sikhs, and Muslims, for example, in East Africa.

From a legal point of view there were two main ways in which effect could be given to such a policy. One, the British way, was to recognize the existence of several different laws of marriage – Hindu, Sikh, Islamic, native customary and what was called 'marriage under the Ordinance' – and let people choose under which law they should marry. Marriage under the Ordinance meant under a law like that of England, committing a person to monogamy and referring divorce cases also to English law (though in practice this often meant an unreformed version of the English law, before the Herbert reforms of 1937). Thus an African could, if he wished, marry under native law and custom, or he could marry under the Ordinance. And, again following English law, marriage in church was, broadly speaking, regarded as marriage under the Ordinance. Those Africans who married in church were – though hardly any of them knew it – thereby committing themselves to legal monogamy and to their divorce (if any) going through the High Court of the colony or a magistrate's court, just like Europeans.

The other possible policy was to divide up the population into different groups for this and other purposes and apply an appropriate law to each group. This was the solution favoured in Portuguese and Belgian colonies. Here the important question became whether an African had the status of *indigène* in which case customary law applied, or whether, as a result of showing that he had reached a certain level of education, etc., and gone through a particular civil procedure, he had become *assimilé, immatriculé,* or *évolué*, in which case he was treated both for marriage and other purposes on the same footing as a European. From an English point of view clear definitions of people's legal status in this way were objectionable. In their favour it was said that they afforded those Africans whose education and style of life fitted them for it the full status of civilized men, on an equal footing with Europeans, together with the responsibilities that went with it and this was better than the colour prejudice which accompanied the British system.

Faced with marital irregularities on the part of their members the churches did not have to rely only on spiritual sanctions. If, for example, a 'ring wife' were deprived of her late husband's property and a clan council gave it to his children by other women, if a man subsequently went through a native customary wedding procedure with another woman, or if one were involved in divorce proceedings in the courts of the colonial power, the churches could and sometimes did intervene, urging their members to take or to abstain from a particular course of legal action. Not that church and state always saw eye-to-eye in such cases. For example, in a case which was related to me in Uganda a woman, married in church to a man who had subsequently gone through the full ceremony of native customary marriage to another woman, prosecuted him, at missionaries' instance, for the crime of bigamy. The district commissioner, sitting as magistrate, had no alternative on the facts but to find him guilty. The district commissioner was, however, angry that such a case should have been pressed, since he regarded the man's only offence as being that of regularizing his second marriage under customary law, instead of taking his second mate as a concubine; he accordingly imposed a quite nominal fine.

Nor was it always the foreign missionaries who brought a Christian influence to bear on marriage. In Buganda, it was African Christians, especially chiefs who were prominent members of the Native Anglican Church, who were responsible for the passing of a law by the Great Lukiiko in 1917 which, in effect, outlawed native customary marriage (regarded as *obukafiri* or pagan) and permitted only the choice between Christian and Muslim marriage – though, as we have seen, many of the same chiefs were lax to the point of hypocrisy in applying the law to their own conduct.

It will have become clear, even from so brief an analysis as this, that extreme confusion prevailed in colonial Africa about marriage, the family and kinship. Different systems of law and custom, different and often incompatible expectations on the part of different people, made many people uncertain and confused about their position and that of their marriages. For example, attempting to satisfy the feelings of traditionally minded kinsfolk, educated Africans might go through rites or practices like bridewealth which, imbued as they were with the ideas of romantic love, they privately found obnoxious. Others might find that marriage in church unexpectedly landed them in unforeseen complications with European lawyers and magistrates if there were to be a divorce later. Missionaries or Christian relatives might intervene to contest inheritance cases against the traditional decisions of a clan council. The church might step in to limit bridewealth payments, or forbid parts of native customary wedding ceremonies as pagan.

THE FAMILY AND SOCIAL CHANGE

What will be the future of marriage, the family, and kinship in Africa? Can we assume that the long-term trend will be towards the weakening of extended clan and lineage ties and the adoption of something more like the western type of family as briefly characterized above, with its nuclear family household and bilateral kindred? The question is an open one.

At present there is a clear association between an industrial economy and a family structure of this type, which following W. J. Goode we may call the 'conjugal' family. At first sight it might seem that this is no more than a coincidence. The rise of modern industry took place first in western Europe, notably England, then in North America and other lands among people with European traditions. These societies also happened to have a Christian tradition and a rule of monogamy; but it might be argued that there is no necessary connection between these facts.

One partial exception to these generalizations could be raised, namely Israel. Here we have a state which clearly does not share the Christian tradition, yet where the family pattern is broadly of the 'conjugal' type. But this apparent exception is not a very strong or conclusive one. Israel shares with the western world the Judaic if not the Christian tradition. Moreover, it has been mainly peopled by immigrants from western Europe and America, bringing with them many of the cultural traditions and ways of life of those countries.

A much more serious exception, and one which is really fatal to the coincidence theory, is Japan. The cultural traditions of Japan are completely different from those of western Europe, springing as they do from different origins and having developed in total isolation from the outside world. There can be no question, therefore, of any general cultural similarities or influences. Moreover, the family and related institutions in Japan are not identical with those of the west. Yet they resemble one another at a remarkable number of important points. Traditional Japanese marriage was monogamous and there was only one mistress of the household, just as there was only one male head. Moreover, the kinship terminology was perfectly bilateral. Japanese is, indeed, unusual among non-European languages in having exact equivalents for those tiresome terms like 'aunt' and 'cousin'. Despite impressions to the contrary among some earlier writers, there were no clans or lineages in traditional Japan, though 'stem' and 'branch' families were linked through ancestral observances. And there was a tradition that non-successor sons – those who could not hope to inherit the father's land or other assets – should leave home and set up independent households elsewhere. This tradition paralleled the neolocal practices of the west, and like them facilitated the transition to industrial conditions. With the rise of modern industry, non-successor sons could move into employment in the growing towns and set up households which in traditional terms were branches of the original stem, the household which was left behind in the country on the family land.[32]

It seems clear, then, that a family tradition approximating to the conjugal type and the rapid rise of a modern industrial economy are related by more than coincidence. In the west, it used to be thought that the conjugal family was the result of industrialization; but as already mentioned it now seems to be established that this was not the case, for the main features of the western family are little different now from what they were before the industrial revolution. So far from being the result of the rise of industry, the conjugal family could have been one of its causes, or at least a facilitating factor.

It has accordingly been argued by W. J. Goode that there is a 'fit' or congruence between the conjugal family and the industrial economy. He further contends that as industrialization proceeds in other continents and areas of the developing world, so their family patterns will tend to converge on the conjugal pattern of the already-industrialized countries. Since their starting points are widely different, this may mean that they will tend to move in opposite directions to converge on the conjugal pattern. For example, in some traditional societies divorce was difficult or even impossible – Hindu society, for instance. In others it was easy – for example under the laws and customs of Islam. So we find that in modern India a start has been made with the introduction of legal divorce, while at the same time some Arab countries are enacting laws which prevent a husband from divorcing his wife simply by saying 'I divorce thee' three times before witnesses, and introducing a form of judicial process. In one case, then, divorce is being made easier, while in the other it is being made more difficult. Yet both are moving towards the position characteristic of the conjugal family in most western countries, where divorce is possible (in order to regularize the breakdown of relations between spouses who prove to be incompatible), yet difficult (in order to safeguard the interests of dependent women and children and the institution of marriage itself).[33]

It may be that the patterns of marriage and family life in Africa, and the actual behaviour of people in this area of their daily lives, will come to converge upon the conjugal model. At present, however, the situation is confused, and it is hard to pick out clear trends. Traditional institutions and attitudes remain strong among large numbers of people. The influence of Christianity and Islam have been considerable, while the period of colonial administration in the newly-independent countries of Africa left a tangle of cross-purposes and conflicting laws and attitudes. It is clear that the governments of these countries have a tremendous task to clear the tangle and enact new unified laws of marriage, the family, inheritance, and the like which will end ambiguities, treat everybody on the same footing, and let everyone know how he or she stands. Two countries which have taken the initiative in this important task are Kenya and Tanzania. It is very much to be hoped that other African countries will follow their lead. Meanwhile there can be no greater challenge to African sociologists of the future than to play their part in educating public opinion in their countries for these urgently necessary reforms.

SUGGESTIONS FOR FURTHER READING

J. Bowlby, *Maternal care and mental health* (Geneva, World Health Organization, 1951). Also published in a slightly simplified form as: *Child care and the growth of love* (London, Penguin, 1953).

M. L. Rutter, *Maternal deprivation reassessed* (London, Penguin, 1972).

A. M. Clarke and A. D. B. Clarke, *Early experience: myth and evidence* (London, Open Books, 1976).

R. Fox, *Kinship and marriage* (London, Penguin, 1967).

T. Parsons, 'The incest taboo in relation to social structure and the socialization of the child', *British Journal of Sociology*, V (1954), 101–7.

A. R. Radcliffe-Brown and C. Daryll Forde (eds.), *African systems of kinship and marriage* (Oxford University Press, 1950). A detailed comparative study of the traditional kinship systems of a number of African tribes; an essential source of material on the traditional starting-point before modern changes.

A. Phillips (ed.), *A survey of African marriage and family life* (Oxford University Press, 1953). Three essays, respectively, by the editor on the legal aspects, Lucy Mair on the sociological perspective, and Lyndon Harries on the missionary point of view of changes in African marriage in the late colonial period.

W. J. Goode, *World revolution and family patterns* (Free Press of Glencoe, 1963 and 1970).

Republic of Kenya, *Report of Commission on the Law of Marriage and Divorce*, 1968.

Republic of Tanzania, *Government's proposals on a uniform law of marriage*, Government paper no. 1, 1969.

wwwwwwwwwwwwwwwwwwwwwwwwwwwwwwwwwwwwwwwwwwwwwwwwwwwwwwww

Technology, economy and society

This chapter explores the relations between technology, economy and social structure. It considers the implications for human society of the different ways in which people make a living and the different forms and extent of their control over the material environment.

It should begin with the broad distinction between primitive, peasant and industrial societies. In earlier chapters it has been taken for granted that some such distinction exists, without very close inquiry, especially in chapter 2. We saw how social anthropology began in the late nineteenth century as the study of 'primitive peoples' and how more recent reconsideration has led to this being amended to 'small-scale societies'.

People dislike the word primitive, especially when they suspect it is being applied to themselves, and it is natural and often right that they should. It has been much misused in the past. Nineteenth-century Europeans, especially perhaps Victorian Englishmen, were rather prone to think of themselves and their societies as the highest products of an evolutionary process in which lower or more primitive forms had been left behind. Nowadays the world situation has changed. Europeans, including the English, can no longer cherish illusions of grandeur and people of the societies they once called 'primitive' now question and resent the term, so, like 'race' and 'class', it has become almost a dirty word, not to be used in polite society.

Yet – like 'race' and 'class' – it is a word we cannot very well do without. In biology it has a meaning free of hidden value-judgements. We do not insult the frog when we say that it is primitive compared with the lizard; we mean only that, though a perfectly effective and viable organism, frogs, like other amphibia, have to go back to water to breed, while lizards, like other reptiles, have been emancipated altogether from living in water. They are thus more advanced; they have a greater independence of their environment. This is one important criterion of evolutionary primitiveness or advancement. The other main criterion is complexity. Primitive forms of life are relatively simple; there is little division of labour between the parts, or organs. More advanced forms develop special organs, such as eyes, lungs and a bony skeleton which enable them to cope with their environment more effectively – and there is thus a connection between the two aspects of evolution.

Much the same can be said of human societies. Recent research has taught us much about the most technologically primitive societies of all: those that depended on hunting and food-gathering.[1] Though few peoples still live in that way, more did so recently enough for competent observers' accounts to be available; they include the Andamanese (See pp. 141–2), the Hadza of Tanzania, the !Kung Bushmen, Australian aborigines, and some Amazon forest peoples. In such societies people live in groups commonly numbering about forty. Men go hunting or fishing, while women and children pick berries, dig up wild edible roots, and cook. Every few weeks the group move as they exhaust the available food within reach of their camp. Contrary to many early impressions, life is not particularly hard. With their impressively detailed knowledge of the environment and skill in utilizing it, hunters and gatherers can subsist with no more than two or three hours' light work a day. The rest is spent in pastimes such as gambling, story-telling, ceremonial, and drug-taking. Dwellings are rudimentary, much use being made of caves and rock shelters; and possessions are necessarily few, since everything has to be carried whenever the group move. Though the diet is usually varied and wholesome, there is little or nothing that can be done to combat disease, and the aged and chronically sick may in the end have to be abandoned. Used in this way, a given area of land can support only a few people; one estimate suggests an average density of eight per hundred square kilometres. Unlike agriculture, such a way of life could not support a settled population with stocks of food, town life, much division of labour, or the highly developed material culture we call civilization.

One way of classifying societies according to their technological basis was that of Hobhouse, Wheeler and Ginsberg, who grouped what they called the 'simpler peoples' – primitive and peasant societies – into seven main classes (Fig. 10).[2]

Hobhouse, Wheeler and Ginsberg's classification, however, intended as it was to apply to what they called the 'simpler peoples', left out the society which is technologically most advanced of all – modern industrial society, as it has emerged in the last two hundred years or so, beginning in England and western Europe and spreading now all over the world. The mastery of the environment which modern technology gives to modern society makes all other societies appear primitive by contrast, and as a rough first approximation we often speak of the broad division between 'primitive' and 'modern' society. Of course, this is really too simple. There are degrees of primitiveness even among non-modern or 'traditional'

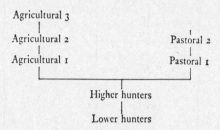

Fig. 10. (After Hobhouse, Wheeler and Ginsberg.)

Lower hunters. Food-gathering and small game hunting; shelters rather than houses; no domestic animals except dog. For example Australian aborigines, Bushmen.

Higher hunters. The chase, substantial houses or tents; sometimes spinning, weaving and pottery; canoes; horses or other domestic animals, but no agriculture and no herds. For example British Columbia tribes, Eskimo.

Agricultural 1. Hunting and food-gathering, nomadism, with some cultivation by women using digging stick. No domestic animals beyond poultry and pigs. No metal; rudimentary pottery. Barter. For example Negritoes, Sakai, Ainu.

Agricultural 2. Subsistence agriculture the main support. Houses, domestic industries. Animals kept but not for draught; hoe digging, no plough. For example Azande, Mayombe.

Agricultural 3. Flocks and herds, draught cattle. The plough. Sometimes irrigation, manuring and rotation of crops. Metals, woodwork, textiles. Regular trade. For example many Asian peasant peoples.

Pastoral 1. Regular keeping of flocks and herds the main support. Little or no agriculture, and but slight development of other arts. For example Tatars, Masai.

Pastoral 2. Flocks and herds the main support, but with subsistence agriculture also, including cases where practised by a serf or tributary people; metal and handicrafts. For example Bedouin, Hima, Kirghiz.

societies, as I have just been showing. Moreover there are two important intermediate cases: peasant societies, which I shall deal with later in this chapter, and those societies which, like many in Africa today, are in the process of changing from traditional to modern, the process we shall call 'modernization'; these societies can be described as 'transitional'.

However, if we accept that the main line of social evolution has been in the greater control over and independence of the environment, a number of important things have to be said about this.

First, command over resources (which is another way of saying control of the environment) goes with specialization and the division of labour. I need say little on this point; most of it was said by that great Scottish economist Adam Smith nearly two hundred years ago and I need only refer readers to the opening paragraphs of *The wealth of nations*. (It has been said that Adam Smith knew about developing countries – he lived in one.)

Secondly, as Adam Smith further pointed out, the division of labour is limited by the extent of the market. 'When the market is very small, no person can have any encouragement to dedicate himself entirely to one employment, for want of the power to exchange all that surplus part of the produce of his own labour, which is over and above his own consumption for such parts of the produce of other men's labour as he has occasion for.'[3]

The sociological implications of this truth are fundamental. In small-scale societies, where the scope for specialization is limited – where people do not limit themselves to one employment – each person tends to occupy few social roles, and the roles themselves tend to be many-sided. Thus being a father may include directing agricultural operations, building a house, taking part in hunting and fishing and teaching boys how to do all these tasks. Moreover, in such societies, many roles are included in, or subsumed under, kinship roles. People cannot avoid being sons and daughters and they seldom manage to avoid being wives or husbands or parents. As we have seen, the role of father may include that of farmer, hunter, builder, etc.; the role of grandfather may merge with those of priest and judge. Equally, it may be difficult to distinguish between kinship, political, military and economic roles.

Nowhere is this shown more clearly than in the contrasting ways in which a labour force is recruited and managed in primitive and in modern society. In many parts of the primitive world it is said that to build a house the first thing to do is to brew beer; people come to drink the beer, and some may stay to help you with the house. Such a method of assembling a labour force, depending on kinship and neighbourhood relations, contrasts sharply with the daily or monthly contract of employment for wages, which is the way modern building firms in African towns recruit men. Among the Bemba in traditional conditions, as described by Audrey Richards, going to work on the chief's gardens was a way of recruiting a labour force that depended on political obligation – it was the duty of the Citimukulu's subjects. It could also be seen as a payment of rent for the right to cultivate one's own land, the Citimukulu being regarded as the ultimate lord of the land. It had educational aspects. While they were at the court the workers listened in to the hearing of cases and extended their knowledge of the customary law; and among the Swazi a similar institution had a strongly military aspect, the word *libutfo* being translated as 'regiment' in English. The roles of subject, worker, pupil and soldier could not be clearly distinguished.[4]

Firth describes in detail the making of turmeric on the island of Tikopia. Turmeric is a pigment extracted from a root crop which also yields a food. The process – part ritual, part manufacture – involved separating the two. It was directed by the Ariki Tafua, a chief and clan head, and the labour and capital equipment (bowls, troughs, moulds, etc.) were contributed by his family and those of the other principal participants. Kinship, locality, political status and ritual considerations all played a part in determining who joined in the process and how and by whom it was directed.[5]

As a contrasting example we may take the English coal mining community described in the early 1950s by Dennis, Henriques and Slaughter.[6] It is worth summarizing in some detail.

Work in the mine went on night and day, being organized in three 'shifts' over each twenty-four hour period. During the night shift about 300 men were at work. The 'machine men' worked a cutting machine which undercut the coal seam for a distance of about 4 to 6 feet horizontally along a 'face' anything from 50 to 300 yards long; coal seams there varied between 3 and 5 feet in thickness. Meanwhile 'drawers-off' were removing the pit props supporting the roof, and replacing them by stone packs or pillars, so that the valuable props could be used again nearer the face.

The biggest number of men – about 900 – worked on the day shift, from early morning to mid-afternoon. Most of them were 'colliers', who worked in small teams to loosen the coal which had been undercut during the night, and load it on to the conveyor belt. The face was divided into portions known as 'stints' and the work was relatively highly paid, each team of colliers being paid under a contract which made it profitable for them to loosen and load as much coal as quickly as possible.

About 500 men worked the afternoon shift. 'Panners' moved forward the equipment – coal cutting machinery, conveyor belt, etc. – left behind by the colliers during the day; while 'rippers' enlarged the two big tunnels or 'gates' leading to and from the face. 'Back-rippers' meanwhile, working in pairs, were expanding old gates, opening new ones, and also from time to time opening up new faces. The last-named work was exceptionally hard and hot, since they were working in spaces not yet ventilated; the other tasks, however, were comparatively easy, and as they were largely unsupervised these were jobs coveted by all and awarded to older men and those who for some reason the management wanted to favour – especially, in this case, trade union officials.

Most face-workers were paid, relatively highly, on the basis of contracts negotiated for each piece of work with the 'deputy', the underground representative of the management – negotiated, usually, with bitterness and acrimony, arguments and rows. By contrast, several other grades of workers were paid an hourly rate. These included the 'haulage men' below ground, who looked after the conveyor belt and the transport of the coal to the shaft bottom by means of railed tubs; and various categories of surface workers who did not go underground at all. These hourly paid jobs were done mostly by the very young and the very old – young men not yet considered equal to face-work, and older men who were past it. A good deal of tension existed between the face workers, paid piece rates, and the hourly-paid workers. Colliers, for example, would accuse haulage men of spoiling their earnings if breakdowns or delays occurred in moving the coal back. The local trade union branch was regarded as being more concerned with the face-workers' interests than with those of men of lower social status, the hourly-paid, and least of all with surface workers. But tensions within the union and between the men were as nothing compared with the hostility between men and management, which had been traditional for a century when the mine was privately owned, and had continued almost unabated after nationalization.

This example could no doubt be paralleled in Africa and a similarly complex division of labour is found in Nigerian coal mines, on the Copperbelt and elsewhere. It will serve as a basis for contrasts with a traditional economy and society. The raising of a labour force by contracts (whether for payment by time or by the 'piece' – that is by the amount produced) involving definite money reward; the specialized structure of managers, foremen, skilled and unskilled workers of various grades, maintenance staff, clerks, and so on; and above all the different conceptions of efficiency in the two cases and the possibility of tensions among workers and between management and workers, all heighten the contrast.

Thus, in traditional societies such as those in Africa, there were no such roles as manager, foreman, clerk, or unskilled worker. All these and literally thousands of others have come into being in recent times in these societies as part of their transition to a modern economy. As we saw in chapter 1, the social structure becomes more complex, with the addition of new roles, as specialization increases. Since specialization depends upon the extent of the market, it follows that larger-scale societies are liable to be more complex. Part of the process of economic development is the growth of complexity concurrently with the growth of the scale of society; this is our third point.

Fourthly, the extent of the market, or the scale of society, critically depends upon a particular aspect of technology – the technology of communications. In modern Africa we are thoroughly familiar with the dramatic rapidity with which new roads stimulate the growth of the market. Cash crops are grown, and can be profitably moved out and sold, where only subsistence agriculture was worth while before. Specialization and the division of labour and the modern economy enter as soon as the road is finished. The large-scale societies of past ages of human history have depended just as much upon communications and when, for example, the collapse of the Roman empire eventually caused its splendid system of roads to fall into disrepair the scale of society in Europe contracted. Trade ceased between countries where it had been commonplace, material poverty and the collapse of cultural achievement followed. We are all familiar with the crucial role of communications in the overseas expansion of European power in the last three hundred years.

Communications and communications technology are vital factors in determining the scale of society because three things flow along them: people, goods and information. The importance of the first two is plain enough, but more needs to be said on the importance of the third.

In the broad distinction between primitive and modern societies literacy is an important factor in its own right.[7] The distinction has even been seen as that between 'non-literate' societies and those in which at least some people can read and write. Writing is the oldest, though not now the only, way in which information can be put into material form and stored, or carried over a distance and read at the other end. Nowadays we also have recording techniques using film and tape. When non-material culture, or knowledge, can take material shape in this way the consequences for society are profound.

First, more people can learn more easily about societies other than their own. Travel alone makes this possible to a limited extent. The increased personal movement that has followed the building of roads in Africa has led to many people getting to know at least something about the life of tribes other than their own. But information technology enormously speeds up that process and allows it to happen on a vaster scale. Through books, newspapers, films, radio and television the inhabitants of modern Accra or Salisbury can gain impressions of what life is like in California or Poland. For those who take the trouble to seek out the books, very full accounts are available of the life and society of peoples all over the world. Thus sociology students in many countries become quite familiar with the life and society of Tikopia, of an American small town ('Middletown'), of an English village named Gosforth, of the Nuer, of tribes in New Guinea and Samoa, and so on.

Through the accounts of social anthropologists, in particular, the culture – or significant portions of the culture – of non-literate societies have become embodied, in written form, into the culture of modern industrial society. The books containing these accounts are not just stored on the shelves of university libraries but taken out and read by sociology students (and their professors) so that a knowledge of other cultures is part of the living heritage of knowledge of at least a small minority in modern society, among whom it is discussed, commented upon, refined and made the basis for further explorations. In some cases this knowledge becomes more widely spread in modern societies. For example, the books of Margaret Mead about New Guinea and Samoa have become quite popular and have been widely read by educated people generally in America and Britain, not just by sociologists and social anthropologists. To some extent the culture of societies in New Guinea and Samoa has become part of the culture of modern Britain and America.[8] The important thing about this statement is that the converse is not true. Because modern society is a literate society it can incorporate other cultures in a way in which the societies of New Guinea and Samoa – in their traditional form – cannot. It is a one-way process.

Secondly, the storing of information in the form of books, or tape, means that the sheer quantity of knowledge in modern society can increase practically without limit. In non-literate societies the quantity of knowledge is limited perhaps to what one man can get into his head – to what one old man can remember. (We must qualify this slightly, for such societies do include, for example, ritual specialists whose knowledge is not shared by old men generally. But, as we have seen, the division of labour is limited in primitive societies and relatively few such specialists are to be found. Most old men know most of the law.) A society which possesses the means of storing information can break through that limitation. Your own university library makes the point plainly enough. It contains vastly more books than you, or any one person, will ever read.

As any librarian will tell you, too, the sheer quantity of knowledge and the rapidity with which it now piles up, creates pressing problems of indexing and retrieval. It means that it is both possible and necessary for people to develop narrowly special interests. There are experts on Africa in the academies of the Soviet Union and specialists on the Soviet Union in American universities. Ease of communication among modern countries drives home, once more, the extent to which the modern world is one. The scale of modern industrial society is virtually the whole earth. It also points up how wide is the range of choice open to people in a fully modern society. This is true in the field of science and scholarship; it is also true of most other aspects of life. As Apter has well expressed it, 'To be modern means to see life as alternatives, preferences, and choices.'[9] In food and drink, for example: in a traditional African society there was little choice of diet; one staple alone, as a rule, bore the name of 'food', while meat, fish, or vegetables were merely trimmings – and there was just one sort of beer. The citizen of a modern society can choose from dozens of forms of alcoholic drink – many different sorts of wine from lands with a Mediterranean climate, or whisky from Scotland or Canada, or beer from England or Denmark. Food continues to have a distinctive national flavour in each country, but in recent years Chinese food has become so popular in England that pre-packed Chinese dishes to take home and cook yourself are now commercially marketed on a large scale in English grocers' shops. A person can choose to cultivate a taste for 'pop' music, or its predecessor – jazz – or the music of the classical composers like Bach, Mozart, Beethoven, or the 'modern' music of Messiaen or Boulez, or none at all.

What one can only call the sheer quantity of culture, then,

which characterizes modern industrial society in contrast to more primitive societies, not only makes choice and specialization possible, it forces them upon us. Life is short and we cannot do everything. Whatever we choose to learn or to do we thereby forgo alternatives. Thus in modern society young people can choose among different ways of making a living, whereas in a traditional society like that of the Nuer every young man had to be a herdsman. But occupational and career choices are only one aspect of the wide variety which young people encounter in modern societies. Choosing among the many different social worlds or sub-cultures that are available, each with its own values and 'lifestyle' (as they call it), has become a matter of bewilderment and even anxiety to many young people, about which they use phrases like 'a crisis of identity' as they wonder with which group to identify themselves.

The diversity of sub-cultures which characterizes modern societies was clearly perceived by Africans in the colonial period, who used to say that there were different 'types' of Europeans – the administrator, the missionary, the trader, the doctor, and so on. It is not hard to understand how the outlook on life, the tastes, the aims, even the manners and the use of language, of (say) an Anglican clergyman long immersed in the sub-culture of the Church of England would differ from those of men whose lives had been spent in the widely different sub-cultures of business, the civil service, or the medical profession, even though they might all be from the same national community.

It would be a very long task to list all the sub-cultures of modern industrial society and I can do no more than indicate some of the more important types. National differences are, of course, very important. France is not England. Language, law, currency, among many factors, constitute important differences. National cultures have by no means yet been submerged into uniformity. However, we cannot simply equate nationality with culture in the modern world for two important reasons. First, as we have seen, there is a rich diversity of sub-cultures within the national cultures of modern states. Secondly, however, there are also very considerable uniformities which transcend their boundaries. Thus English is the language not only of England but also of the United States and of many nations that have historical associations with Britain. There is an increasing trend for most world communications to be in one or other of a handful of world languages – English, French, Spanish, Chinese and Russian. Engineering practice, town planning, the organization of industry (factory, manager, foreman), clothes, cars, the style of life of political and business leaders – these are more or less indistinguishable throughout modern industrial society. If you were to arrange a meeting of (say) experts on urban sanitation, or television producers, or airport security officers, from any of the different countries of the modern world – America, Ghana, Japan, Hungary – and overcame language barriers by installing simultaneous translation, you would find that their lives, their problems, their attitudes, were closely similar. The fact that they practise a common occupation would create similarities, despite the national differences among them. Indeed, some of the institutions of the modern world are international in character, and would not be what they are if they were not international. One important institution of this kind is science; another is sport. Some formal organizations are explicitly international in character, and create a world of their own transcending national boundaries. The most important of these is obviously the United Nations and its associated organizations, together with other international bodies like the World Bank. Another class of international organizations are the so-called 'multi-national corporations', business enterprises whose interests and management extend over many countries. In a complex society religion is to some extent a specialized activity with its own sub-cultures, and many of these too are international – the Roman Catholic Church, for example, the Anglican communion, and some Islamic sects like the Shia Ismailia Khoja.

The arts and a wide range of recreational and leisure activities in modern society are each characterized by its own sub-culture into which newcomers are initiated. Age differences may be associated with sub-cultures as in the case of the 'youth sub-culture' of American society. It is even possible to discern a criminal sub-culture. Perhaps most important, there are marked cultural differences among social classes, as we shall see in the next chapter.

Thus it is possible to arrive at a view of modern industrial society as a single interdependent system of institutions. It is enormously complex and divided into a rich variety of sub-cultures. But it can be seen only as one single interlocking whole. It is one world against the many small worlds of traditional societies.

Perhaps I can set out the broad contrast in the form of a table.

Traditional societies	Modern industrial society
Technologically primitive.	Technologically advanced.
Poor.	Affluent.
Small scale.	Large scale.
Little division of labour, specialization.	Complex division of labour, much specialization.
Many if not most other roles subsumed under kinship. Each individual occupies few roles.	Kinship roles of less importance, out-weighed by others. Complexity of structure; each individual occupies many roles.
Kinship the dominant institution of the whole social structure.	Kinship, though vital, only a relatively small part of the whole social structure.
Pre-literate, non-literate. Mass media absent; communication by word of mouth.	Literate. Mass media important.
Oral tradition.	Knowledge stored in books (also tape, film, etc.).
Predominantly rural.	Predominantly urban.
Small communities, self-contained, culturally uniform. Diversity between local cultures, but not within them.	Large communities, interdependent. Rich variety of sub-cultures within ONE WORLD.

Now consider the intermediate case of peasant societies. As the term is generally understood, peasants make a living from the land with simple equipment and mostly with family labour (though some latter-day peasant communities have modernized their agricultural methods). Peasant communities are accordingly small in scale, most needs being met within them. The division of labour is limited and the occupational role structure is simple. Kinship is the dominant institution, and as in primitive or traditional societies other roles are subsumed under those of kinship. The relative isolation of peasant communities makes for cultural differences between them, so that over quite small areas there may be wide differences of language, kinship systems, inheritance customs, and the like. For all these reasons, peasant societies can be well studied by the field methods of social anthropology. Such studies have been done, for example, by Arensberg and Kimball in Ireland, by Miner in Quebec,[10] and by several authors on Chinese peasant life.[11]

Peasant communities, however, characteristically occupy a subordinate or 'underdog' position in wider systems of economic, political, and social relations.[12] There is some trade with towns and market, while much of what peasants produce from the land they occupy is yielded up as rent, tribute, tithe or tax to higher authorities such as a landowning nobility, monarchy, religious hierarchy, or bureaucracy. Peasant communities are subject to the power of those authorities, to which their loyalties may be less than heartfelt. They often regard a change of regime as merely exchanging one oppressor for another. Moreover, they may be forced to yield up their young men for military service. Many an empire's army has been made up of peasants in uniform, and many a regime has extended its sway over culturally diverse communities by posting soldiers from one ethnic area to keep order in another, where they have no kin, no common language, and little fellow-feeling with the local people.

Culturally, too, peasants have often been the underdogs. Their languages have been despised as mere dialects, just as peasants themselves have been regarded by their betters as uncouth, stupid, and obstinate. Peasant languages, often unwritten, have not been those of the centralized political institutions, of trade and law, or of the literate minority, the *literati*, with access to a world of learning. For example, the diverse languages of mediaeval Europe were long overlaid by Latin as the language of the church and of written communication among educated people, while French was the polite language spoken in the royal courts and by the nobility in many countries, including Germany, Russia, and for a time England.

ECONOMIC DETERMINISM

We now come to the question of how the technology and economy of a society are related to other aspects of the social structure. According to one view all social relations are determined by the mode of production that prevails in a particular society. The economy is seen as providing a substructure and all other institutions as a superstructure built upon it and wholly shaped by it. This view is particularly associated with Marxist thought and Marx himself wrote:

Men make cloth, linen, or silk materials in definite relations of production
. . . These definite social relations are just as much produced by men as
linen, flax, etc. Social relations are closely bound up with productive
forces. In acquiring new productive forces men change their mode of
production; and in changing their mode of production they change their
way of earning a living – they change all their social relations. The
hand-mill gives you society with the feudal lord; the steam-mill, society
with the industrial capitalist.

The same men who establish their social relations in conformity with
their material productivity, produce also principles, ideas, and categories,
in conformity with their social relations.[13]

It has been the strong tendency of Marxists to attribute political
ideas and relations, and characteristic expressions in art, literature,
science and scholarship in particular classes, to economically
determined class differentiations in society. This tendency of
thought is given the name of economic determinism.

Generally it is criticized for rather over-stating a good case. The
way of making a living which prevails in any society is certainly
liable to be closely related to all its institutions and needs to be
considered fully, whether we are concerned to analyse a society at
a point in time, or to study social change. But 'determine' is too
strong a word and we should rather use some less absolute term
such as 'influence'.

Two main objections may be raised to economic determinism in
its extreme form. First, it is a mistake to think of 'the economy' of a
society as if it were a single institution, or institutional complex, to
be separated from other institutions such as government, education, religion, or kinship. If economics is concerned with the way
in which scarce resources are allocated among different alternative
uses, then all institutions have an economic aspect and not only
those concerned with material production. Secondly, those institutions which are concerned primarily with satisfying material
wants – producing food, houses, clothes, etc. – are themselves
liable to be influenced by the other institutions of society. Religious beliefs and practices, for example, can affect the way in
which people make a living, as well as the other way round. It is
not a one-way process.

To illustrate the relation we may take, as an example, the
Ankole people, of Uganda, as described by Kalervo Oberg.[14]

Traditionally, they were divided into two groups, or classes; the pastoral
Ba-hima, who made up rather less than ten per cent of the population,

and who dominated the Ba-iru who lived by hoe agriculture. Economic exchange took place between them, the Ba-hima giving cattle and milk products in exchange for spears and other ironwork, wooden milk pots, and other products.

In terms of political organization, the pastoralists needed a strong central government more than the peasants. Their large herds were a constant temptation to aggressive attack both from within and without; and the daily life of Hima men, which sent them out on the hillsides, armed with spears to defend their herds against lions and other wild beasts, made them alert, tough, and warlike. A strong central power was necessary, therefore, to check fights and cattle-raids between lineages, and to organize the defence of the rich herds against raids from neighbouring tribes. The king was accordingly a Hima noble, and the central government and the ritual life of the king and his court were traditionally regarded as strictly matters of the Ba-hima. (Great was their consternation when, under British rule, a Mw-iru became prime minister of the Ankole kingdom.)

Important differences in the kinship systems, too, were related to the two different modes of livelihood. Relatively to their means, bridewealth was far more onerous among the Ba-iru. It was necessary to borrow goats and cattle to raise the customary two heads of cattle, or equivalent in goats, and a man might be burdened by his bridewealth debts for many years. For a Mu-hima, the customary four heads of cattle were a trivial payment out of a herd that might number scores or even hundreds. Nevertheless, polygyny was more widespread among the Ba-iru; Oberg estimated that, on the average, married men among them had 1·5 wives, while among the Ba-hima the average was 1·1. Ba-hima spoke disdainfully of the great desire of the Mw-iru for wives, and told him that once they used to practise monogamy, like Europeans.

This difference was clearly related to the nature of women's work in the two classes. Ba-iru women not only bore and reared children, but also carried out agricultural production. They were in a strong position in the home, and could in a quarrel neglect to cook or run home to mother in order to bring a husband to terms. It was in a husband's interest to keep on good terms with his wife on whom he depended. Among the Ba-hima, however, apart from bearing and rearing sons, women were regarded as more or less useless. They were excluded by ritual beliefs from making themselves useful with the cattle, which were kept very strictly a man's affair. Where the Mw-iru wanted both sons and daughters, therefore, the Mu-hima wanted only sons – men to build up a strong lineage, upon which, with the king, he depended to secure his rights. The kinship structure of the two groups accordingly differed, with a richer terminology and a stronger tendency among the Ba-hima to a patrilineal clan system.

In Ankole, then, the influence of the two ways of making a living upon the kinship and government of the two classes was plainly both important and pervasive. But Ankole is still some way short of a case of economic determinism. It was for magico-religious reasons, not rational ones based on technical necessities, that Hima men insisted on handling everything to do with the cattle themselves; in other societies, women are allowed to help with cattle, and show themselves perfectly competent at it. There was no reason in the basic technology of Hima life why women should be regarded as more or less useless apart from their reproductive function. Thus, in this respect at least, the traditional magico-religious beliefs and practices of Ankole do not seem to have been very closely related to their material way of life and on this point Oberg plainly stated: 'I do not know why the Banyankole have totemism, and the ancestor cult, why they do not have age-classes and circumcision rites.'

Other pastoral people in Africa (e.g. Masai) had age-classes and circumcision rites; the Hima did not. Some peoples, whose basic economy was that of hoe agriculture, had age-classes and circumcision rites (e.g. Kikuyu); the Iru did not. Hoe agriculture seems to have been an extremely poor determinant. It supported every variety of political and kinship structure in traditional Africa. Matrilineal clans (Bemba), patrilineal clans (Gisu, Kiga), patrilineages (Nilotic peoples), age-grade systems (Kikuyu), and a wide variety of chieftainship systems (Ganda, Bemba, etc.) were all among the 'superstructures' based upon the same 'substructure' of the woman with the hoe. There could hardly be a clearer refutation of the extreme claims made for economic determinism.

But a comparison of traditional economies and societies, as they once were, is not enough. To complete this discussion we must bring in some consideration, however brief, of social and economic change.

ECONOMIC DEVELOPMENT AND SOCIAL CHANGE

No one who lives in modern Africa can be unaware that economic changes bring social changes in their train. This makes it, perhaps, all the more important to stress that economic changes can occur only when the social conditions are favourable. For most of human history, over most of the world, they were not. After the first great technical revolution in human history, the invention of agriculture some 8,000 years B.C. or thereabouts, and after the rapid social changes that this entailed – population growth, the rise of the first cities in the Middle East, India and perhaps eastern Europe – there followed long periods of technical stagnation, so that it is not much too simple to say that until 300 years ago man's basic technology was still Neolithic all over the world. In places it still is. The second great technical revolution, in which we are still living, began in western Europe, especially England, roughly 200 years ago. (In more than a manner of speaking, it began among the coal-laden hills and valleys of northern England which I see from my windows as I write these words.) Just what was the unique combination of circumstances in western Europe in the seventeenth and eighteenth centuries that started off the staggeringly rapid processes of technical and economic change that now overwhelm us? This was, of course, the question to which the great scholar Max Weber addressed himself. It is a vast question, and we can do scant justice to the richness and complexity of his answers.

It was not climate, nor geology; North American Indians and other people inhabited lands with similar climates and with coal and iron deposits, without showing the slightest sign of industrial development. It was not the general structure of society. Inequalities of wealth and power in feudal Europe were fairly closely paralleled in India, China, Japan and other countries with a military nobility lording it over an oppressed peasantry. It was not even 'the state of the industrial arts'; in the traditional crafts of weaving, building, etc. Europeans 300 years ago were not noticeably superior to Indians and Chinese; indeed in some crafts, such as silk weaving and ceramics, the Chinese were superior, while gunpowder had been introduced into Europe from China at a somewhat earlier period, though Europeans had possibly carried the art of building and navigating wooden sailing ships to a slightly higher pitch than others. Why, then, should the industrial revolution have started in Europe and not India, China, or Japan?

Weber's is a complex analysis; at risk of over-simplifying, the one factor to which he gives somewhat greater weight than others was, surprisingly, religion. It was 'the protestant ethic' which for him was closely linked with 'the spirit of capitalism'. The Roman Catholic church had preserved the Roman and Greek scripts and with them access to the classics of early scientific and philosophical thought; but the renewal of scientific inquiry into the nature of the universe, which was an essential pre-condition for technical development, ran counter to religious dogmatism. At the same time, many of the personal traits of early Protestants – their honesty and trustworthiness, their diligence, their sobriety, the modesty of their personal tastes, and their consequent ability to save – made for the success in business of a class of people who, though scrupulously law-abiding, were impatient of authority, whether political or religious, and felt themselves answerable ultimately only to conscience as the inner voice of God. Not without struggles against the old order, therefore, the new puritan middle classes established both freedom of inquiry, and the right of economic innovators to the rewards of their enterprise – both of which were essential features of industrial capitalism as it developed in the nineteenth century in England, Europe, and America. It could not have happened elsewhere. In India, for example, its emergence was fatally blocked by the caste system, which led to the conservation of traditional crafts in closed hereditary groups, each satisfied with its due reward in a supernaturally sanctioned system of division of labour; and industrial development, when it came, came later and from outside, as the result of the activities of European foreigners (says Weber, though others dispute this).

We could, of course, apply the argument of economic determinism to seventeenth-century puritanism in Europe, and say that it was no more than a rationalization of the economic interests of the urban trading class. But there were urban trading classes in India and China too – why were they not Puritans? We can hardly explain economic development (which is what Weber was trying to do) by saying that it was due to economic development. In this case it seems clear that economic, religious, and scientific and technical changes took place together and reacted upon one another. There is no reason to say that the economic changes came first and determined the others; on the contrary, if any one of them did take the lead, it was the religious factor. Most fundamentally, economic development depended first and foremost on a change in men's minds – a change in men's view of the world and their place in it. It was this that led to a rational scientific attitude, a readiness to experiment, the acceptance of experience (or sense-data) as the only test of the truth or falsity of ideas about the world. It was associated also with an acceptance of individual responsibility, individual risk and individual reward, which were essential to the spirit of capitalist enterprise. This entailed in turn a disposition to accept change – an acceptance that changes will occur, and a readiness to accept the dislocation and re-arrangement of social relations which always go with technical and economic change.

TOWARDS A SOCIOLOGY OF DEVELOPMENT

The sociological study of economic development, and in particular the sociology of present-day developing countries, is a large and complex subject which is itself developing rapidly, and I can hope to do little more here than outline its scope. If change begins in people's minds, it follows that an important aspect of change is the communication of ideas. In the modern world, institutions con-cerned with communication include, notably, the education sys-tem and the mass media of communication – the press, film, radio and television. Thus one part of the sociology of development is concerned with the information system of society, if I may use the term. Secondly, change has personal and psychological aspects. Thirdly, technical discovery and economic innovation result in changes in the social structure, often accompanied by conflict. Fourthly, economic development is usually closely associated with the growth of towns. Finally, however, it is important to dis-tinguish between the processes of change in those countries in which economic development was endogenous (that is, those countries in which it began of its own accord, which 'pulled themselves up by their own bootstraps' as the Americans say) and in those in which it has occurred under the stimulus of outside forces and the activities of foreigners.

EDUCATION AND THE MASS MEDIA

Readers of this book will not need to be reminded of the effect that modern education has in widening people's mental horizons. When people can read, and learn that things can be done differ-ently, they are presumably more ready to imagine the effects of change in their own lives, and to work for changes that they think will benefit them. The educated elites of developing countries are, moreover, in touch with a wider world than their less educated kinsmen and fellow-citizens; their mastery of one or more of the major world languages alone is sufficient to open their minds to an awareness of the modern world, and in addition the education they have undergone is in most cases linked to the cultural and scientific traditions of one or more of the developed nations – American, British or European. As I have pointed out elsewhere:[15]

Those Africans who reached the highest political positions under British rule were almost all highly educated men, while the members of legislative councils were mainly at least secondary-educated . . . The language in which parliamentary business was conducted was English; and a command of English sufficient to ask a nimble supplementary question or seize on ambiguities in the words of a Government speaker is possessed by few but the secondary-educated . . .

The world of educated Africans spans huge contrasts – from areas of life in which people dress in skins, live in grass huts, and fight with spears over cattle, through the milieu of the mission station and the tin-roofed trading settlement, to another area of life in which people fly to New York to attend meetings of the General Assembly and negotiate dollar loans . . . Yet the world is one. The dollar loans have a bearing on the cattle-raids. If we think of two worlds, or two social systems, now impinging upon one another . . . then educated Africans are at the points of impact.

It is not only the formally educated through school and university whose minds are open to the wider world. In his book *The passing of traditional society*, the American sociologist Lerner lays particular stress on the importance of the mass media in bringing about what he calls 'empathy' (a slightly unfortunate use of a word borrowed from psychology), or a capacity to imagine things otherwise than they have always been. Lerner and others accordingly regarded the mass media as prime movers in modernization. Inkeles and Smith, who carried out a study in the 1960s in six developing countries, found that media exposure was indeed a strong and consistent influence for individual modernization. Even stronger, though, were two other influences: going to school, and working in a factory or some other modern economic organization including a reorganized co-operative agriculture. And while schooling is costly, whether to parents or to the state or both, the transformation of people's outlook on life that occurs in the course of their work costs nothing.[16]

INNOVATORS AND INNOVATIONS

Looked at in another way, the process of social change raises the question of why some people in a changing society are innovators while others are more conservative. What personal and psychological characteristics are associated with a readiness to accept new ideas? The American sociologist Rogers, summarizing a large number of studies (including his own) on the diffusion of innovations, especially among farmers, found that farmers who were prone to adopt new agricultural practices were more exposed to impersonal sources of communication such as radio, newspapers and technical journals; they travelled more, and they tended to have friends over a wider area than their own neighbourhood.[17] Rogers is careful not to assume that all new ideas are good, and indeed lists a number of innovations which deservedly failed to gain acceptance. The character of the innovation itself makes a difference, so that, for instance, an idea is more likely to be tried out if trials are possible on a small scale first, less likely if it means going over to it completely. It was, however, interesting that the one innovation that was widely adopted by American farmers who were *not* otherwise very innovative was one (the grass incubator) which was not recommended by official or expert opinion; farmers learned about it from the commercial concerns that sold it. Rogers, and some other American social scientists such as Lazarsfeld,[18] goes on to suggest that there is a 'two-step flow' of information, opinion, and new ideas; some people, more aware through the mass media of what is going on in the world, become 'opinion leaders' whose ideas are taken up by their neighbours and acquaintances. It may be that this is true of American society; but it cannot be assumed to be so elsewhere.

In Britain, for example, although Trenaman and McQuail looked for opinion leaders and a 'two-step flow' in the formation of political opinion at the time of the 1959 general election, they did not find them.[19] Some people discussed politics more than others, but the 'discussers' did not influence others, and were not themselves influenced by the mass media.

Not enough is known about the social and psychological factors which make some people in developing countries embrace change and put themselves into social situations which involve change (as for instance by moving to town), while others continue to follow more traditional practices. However, a study by Doob based on work in Africa and Jamaica raised a number of suggestive hypotheses.[20] Another social psychologist, Ogionwo, made a detailed study of 'progressive' farmers in Nigeria and compared them with their more traditional counterparts. Progressive farmers were found to have higher incomes and living standards, but that might equally well work both ways. No doubt they were better off because they adopted new farming practices, but it could also be that their greater resources made them more ready to experiment with new practices, knowing they had something to fall back on if these failed. Education, social participation, and contact with the information media were associated to some extent with readiness to adopt new methods. However, those who adopted the new ways were just as likely to be traditionally-minded as others, and they took their family and kinship obligations just as seriously. This last finding casts considerable doubt on the view, often taken for granted in discussions of development, that there is an intrinsic opposition between the 'traditional' and the 'modern', and that innovators are people who have been in some way freed from their traditional obligations such as family ties.[21]

STRUCTURAL CHANGES AND CONFLICT

I have already pointed out the changes in the social structure that accompany technical discovery and economic innovation. New social systems and sub-systems are created, like business firms and trade unions, political parties, religious denominations and recreational associations, and added to the more traditional social system of kinship. In this way people come to occupy new roles which did not exist traditionally, like labourer, clerk, foreman, branch secretary, or churchwarden; and many if not all people occupy a number of roles, in some cases a large number. As with innovativeness, people differ in this respect; some are 'joiners', others are not, and it is possible to study the social and personal factors making for high or low social participation, as it is called.

There is in a complex society also a greater possibility of conflict between sub-systems. For example, business firms, in addition to competing with one another in prices and sales, may also compete for scarce resources of capital and skilled labour. Furthermore, either individually or in concert they may act as pressure groups upon the government, for example to change the law so as to favour enterprise, to adopt tariffs or taxes in their favour, or to manage the currency so that business is stimulated. In this they may be resisted by other interests such as trade unions, whose view on such a question as the labour laws is not likely to be the same as that of employers. However, both employers and unions may have a common interest in raising the prices of industrial products and thereby increasing the profits of industrial firms (so long, that is, as the unions are able to get wage increases to match rising prices). In this they may be opposed by farmers, housewives, civil servants, and pensioners, who have an interest in stable prices. In the same way, universities and schools may be at logger-heads about examinations and entry requirements, the army and the treasury may be locked in bitter conflict over the annual estimates, and so on. In a complex society, government may be regarded as an exercise in 'tension management' (as American social scientists call it) rather than having any more positive purposes of its own.

Such conflicts are not only the result of the growth of scale and complexity; they are, in turn, likely to bring about further changes, depending on how they are resolved, and in whose favour.

TOWNS AND SOCIAL CHANGE

Fourthly, economic development is usually closely associated with the growth of towns. Adam Smith realized this when he wrote that 'the division of labour is limited by the extent of the market . . . There are some sorts of industry, even of the lowest kind, which can be carried on nowhere but in a great town.'[22]

The market is literally the central institution in any town. In-separable from the idea of a town is a way of life in which people do not produce their own food, but produce other goods and services and exchange them for food. Every town must therefore have a food market, to which the people from the surrounding country-side bring food for sale or exchange for the characteristic products of the town. These include, of course, the goods that are traded or made in town and bought by countryfolk; less obviously they include certain services that are provided at the centre of a dense population and consumed, as it were, over a wider area. Examples of these are government and administration – an example, pre-sumably, of a 'compulsory good', something which people have no choice but to 'consume' and pay for in taxation. Another example is religion. Many towns are, among other things, centres where a large temple, mosque, or church attracts the faithful, out of whose contributions clergy, cathedral staff, or a high priest are maintained. Other examples are healing and education, when large hospitals or schools and a university are situated in or near a large town, which accordingly becomes, as it were, the site of the 'industry' of health or education. As the division of labour becomes finer and the economy becomes more complex, it depends more and more on the density of population and the ease of communication which a town affords, to sustain a large enough market for the more complex and advanced kinds of activity which characterize a modern economy.

It is no accident, therefore, that economic development has taken place in and through the growth of towns. In recent times, indeed, the growth of the world's urban population has been even more rapid than that of the population as a whole. Thus between 1900 and 1960, while the world's population rather less than doubled, the urban population increased by well over five-fold, and most of this increase took place in the towns and cities of the newly developing countries.[23] In a close and detailed analysis, the American economist Hoselitz has compared the growth of towns in present-day developing countries with that in Europe and America in the early stages of their industrial revolution.[24] It seems that there are many parallels or features common to all towns in periods of economic growth, and these include the following. First, the emergence of a business class of people motivated to engage in risky enterprises. Secondly, the immigration of large numbers of people from the countryside, even in some cases from far afield, as in the case of the Irish in nineteenth-century Liverpool, or the immigrants of many different European nationalities into Chicago in the period 1880–1920; there is a parallel here to the multi-racial composition of modern African towns like Nairobi. Thirdly, the problems of physical squalor associated with this immigration of poor country-folk – low housing standards, water supply, drainage, street lighting and paving, illicit brewing and distillation, prostitution and crime. From this it follows that the contrast between wealth and poverty, the difference in the standard of living between those of the business class who succeed (and by no means all do) and the poorest of the immigrant labourers becomes extreme. A most striking instance of this is modern Hong Kong.

Towns, however, are not only centres of economic activity but also of politics. From the economic point of view it may make sense, as it were, to raid the town in the course of a short visit, get what you can out of it, and come away – return home, to the country, where your real life is lived. But to engage in politics means being in at the centre of things, and this in turn implies a more definite commitment to town life over a longer period. Even in the colonial period, African towns were the natural centres for political party headquarters and the editorial offices of vernacular newspapers; such things, indeed, could hardly have been any-where else but at the centres of transport and communication with ready access to post and telegraph offices, bus centres and the like. Since independence, it must follow that more Africans in the highest positions of political power will become townsmen, along with many more civil servants, business men, traders, and so on. Urbanization, that is, must be an important aspect of social change, however much some people may cling to country life as an ideal and retain their country houses if they can afford them.

ECONOMIC DEVELOPMENT – ENDOGENOUS AND INDUCED

In the last few paragraphs I have been dealing with some ways in which the development process in present-day developing countries has been like that undergone by the modern industrial states at earlier periods in their history. I must now point out that there are certain important differences between 'endogenous' de-velopment (that is, development which is stimulated and carried through inside a national community with its own resources, in a self-generating manner) and development that occurs as a result of outside influences.

One important difference is that a society undergoing develop-ment at the present day need not go through the painful, even cruel, process of accumulating its own capital. In a country starting with only the resources of a subsistence economy, the initial saving necessary for capital accumulation must for a time reduce still further a standard of living which is already low. Thus in England it was the best part of a century before the working class began to benefit from industrial development. In other words, some three generations of workers were forced to live even poorer and more precarious lives than they had as peasants before their descendants at last began to reap the benefits of their sufferings and enjoy higher real incomes. The legacy of that period is still with us in the form of the class bitterness and industrial strife which have become traditional. By contrast, a country which undergoes its industrial revolution in the twentieth century can, in principle, borrow the capital to do it with, repaying later out of the increased income which the capital generates – whether it takes the form of investment in particular units of industrial machinery, land improvement, mining, and so on, or in the more public and general development of the country through such things as roads. It is only where there are political barriers to the lending of capital from rich to poor countries that the English history of a harsh 'forced saving' need be repeated; the Soviet Union in the 1920s and 1930s was such a case.

In the same way, not only can the money capital be borrowed from the already-developed countries; so also can the knowledge, the techniques, and even the personnel necessary for development. We are familiar enough with the presence of expatriates of all kinds – business managers, technical experts, teachers, missionaries, and so on – in developing countries.

The borrowing of capital and personnel for development, however, inevitably means that development itself begins to seem an alien intrusion, whereas when development is endogenous, the new social institutions that accompany it are indigenous or native to the society in question. Thus, for example, in England during the industrial revolution of the eighteenth and nineteenth centuries, there took place the emergence of a business class, the rapid growth of towns, the development of a system of universal primary education, the growth of the newspaper as a popular medium of communication, and political reform in which the power of the landowning gentry and aristocracy was reduced and a more democratic system instituted. It is true that all these changes could be paralleled in the history of an African state such as Kenya in the twentieth century; but there is one important difference at every point in the comparison. In England the business class were English; whatever the difference in terms of wealth and power between them and their labourers, they were of the same nation and culture; they spoke the same language and they could be appealed to in the same terms by symbolic loyalties to (for instance) queen and country. In Kenya, by contrast, the business class were foreigners, people of European and Asian descent, lacking a common culture and responsive to a different set of symbols from those of the mass of the population. Thus, when conflict occurred between employers and workers in England, the possibilities of finding common ground were greater; and the problem could, in the end, be largely solved by the growth of a trade union movement which became established and incorporated into British life as a whole; by the emergence of a Labour Party, destined eventually to take over, from time to time, the government of the country, and to participate in Parliament along with traditional Liberal and Conservative parties; and by a redistributive approach, aiming to integrate the labouring class into the common society and culture of the nation.[25] In Kenya, by contrast, the sense of injustice aroused by an overwide difference between rich and poor was not resolved by integrating the poor into the life and culture of the rich. It rather took the form of anti-foreign sentiments, in which the settlement of land by European farmers, and Asians' dominance in business, were the targets of African antagonisms. In the same way, at other points in the comparison, the growth of towns in England was not viewed as the intrusion of something alien, dominated by foreigners, as it was in Kenya. When English children went to school, it was not to be instructed in a foreign tongue and taught techniques of a foreign culture as an essential qualification for participation in the new life. If there were missionaries in England in the nineteenth century, their mission was to recall men to a long-established faith, not convert them to a new. And, crucially, in the political arena the overthrow of the rule of a privileged and powerful minority was not viewed as a successful claim by the majority to their rightful *share* in government; it was, quite simply, the end of foreign rule.

It follows from this that nationalism and socialism are related in the present-day developing countries in a quite different manner from the societies of nineteenth-century Europe in which socialism first grew up, and in the next chapter I shall go on to analyse this difference further and to give some account of African socialism. It also follows that the sociology of developing countries must be concerned with the relation between rich and poor nations, with the idea of aid taking the place of redistributive taxation and social welfare schemes. And finally, there is a racial element in the subject. Because of the circumstance that the rich industrial nations are inhabited by pale-skinned peoples, while the developing countries' populations are on the whole darker-skinned, the relations between them are affected by the same sort of attitudes and practices as those which affect the relation between 'whites' and 'non-whites' within multiracial countries.

Thus the aspirations for economic development in the developing countries may come to include the emulation of the rich industrial states for its own sake, quite apart from the material benefits to be gained in terms of higher living standards and a richer, fuller life. This desire to show a mastery of the modern world and so assert equality with its dominant groups poses serious dilemmas for the leaders and the educated elites of the new states of Africa and Asia. The more thoroughly they learn metropolitan languages like English and French, master science and technology, and practise the administrative skills that are universal in the modern world, the more different they become from their less westernized fellow-countrymen, neighbours, and kinsmen. Rather than being content to become merely 'black Europeans', many of the intellectuals of modern Africa have stressed the distinctiveness of their cultural heritage under such names as 'negritude' and 'the African personality', and justified the policies of the new African states by reference to traditional images such as *ujamaa*. Such sentiments too have a good deal to do with the rise of African socialism, to which I return in the next chapter.

SUGGESTIONS FOR FURTHER READING

Adam Smith, *An inquiry into the nature and causes of the wealth of nations*, (1776, and many subsequent editions), especially chs I, II, and III.

Emile Durkheim, *De la division du travail social*, English translation by G. Simpson, *The division of labour in society* (Free Press of Glencoe, 1947).

Max Weber, *The Protestant ethic and the spirit of capitalism*, English translation by Talcott Parsons, (London, Allen & Unwin, 1930); see also Reinhardt Bendix, *Max Weber: an intellectual portrait* (London, Heinemann, 1960), ch. II.

Ferdinand Tönnies, *Gemeinschaft und Gesellschaft*, English translation by Charles P. Loomis, *Community and society* (Michigan State University Press, 1957).

Teodor Shanin (ed.), *Peasants and peasant societies* (Harmondsworth, Penguin, 1971).

Talcott Parsons, *Societies: evolutionary and comparative perspectives* (Englewood Cliffs, Prentice-Hall, 1966).

Gerald Breese, *Urbanization in newly developing countries* (Englewood Cliffs, Prentice-Hall, 1966); *The city in newly developing countries: readings on urbanism and urbanization* (Englewood Cliffs, Prentice-Hall, 1969).

In addition there is a large literature on African towns, of which the following represent no more than a small selection:

M. P. Banton, *West African city* (Oxford University Press, 1957).

V. G. Pons, *Stanleyville* (Oxford University Press, 1969).

Cyril and Rhona Sofer, *Jinja transformed* (East African Institute of Social Research, 1956), East African Studies no. 4.

A. W. Southall and P. C. W. Gutkind, *Townsmen in the making* (East African Institute of Social Research, 1956), East African Studies no. 9.

David J. Parkin, *Neighbours and nationals in an African city ward* (London, Routledge and Kegan Paul, 1969).

J. A. K. Leslie, *A survey of Dar es Salaam* (Oxford University Press, 1963).

Hortense Powdermaker, *Copper Town, changing Africa* (New York, Harper and Row, 1962).

Pierre L. van den Berghe, *Caneville: the social structure of a South African town* (Wesleyan University Press, 1964).

Monica Wilson and A. Mafeje, *Langa: a study of social groups in an African township* (Oxford University Press, 1963).

vw

Social class

The institutional cluster with which this chapter is concerned is on a slightly different footing from the others, since social class, social differentiation, or inequality does not arise in quite the same direct way from any basic human need, nor is it quite universal in all human societies. As we shall see, however, the only known societies which can really be called classless are extreme cases. Inequalities are found in almost all societies, and even though not quite inevitable they offer a wide range for comparative treatment.

In nearly all societies the good things of life, the things that people desire, are unequally distributed; some have more, others less. When we ask – what good things? – the answer that sociologists have given, since Max Weber, is that they are to be thought of under three main heads: wealth, prestige and power. Wealth may be subdivided into income and capital. A person's income gives him a flow of wealth, that is command over goods and services, over time, while his capital means the stock of wealth which he possesses at a particular moment of time. Prestige means the extent to which a person is looked up to or looked down on, regarded as a sort of person to be admired or emulated or, on the other hand, treated with contempt. Power refers to the extent to which a person can influence or command the actions of others, make his will effective and make decisions. Clearly these three aspects of the matter are related to one another. A person who has wealth has power, because he can, if he wishes, use his wealth to employ others, to pay them to do what he wants done. In the same way, people who have wealth are admired and usually enjoy high prestige. So are people with power. Nevertheless they are partly separable from one another. A high government official or minister may have less wealth than many rich business men, over whom he nevertheless exerts power. Someone who has great wealth may not be admired if it is thought that he got it in a disreputable way.

What we are concerned with is the distribution – the usually unequal distribution – within societies of wealth, prestige, and power. The widest terms used to cover this subject are social differentation and inequality. Social class, a common phrase in ordinary English, is associated in sociology with the question of whether, in a particular society, there are groups which can be called classes – groups, that is, which are marked off from one another by definable boundaries and which are importantly different from one another in wealth, prestige, and power. Some sociologists, especially Marxist sociologists, tend to look for the existence of such groups in the societies they are studying.

In the study of modern industrial societies the social class view is opposed by non-Marxist sociologists who tend to see those societies as ranked into a series of layers or strata in a continuous manner without clearly marked boundaries or divisions between classes. Such sociologists accordingly use the term social stratification for the subject we are talking about. In the technical language of sociology, therefore, social stratification and social class have come to be associated with two different, and even opposed, ways of looking at the matter. It is a pity that so useful and commonly understood a phrase as social class should come to have so special a meaning; without commitment to a particular school of thought, I propose to go on using it in a general sense for the whole phenomenon of inequality or social differentiation.

Four case-studies – two from Africa, two from elsewhere – will be taken to illustrate the range of different systems of inequality in traditional societies. We shall then deal in more detail with social class in modern industrial societies before considering the changing picture in Africa.

FOUR CASE-STUDIES OF TRADITIONAL SOCIETIES

1. *The Andaman islanders*[1]

About the nearest thing to a classless society, of which we have an account, is that of the Andaman islanders, described by Radcliffe-Brown early in this century. It is not just a coincidence that this was technologically one of the most primitive societies known.

There was neither agriculture nor the keeping of herds and even the dog had been a recent introduction from outside. The Andamanese made a living by fishing with dug-out canoes, and gathering the products of the sea, such as shellfish, and by hunting and gathering the products of the forest – wild fruits and edible roots. Since food was not stored it was literally the case that no one knew where each day's meal would come from and the whole energies of the people were devoted to finding food day by day. This permitted no division of labour save that between the sexes – the men hunted and fished, the women gathered food in the forest and along the shore. There were no slaves, for there was no menial work for them to do that was different from the ordinary men's and women's work; in the same way there were no chiefs or nobles, for there was no possible way in which people could be exempted from ordinary work. Private rights in land did not arise since there was no cultivation and all had access to land and sea. Houses were the simplest shelters and there was a minimum of personal property – the biggest items were canoes and though they were privately owned they were very freely lent. The other artefacts included only the weapons of the chase, fishing tackle, cooking pots, and personal ornaments. Moreover, there was hardly any idea of social rank. The Andamanese language included words equivalent to Sir and Madam, which were used by the young in addressing their elders, but there were no chiefs. There was no clan system, so clans could not be ranked, and marriage was monogamous, so that a successful man could not even take more wives than another. Some men and a few women had a reputation as magicians and some men, who were popular and respected as hunters, had something of a personal following, in that young men would try to settle in their encampment and gain their favour by bringing them gifts. There was, therefore, what might be called leadership, but this hardly amounted to even the most rudimentary system of social class. Andaman society was as near to being classless as any we know – at the price of the barest and most precarious subsistence economy possible.

2. *The Kikuyu*[2]

Though not quite so classless as Andaman society traditional Kikuyu society was based on a differentiation, according to age, in which each man has much the same chance of becoming an elder with prestige and power.

From an early age boys set up informal groups who played and herded goats and, later, cattle together while girls also formed neighbourhood groups. Such one-sex peer groups (as Parsons has called them – see chapter 4) are probably to be found in all societies. Kikuyu society was unusual in formalizing them and making them, along with descent groups, the most important groups in the social structure. Both boys and girls were circumcised, traditionally at the age of about 18–20, and initiated into an age-set, that is a group of those initiated together, who remained a group with rights and duties to one another as they passed successively through the different stages of life. Sometime after initiation the young men were (so to speak) called up into a military organization, forming warrior bands under the leadership of one of their own number. The choice of captains, though magically performed and sanctioned, was probably related to personal qualities of leadership and courage. The authority of these warrior captains was strictly limited to the conduct of military operations and they had no power to make laws, settle disputes, or give orders to people outside the warrior bands – a point which seems to have been misunderstood by some early Europeans, who treated these men as if they were chiefs.

After his time in the warrior grade the next stage in a man's life, when he settled down to marry, cultivate, and bring up children, was a comparatively humdrum one and his ambitions would no doubt turn to the time when he might become one of the elders, whose fire he tended and whose errands he ran. Entry to the grades of elder (there were more than one) was not an automatic matter of attaining the requisite age. The acceptance of one's age-mates had to be gained by personal qualities shown throughout life. Courage and fortitude under the initiation ordeals and as a warrior, generosity and even temper, knowledge of the customary law and sound judgement – these were the qualities which counted. This system ensured, therefore, that those who eventually served as judges and priests had the requisite qualities but it also meant that they were relatively old. It was not just a matter of waiting one's turn but everyone had much the same chance to prove himself. There was, that is, equality of opportunity. The system was also intensely conservative, for one proved one's self by conforming to traditional values, and might have the opportunity in old age to ensure that everyone else did so too.

3. *The Ganda*[3]

Though not very far away in distance – only some 400 miles or so – the traditional social organization of the inter-lacustrine Bantu was in complete contrast to that of the peoples just described. In contrast to the Kikuyu assumption (so taken for granted as rarely to be stated) that all men were, at any rate potentially, equal these societies were based on what the anthropologist Maquet has called 'the premise of inequality' – the taking for granted, that is, that men were unequal and the consequent concern to be sure who was above whom. This group of peoples, including the Rwanda and Rundi, Nyoro and Toro, were well exemplified by the Ganda.

As is well known, the supreme individual at the top of this system of inequality was the king or Kabaka. Traditionally his supremacy was based on three things. He was head of the clan system – Sabataka, or chief clan head, being one of his titles. He was head of an almost bureaucratic system of county chiefs, whom he appointed, dismissed, promoted and transferred, and also of a military organization with specialist leaders – generals and the admiral of the canoe fleet. While remaining somewhat aloof from the priests of the traditional religion, he also owned and controlled a number of powerful magical objects known as *mayembe*, literally horns, sometimes translated fetishes. He reigned by both physical and supernatural terror. His court, thronged with thousands of followers, courtiers, wives and people up from the country, was a place of danger, intrigue and opportunity. Danger, if one displeased the Kabaka, of meeting a horrible death, but opportunity also, for if one pleased him and gained his favour there was the chance of power and privilege, for one's self and for one's relatives. Clans vied with one another for the royal favour and for information about what was going on, which might lead to warnings enabling relatives to escape, or advance notice of favours. The clans jealously guarded the privileges they traditionally enjoyed of supplying the Kabaka with particular officials, such as his butler, his blacksmith, his litter-bearers (in modern times they became his chauffeurs) and his wives. The chieftainship of particular counties was associated with particular ceremonial court office. For example, the Kago, chief of the county named Kyadondo, was the king's *sabaddu* or supervisor of the servants. The Mukwenda, county chief of Singo, was the royal shield-bearer.

The intrigues, the jostling for favour and the intricate hierarchy of traditional offices were reproduced in miniature at the courts of the county chiefs, of clan heads, or of any person of consequence. So, by the time one had reached the last court of the smallest territorial chief or lineage head, with his *sabaddu*, his shield-bearer and so on, one could almost reach the conclusion that no-one in traditional Buganda was just an ordinary commoner. And if there were, a man could always make his own family into a court, and lord it over his wives and children. Indeed fathers were said to rule their families, towards whom their traditionally expected behaviour was haughty and autocratic. Children, after punishment (and punishments were severe), were supposed to thank their fathers for teaching them how to behave, in the same way as criminals at the court of the Kabaka were expected to thank him for correction when sentenced. In short, the all-important principle pervading the whole of Ganda life was to see where power lay and align one's self with it; seek favour from one's superiors and lord it over one's inferiors.

4. *Caste in traditional India*[4]

If the Ganda system represents an extreme of inequality between *persons*, the caste system of traditional India represents extreme inequality between *groups* delineated by birth. A caste is a group, normally endogamous and often associated with a traditional occupation, which is regarded as occupying a rank in a system of ritual inequality. The highest castes were those regarded as holiest according to Hindu religious ideas and were grouped together as Brahmins. Next came the castes of landowners, military leaders, and secular administrators, grouped together as Kshatriyas, and including for example the Rajputs. Then came a very large number of castes of cultivators, craftsmen, and traders; hundreds of castes were associated with nothing more specific than farming, but this group, the Vaisyas, included also the castes of specialized workers such as gold- and silversmiths, leatherworkers, etc., ranging down to the castes who performed such menial or unenviable tasks as disposing of corpses or removing night-soil. The term Sudra is sometimes taken to mean the practitioners of unclean occupations like this, but in fact it is a rather vague and relative term. From the point of view of a Brahmin, everyone else is unclean or Sudra.

Not all tasks were rigidly confined to one caste; as we have seen, many castes were peasant cultivators, while Brahmins and Kshatriyas might be found doing many different kinds of work. It is most accurate to speak, as Ghurye does, of a 'lack of unrestricted choice of occupation'. Some kinds of work or business, for example those of the handicrafts workers, were reserved to members of those castes as a protection of their economic position. It was rather like the closed shop of modern trade unionism; no one might ply the trade unless he was a member of the union, except that in the Indian case membership of the 'union' was by birth. At the top of the system a similar idea prevailed. Though they might do other jobs also, Brahmins had the exclusive right to perform most ceremonies of Hindu ritual, being called in and rewarded by people of all castes for doing so. Many other aspects of the caste system follow from this. Since Brahmins alone might carry out the occasional rituals on which all depended, all had an interest in maintaining them in a state of ritual purity. Accordingly there followed an elaborate system of avoidances to that end. Near the top were those castes from whom a Brahmin might accept food without pollution. A little lower came those from whom he might take water. Lower still were castes whose touch and even proximity would make a Brahmin unclean. After giving instructions to his low-caste labourers, a Brahmin farmer would carefully wash himself all over. Villages might have two wells, one for high-caste and the other for low-caste people. Even the shadow of a low-caste person might pollute a Brahmin's person, house or food, while in some parts of India low-caste men had to wear a brass pot on a string round their necks to spit into, lest they should pollute a road on which a Brahmin might tread. What is important about these observances is that – as all authorities agree – in traditional India they were not forced by a powerful and privileged group upon resentful lower orders; on the contrary, they were accepted and upheld by all, Brahmin and Sudra alike.

Moreover, through a belief in re-incarnation, members of a low caste could hope that if they faithfully performed the tasks of their caste and obeyed its particular rules, they might be rewarded in the next life by being re-born in a higher caste. The punishment for an impious life was re-birth in a lower. These beliefs contributed to the feeling that the system was in everybody's interest and help to account for the extraordinary way it has resisted change for well over two thousand years.

SOCIAL CLASS IN TRADITIONAL AFRICA

The two African examples in the previous section should warn us against any simple-minded view of the uniformity of traditional systems of social differentiation in Africa. Even in comparatively limited regions of the continent like East Africa, there was (as I have tried to show elsewhere)[5] wide diversity. Besides the egalitarian age-system of the Kikuyu and the highly despotic kingship of the Ganda, there was at least one system which combined both – the Chagga – besides a more open system among Nilotic tribes like the Lango in which an ambitious man could achieve importance by setting up a new lineage on new land, and simple systems like the Gisu in which clans were the main form of local organization and it was clan heads who were important. In Africa as a whole the diversity was enormous.

Nevertheless, two general statements can possibly be made about these traditional African systems. Traditional technologies were primitive and the old Africa was hostile to the accumulation of wealth except in the form of cattle. Where all were poor and there was little surplus over the immediate needs of subsistence, even chiefs went hungry along with their people when food was scarce. True, in some areas chiefs had large food stores; the prestige and importance of a Bemba chief, for example, was reflected in the number of his granaries. But the grain they contained was meant to feed his courtiers and the subjects who came for a few days at a time to render tribute labour. To be stingy with food would at once reduce his standing with his people. And in times of famine he was expected to feed all comers.[6] The general material circumstances of chiefs and other men of high status were not very different from commoners'. Besides eating the same kind of food – and sometimes going hungry – they wore similar clothes and lived in the same kind of houses, if usually bigger and better built. There was, among African chiefs, nothing remotely like the bejewelled displays, the palaces and elephants of traditional Indian princes, for example, or the great houses, carriages, and private parks of the

English gentry and nobility. Traditional African social differentiation, that is, was along the dimensions of power and prestige rather than wealth. It follows that (again, always excepting cattle) where a prominent man had little or no permanent store of wealth, his power and prestige depended more on the acceptance of his standing by his people from day to day. Without a store of wealth to fall back on, a chief whose people deserted him was nobody. Perhaps more than in other parts of the world, therefore, in the old Africa chiefs relied on maintaining their position by a mixture in varying proportions of popularity, intrigue, and terror.

Secondly, and not unconnected with this, African traditional systems were marked by an absence of social distance between chiefs and people. Where Chinese mandarins, Indian princes, and English gentlemen lived in secluded privacy behind high walls which ordinary people (except their own servants) were not allowed to penetrate, African chiefs were accessible to all, their houses and courtyards being usually thronged with people – messengers, courtiers, chiefs, wives, servants, and dependants, from whom a chief seldom escaped by day or night. When they went on safari it was on foot, or litter. When in modern times some African chiefs (educated, it might be, in western countries) began to adopt the new sort of privacy in their private lives this represented an abrupt breach with tradition, often resented by traditionally minded people. Even the wearing of western dress sometimes served to cut them off from their people, while to go on safari by car meant that they could not be addressed, praised, or petitioned as they passed.

Thirdly, the wide kinship groups of traditional Africa meant that even when there were mighty chiefs they usually had poor relations. True, there were royal clans in some tribes; but these were large and included humble cultivators or herdsmen whose only claim to distinction might be a distant kinship to the king.

It seems likely that these three aspects of rank in traditional African societies have a good deal to do with the attitudes to social class differences in modern conditions which are found in African socialism, to which we turn in the next section but one. Before discussing this, however, we must outline the western system of social class against which socialism is a reaction.

SOCIAL CLASS IN MODERN INDUSTRIAL SOCIETY

As with other institutions we must now consider in some detail the system of social differentiation that characterizes modern industrial societies, since this is the most important influence which is changing modern Africa. It is not easy to do so, since social class in those societies is a vast, vague, and all-pervading phenomenon, exceedingly difficult to grasp in all its aspects. It is, accordingly, a phenomenon which has been very extensively studied by western sociologists and the literature on it is vast. A third difficulty is that there are, as I have hinted, two opposing views about it among sociologists – which I must begin by briefly expounding.

In the Marxist view, the social structure is economically determined in all societies. Social differentiation arises spontaneously in society because of the gain in efficiency when people specialize in different kinds of production. The form of specialization which crucially affects capitalist society is the division of labour between those who own and manage the means of large-scale production on the one hand, and those whose contribution is their labour on the other. In capitalist society, that is, the important distinction is between the owners and the non-owners of the means of production, and since handicraft methods are less efficient than large-scale methods involving the use of large and costly machinery, hand workers are undercut and the workers have no alternative but to sell their labour to those who own the machines. They are deprived of the means of production; they produce goods which they do not own and of whose ultimate use they may even be ignorant; they are, that is to say, alienated – at best apathetic, at worst hostile to the whole system. The division of labour, then, though it arises spontaneously and is more efficient, has undesirable effects also.

According to this view, a class is a group of persons with a common relation to the means of production. Though there may be several classes (e.g. peasants, independent handcraftsmen, and professional men as well as capitalists and workers), there is a strong tendency in capitalist society for the other classes to disappear, leaving a sharp division between the capitalists or the bourgeoisie on the one hand and the workers or the proletariat on the other. These two classes' interests conflict, and class conflict therefore characterizes the capitalist system. As more and more men are drawn into one or other of the two great opposing camps, the conflict tends to grow sharper and there is likely to be a crisis in which the workers, organized as a political party, will seize the instruments of production, 'expropriate the expropriators', and usher in the communist millennium. In capitalist society, that is, class conflict is the main, and finally the only, sort of conflict.

Opposed to this view, functionalist sociologists especially in the United States take what is termed the social stratification view. Disagreeing fundamentally with the Marxists, they see the social structure as based, in the last resort, upon the integrating factor of shared values, and – as we have seen – take the view that it is to the extent to which people share mutual role-expectations that they constitute a society. In the case of social class, therefore, the functionalists point to the empirical evidence that if you ask people to arrange in rank order a list of occupations, they invariably show close agreement. Specialization makes for efficiency (and here the two views agree), but since different roles are differently evaluated by common consent (that is, for example, everybody always agrees that medical men have high prestige, unskilled labourers low, and policemen and primary teachers somewhere in between) then the system is sustained by agreement, not conflict. Specialization is viewed, then, without regrets.[7]

On this view, the basis of the social hierarchy is the different value which is put on different people's work. A class consists of families whose breadwinners have similar jobs and similar rewards, and who in consequence share a similar material standard of living and style of life. Classes, however, are not sharply divided from one another; there is a continuum from top to bottom, with no breaks, and any divisions that are made – for example into 'income brackets', or between manual and non-manual workers – are arbitrary lines drawn for convenience anywhere one wishes. Here again, there is empirical evidence to support the view. American sociologists' interview subjects, when asked to divide people they knew into classes, showed no agreement about the number of classes they needed, and indeed displayed confusion and bewilderment, and some even ended by asking 'How many classes do you want?' On the other hand, there is also some research evidence (by Lenski and Landecker)[8] of a certain isolation of the topmost groups in American society, with a boundary between them and the rest which, though not insurmountable, is not crossed with perfect ease.

The fact of class conflict is not denied by sociologists who take the functionalist view, but it is seen in relation to other sources of conflict in society. True, there can be and often is tension in industry between workers and management; but there are also numerous other sources of conflict, for example between skilled and unskilled workers in industry, and between urban industrial workers and peasant farmers. The interests of the employed, self-employed, unemployed, and pensioners seldom coincide, the public and private sectors often clash, and there are competing claims on public resources for health, education, and defence. Just as there are numerous sources of conflict – class conflict among them – so there are numerous institutions for containing and resolving conflict – industrial tribunals and conciliating courts, Parliament, the law, and so on.

Possibly the greatest advantage of the social stratification view, however, is that it takes account of the fact of mobility. There is little room in the Marxist system of ideas for the possibility of people rising or falling in the social scale, and for there to be movement on a substantial scale between the capitalists and the workers would be quite alien to it. In fact, however, mobility exists on a wide scale apparently in all modern industrial societies. In Britain, the survey by D. V. Glass in 1949 showed that about one in three men had moved up in the world compared with his father's occupational status, about one in three had moved down, and about one in three had stayed at the same level.[9] Similar findings were reported from other industrial countries, including communist states as well as those with private-enterprise market economies.[10]

The findings of J. H. Goldthorpe in a survey carried out in the 1970s were somewhat different, and showed that among the sample of men then interviewed there had been far more upward than downward movement. Comparing those men with their fathers, the whole class structure had changed, with the working class shrinking from 55 to 44 per cent of the male working population, while the business, professional, and administrative classes (which together Goldthorpe called the 'service class') had nearly doubled in numbers. In one sense, then, British society had been very 'open' indeed during the experience of that generation, with the top class recruiting new members heavily from other social classes. The social origins of the 'service class' were accordingly very mixed, and Goldthorpe's class 2 in particular were remarkably like a microcosm of the nation. However, all classes were to a large extent self-recruiting, and class 1 most of all so. In another sense of the term, then, Britain's was not a very 'open' society, since it was marked by considerable inequalities of opportunity. While a working-class boy had some chance of going to the top, a boy born into class 1 was virtually certain to stay there.[11]

But though there were inequalities in Britain in the 1970s, they were not wide compared with those in other countries. As a simple measure of inequality (it is not the only one) we may take the share of all household income which is received by the top ten per cent of households. According to the World Bank's statistics, the least inegalitarian countries were Sweden and Norway, where the top ten per cent of households received 21.3 and 22.2 per cent respectively of all household income; and among communist countries Yugoslavia, where their share was 22.5 per cent. In Britain the figure was 23.5 per cent, and in the United States 26.6 per cent. Somewhat greater inequality was found in some other western countries, particularly France, West Germany, and Italy, in all of which the top ten per cent of households received just over 30 per cent of all household income.[12] Exact figures for the Soviet Union and other Soviet-bloc countries were not available, but published figures of the wage- and salary-scales in state employment there, together with the estimated incomes of collective farm members, suggest income distributions about as unequal as those in the western industrial countries.[13] Far wider inequalities prevail in some newly-industrializing countries. According to the World Bank, the top ten per cent of households in India received 35.2 per cent of all household income; in Malaysia, Turkey, and Peru their share was around 40 per cent; while the country with the greatest inequality was Brazil, where the top ten per cent of households received just over half of all household income, leaving less than half for the remaining ninety per cent. It should not be thought, however, that extreme inequality always or necessarily accompanies rapid economic development. Some countries had achieved redistribution with growth, notably Taiwan and South Korea, where the top ten per cent of households received respectively 24.7 and 27.5 per cent of all household income.[14]

Inequality in industrial societies arises primarily because different occupations are differently rewarded. A private-enterprise economy particularly tends to pile up inequality; it is rather like a game in which the winner of each round thereby gets a better hand for the next, while losers find it hard to get back into the game at all. Further, in all industrial societies, not only those with market economies, it is common to find workers rewarded for extra output (by way of piece rates, bonuses, etc.) and extra skill, while incentives are also afforded for extra responsibility. Few exceptions indeed can be found to the rule that if one person supervises the work of another, the first person is paid more than the second. The larger the organization, and the greater the number of steps or ranks in its hierarchy, the wider must the difference be between the pay of people at the top and at the bottom. This is as true of public organizations such as armies and state industrial enterprises as it is of privately-owned business corporations.

Industrial societies generally are accordingly characterized by inequalities among families, especially nuclear family households (see chapter 4), according to the occupational status and earnings of the chief income earner or breadwinner. Hitherto that person has normally been the husband/father, though in future more account may have to be taken of married women's employment and their contribution to family income. Those earnings have determined the style of life which the family can enjoy, and its access to consumer goods, in ways which significantly affect the life chances of all family members.

Associated with these inequalities are class-related differences in families' characteristic attitudes and practices concerning child care and education. Because they live in bigger houses, the children of better-off families are more likely to have rooms of their own in which they can do their homework undistracted. There are more likely to be books in the home; and better-off parents are more likely to take an active interest in their children's schooling, visit the school, attend school functions, and join the parent–teachers' association. Generally they ensure that what is taught in school is reinforced at home and vice versa. Thus better-off parents usually speak literally the same language as teachers, while the children of less priviliged families may hear the 'correct', officially-approved language of the state at school but some other variant at home. And while better-off parents exert themselves to arrange the best possible education for their children from the state schools, in many industrial countries they have the option of paying for them to go to schools in the private sector. Thus children of the better-off and relatively privileged classes have better chances of doing well at school, and so gaining professional qualifications and other educational diplomas giving them access to more highly rewarded occupations in their turn.[15]

Families of similar social class status, occupying as they do housing of a similar type and standard, tend to be neighbours. Gradations of occupation and income are reflected in the different residential areas in which people live, with the well-to-do suburbs keeping their distance from the slums of the city centre and the housing estates of the affluent working class. Living in different areas, the children of the different social classes naturally attend different schools. Even where, as in the United States, there is an egalitarian tradition of everybody mingling in 'the neighbourhood school', neighbourhoods correspond to social classes closely enough to make this largely an empty phrase. What the English call the 'old school tie' and the 'old boy network' – friendships between classmates conferring later advantage – are not without their importance in other industrial countries too. And, as we saw in chapter 4, since children of similar social class origins meet one another as neighbours and at school, it is not surprising that as they grow up they tend to marry one another. We must therefore add neighbourhood, friendship, and homogamy to the list of factors tending to perpetuate inequalities among families in industrial societies.

Finally, in some industrial countries these tendencies are yet further enhanced by the private ownership and inheritance of capital. Over and above personal possessions – house, car, clothes – some people in non-communist countries own assets such as land, buildings, and shares in industrial and commercial companies which can be a source of income over and above that which they derive from their occupation. Such capital wealth is usually jealously conserved in families upon whom it confers great and obvious advantages; and it is very unequally distributed, much more so than income. Most families indeed have no capital in this sense of the term.

Too much should not be made of this aspect of the matter, however. For one thing, not all the productive assets of any nation are privately owned, and there is an appreciable public sector in the economy of even so 'capitalist' a country as the United States. In a country with a mixed economy such as Britain, the public sector is substantial and includes such major industries as coal mining, gas, electricity, iron and steel, shipbuilding, railways and air lines. The scope for private capital is correspondingly limited, and indeed it may be doubted whether such a country can properly be called capitalist at all.

Further, in some other industrial countries, notably of course the Soviet Union, the private ownership of the means of production has been abolished altogether, while engaging in trade for private profit and employing other persons have been made crimes. But the result has certainly not been the end of inequality. In theory, the means of production belong to the people as a whole, their management being vested in state enterprises which alone have the right to employ and to trade. As we have seen, though, earnings in those enterprises, and the distribution of incomes in the Soviet Union as a whole, are about as unequal as they are in western industrial countries. It seems clear that the other factors making for inequality work in much the same way there as they do elsewhere, and irrespectively of the ownership of the means of production. Thus most students in Soviet universities come from the families of the better-off minority of non-manual workers, reflecting the advantages there too of an educated home background in gaining the qualifications for careers in the professions, administration, and management. Advancement in a career, moreover, depends on membership and good standing in the communist party, and some accounts suggest that personal influence and 'old boy networks' are of great importance. And it has been argued that though the means of production are in theory owned by the people as a whole, in practice they are controlled by a small elite of the party, who through their command of the apparatus of central planning effectively determine 'who gets what', the whole structure of income and rewards, throughout the Soviet state. Whatever may be said about the unequal distribution of capital in some other countries, the distribution of power in the Soviet Union is clearly very unequal indeed.[16]

People in western countries are deeply divided in their attitudes to the social class system. This is indeed one of the most important things about it: it certainly does not rest on consensus. Some people defend inequalities, others condemn them as unjust. Four views may be distinguished.

There are first those who accept inequalities as natural, normal, and even desirable. Two main lines of thought converge on the 'Right' or conservative side of opinion in western countries on this issue. What may be termed the truly conservative view is that there is a natural hierarchy of skills and talents in which some people are born leaders, whether by heredity or family tradition. It is wise for the rest of us to accept their authority, and not begrudge the rewards that are rightly their due. This view is not confined to those who enjoy privilege. Like Weber's traditional authority (see chapter 7), it has something to do with the magic of royalty, and much to do with the respect shown for members of distinguished families who have rendered great services to their country over the generations. It is, however, now less often expressed; and the more usual right-wing view, which may be called 'liberal-conservative', is that unequal rewards are right and desirable so long as the competition for wealth and power is a fair one. There have to be genuine prizes to strive for if everyone is to give of their best. Thus most Americans maintain that anyone can get on in the world given ability and energy. Such a view is in one sense egalitarian, since it implies that everyone should start the race at or near the same starting point, so that hereditary privileges are wrong and should be abolished. (This may incidentally explain why Americans regard British society as class-ridden compared with their own, though in fact there is even less inequality in the latter; but Britain has a royal family and a titled nobility, which were rejected from the first by the United States.)

By contrast, the egalitarianism which inspires the socialist tradition, especially in Europe, takes the form of a protest against excessive inequality and a call for redistribution from the rich to the poor.

Socialism is a very large subject, and the very meaning of the word itself is disputed. In introducing it, we may well distinguish with Berki between socialism, body and soul;[17] between the spirit of socialism on the one hand, and on the other the body of economic, political, and social institutions that have come into being in those states which, following communist revolutions, include the word in their official titles, like the Union of Soviet Socialist Republics.

The spirit of socialism has been characteristically expressed in slogans embodying double negatives, such as 'the end of inequality' and 'expropriate the expropriators'. The wrongs that people have suffered, the grievances and injustices and social evils against which they have struggled, have been attributed to the economic system identified as capitalism, which as generally understood combines two elements: the private ownership of the means of production, and a market economy. The socialist dream is of a utopia in which people co-operate, not compete, and production is for use and the common good, not for private profit; in which all share equally in bearing the common burdens of sickness and adversity; and in which all have access to their cultural heritage.

Socialism as a political movement has been immensely successful, not only in the countries that have undergone communist revolutions. Notably, it has inspired public enterprise, the taking of assets into public ownership, and redistributive fiscal and social welfare measures in countries that have had labour or social-democratic governments such as Sweden and Britain. Socialists have long been deeply divided, however, both about the economic ends to be pursued, and the political means for achieving them.

Thus the means of production, if not privately owned, need not necessarily be managed by state enterprises whose activities are co-ordinated by a central planning organization as in the Soviet system. Other possibilities include local government control, as in the 'gas and water socialism' of the days when the British Labour Party won elections to city councils and set up municipal enterprises before it won national elections and formed a government. Another is the co-operative management of enterprises by those who work in them. Private ownership may be largely eliminated yet some features of a market economy retained, thus avoiding Soviet-style central planning; and it may be possible to combine co-operatives in some parts of the economy, some state corporations, and even some small-scale private enterprise, as possibly in Yugoslavia. Or a socialist government may decide not to incur the odium, and the bureaucracy, involved in nationalizing industries, but leave them in private hands while exercising the control they need and redistributing the benefits through a form of central planning in co-operation with managements and trade unions, which was the policy of the Swedish social democrats.

Most fundamentally of all, though, socialists are divided about whether realizing the dream of a socialist society necessitates the unchallenged leadership of a single socialist party, or whether it is compatible with a multi-party political system in which people enjoy the fundamental freedoms of expression and association. Broadly, those who take the first view are termed communists. Those who take the second are now called democratic socialists, or social democrats, though there have been shifts of meaning and subtle differences here, and communists too claim to be democratic.

A key issue on which the two traditions are divided is whether taking assets into public ownership should be carried out with or without compensation. Communists would say 'Expropriate the expropriators!' Compensation does nothing to reduce the inequality of wealth, and merely perpetuates a capitalist class. And since it is not to be expected that those with lawful rights would surrender them without a struggle, force must be used. After the revolution, too, the attainment of socialism involves an irreversible, once-for-all transformation of society. To allow political dissent, freedom of expression and association, which might lead to the formation of a non-socialist political party; and to allow free elections which that party might win, and bring back capitalism; all this would be, in their chill phrase, 'failing to control the forces of reaction'; in no way could it be permitted. By contrast, democratic socialists like the British Fabians have always sought to attain socialism by evolution, not revolution; by persuasion, not force; by methods not viewed as immoral by the great mass of the people; and so by peaceful, constitutional means, including compensation for assets taken into public ownership. Where there is a tradition of representative government, with freedom of association, a multi-party political system, and genuine elections, socialists should work within that constitutional system, even if from time to time 'the people's choice' is of a government that reverses their cherished reforms, sells nationalized industries back to private ownership, dismantles the state welfare system, and allows the market economy once more to pile up inequalities.

SOCIAL CLASS IN MODERN AFRICA

With traditional systems as a starting-point, social differentiation in modern Africa is undergoing changes in which the influence of systems arising from the modern economy is of leading importance. Moreover, prominent Africans, who now move in a society whose scale is international, increasingly tend to live a style of life like that of the rich and powerful anywhere. They wear the same clothes, live in similar houses, drive (or are driven in) the same large cars, keep their money in banks, sit at desks and use telephones, and generally display their wealth and power in the same way as the rich and powerful in America, the Soviet Union, Japan, or anywhere else. The international society of the rich and powerful, that is, has become the reference group for everyone everywhere. Its culture sets the standard to which the ambitious aspire, and by which the poor and deprived measure their poverty and deprivation.

Thus the achievement of independence by African states has in many cases led to the enhancement of inequalities. Extreme examples of this are symbolized in incidents like the purchase in 1962 of a gold-plated bedstead for £3,000 by the wife of the former Minister of Agriculture in Ghana, or the lavish wedding of the Prime Minister of Uganda; the Rolls-Royce cars of the Kabaka of Buganda, or the costly palace of the President of the Ivory Coast. From the standpoint of European socialism, such expenditure seems morally wrong in countries whose living standards are low, and organizations like the British 'War on Want' have been known to react sharply to such extravagance. From an African point of view, however, as Worsley has put it, 'Much of this behaviour is merely an understandable assertion of the right to do things Europeans do'.[18]

Not all African leaders have reacted in quite this way, however. Notably, Dr Nyerere's government in Tanzania imposed sharp restrictions on the rewards and life-style of senior officials and ministers, while raising wages at the lower levels of government departments and the nationalized industrial and commercial concerns. Along with policies for the active development of rural areas and the provision of basic health and educational services there, it is regarded as having achieved genuine redistribution together with at least a modest rate of economic growth.

Symbolic equality with the world elite apart, there has been, in recent years, a general African reaction against the western social class system, and some African leaders and intellectuals seem concerned that it should not be allowed to grow up in Africa. What has been called African socialism has a good deal in common with the two rival socialisms of Europe. Many African leaders have been influenced by Marxist thought, while the democratic socialist approach has also had its influence. Yet there are subtle differences. Following Friedland and Rosberg, we may discern three important strands in African socialism.[19] First there is an acute awareness of the poverty and backwardness of the new African states and a heavy emphasis on the need for rapid economic development. The war on poverty, disease, and ignorance, however, seems to come only in part from a humane concern for the welfare of the poor, and in part from a sentiment which is lacking in European socialism – a sense that poverty and backwardness are somehow shameful and a desire to emulate the affluent societies as an assertion of equality with the former colonial masters. It is a matter of pride at least as much as compassion. Where the development of capitalism in its original form led to the alienation of some men, a class, within European nations, in the twentieth century the more important alienation is of whole peoples, namely those recently or still under colonial rule. Mamadou Dia thus writes of 'the revolt of the proletarian nations, or the twentieth-century revolution';[20] while President Senghor has expressed the same idea in the following passages:

In Europe, it is a question of eliminating inequalities arising from the formation of classes. In Africa, it is a question of eliminating inequalites arising from the colonial conquest, from political domination ... The proletariat of the nineteenth century was estranged from humanity; the colonized people of the twentieth century, the coloured peoples, are estranged even more seriously.[21]

Secondly, there is a concern that the process of economic development should not lead, as it did in nineteenth-century Europe, to extreme differences of wealth and poverty. For one thing, such wide social differences would be hard to reconcile with the widely extended kinship systems of traditional Africa, which, as we saw in chapter 4, contrasted sharply with the conjugal family system of traditional Europe. Indeed, members of the new African elites have already experienced the social strains and role conflicts which go with the wide differences between their expectations and style of life and those of their less educated kinsfolk. This

became very plain during my own studies of forme.
students.[22] This concern to avert class formation leads t.
deal of myth-making. Many modern African leaders assert
social differences are foreign to the African tradition, which, as we
have seen, is certainly not universally true. To link African socialism to a traditional kinship image may account, too, for the use of a
word like *ujamaa* by President Nyerere in his exposition of African
socialism.

Thirdly, there is an insistence that the needs of the new African
countries are not to be met by the slavish imitation of capitalism
(already discredited by its association with colonialism) nor European socialism, but by something distinctively African. African
socialism is thus to be linked with the search for negritude or the
African personality. To quote President Senghor again:

In the final analysis, our task is to realize a symbiosis of our Negro-African
(or, more precisely, Negro-Berber) values and European values – European values because Europe contributes the principal technical means of
the emerging civilization. Not all the values from either side are to be
retained; some are negative; others, belonging to the past, are interesting
only as folklore. In a word, sub-Saharan man must realize his full potential
as a man of the twentieth century, and at the same time make his
contribution to the Civilization of the Universal.[23]

The situation in newly independent African states, to which
African socialist ideas are related, was, of course, different in
fundamental ways from that in Europe of the early industrial
revolution. To a large extent what was objectionable about the
great concentrations of wealth and power was not that they were
in private but that they were in foreign hands. Outrage at that
state of affairs, the same general sentiments which in Europe were
anti-capitalist were in Africa anti-foreign, and account, for example, for the persistent hostility to Asians in East Africa both
before and after independence. Africanization rather than
nationalization accordingly became the major aim of the nationalist parties, and, after independence, of the new governments. It is
not uncommon, for example, for them to require foreign private
businesses, as one of the conditions for operating in an African
country, to train local men for senior posts. Thus the Kenya
government's white paper on African socialism states:[24]

Foreign investors should therefore be prepared to accept the spirit of
mutual social responsibility, for example:

   (i) by making shares in the company available to Africans who wish to buy them;

  (ii) by employing Africans at managerial levels as soon as qualified people can be found: and

 (iii) by providing training facilities for Africans. (para. 38.)

The same document even states elsewhere:

Enterprising Africans should be encouraged to develop indigenous commercial banks so that Kenya's dependence on monetary policies abroad can be reduced. (para. 92.)

It may be readily understood why this should be so. Yet there are dilemmas and even dangers in this approach. As the American economist Morse has pointed out, the more successful local business capital and enterprise is the more it will result in the building-up of a group or class with capitalist ideas and a vested interest in defending its privileges.[25] In the same way, the more successfully foreign enterprises are induced to Africanize their managements, the greater will be the number and strength of indigenous business men who are not only capitalist in outlook but have a vested interest in the continuation of foreign business enterprises in their country – a situation of which there are some examples in South America which from a socialist point of view are to be regarded as awful warnings. It is possible that a solution might be to insist on government participation in all large foreign businesses, so that the African managers and directors become government nominees and think of themselves more as civil servants than business men. But meanwhile it seems a rum sort of socialism that positively encourages the growth of an indigenous capitalist class!

SUGGESTIONS FOR FURTHER READING

André Béteille, *Social inequality* (London, Penguin, 1969 and 1978).

Melvin M. Tumin, *Social stratification* (Englewood Cliffs, Prentice-Hall, 1967); *Readings in social stratification* (Englewood Cliffs, Prentice-Hall, 1970).

David Lane, *The end of inequality?* (London, Penguin, 1971).

R. N. Berki, *Socialism* (London, Dent, 1975).

W. H. Friedland and C. G. Rosberg, *African socialism* (Stanford University Press, 1964).

Aggression, conflict and social control

Social control, the subject of this chapter, has a number of inter-related aspects. We consider first the control of aggression. This leads us into a discussion of conflict and the two great rival views of the nature of human society itself, the 'consensus' view and the 'coercion' view. We then consider how culture, the distinctively human characteristic, involves particular modes of settling disputes and resolving conflicts. Among these we specially consider the nature of authority and the sanctions that sustain it; and this in turn brings us to look at the nature of the communities which are united by subjection to a common authority. Finally, we return to a more detailed consideration of the institutions – military and police – through which violence is controlled in modern societies; 'the police idea', and military rule.

THE CONTROL OF AGGRESSION

In his book *On aggression*,[1] the biologist Konrad Lorenz examines the functions of intra-specific aggression (that is, attacks on members of the same species) in the animal kingdom generally, and ends with some consideration of the same question in man.

Intra-specific aggression is by no means universal among animals, but it is found in so many species as to raise the question 'What is it good for?' A behaviour pattern so common is clearly not to be thought of as a merely negative destructive force; the presumption is that it must be good for something, that is, it must have a function. If it were a disadvantage to a species in the struggle for survival, presumably both the species and the behaviour would have died out. (It will be noted that, like other biologists, Lorenz uses the idea of 'function' in very much the same way as sociologists.) According to Lorenz, aggression may have four functions.

(1) Territory formation. By chasing off other birds from a 'territory' round the nest, the male in many bird species ensures control of an area big enough to provide a food supply for the brood of chicks. Aggression spreads the population of a species out more or less evenly over the land or habitat that is suitable for its needs.

(2) Selection. Fighting between males ensures that the biggest and strongest mate with the females, and pass on the most vigorous strains to their offspring. Such fights are seldom fatal, however; defence mechanisms (see below) usually ensure that they stop before the winner kills or badly hurts the loser.

Beyond a certain point, however, this sort of selection may be harmful to the species (more precisely, have negative survival value). For example, an extinct lizard named Triceratops developed such heavy armour for these intra-specific fights that its movements were seriously handicapped; indeed that may be partly why it became extinct.

(3) Aggressiveness, especially in males, may be related to sexuality. Lorenz cites a species of Cichlid fish in which there is no visible difference between males and females – they look exactly alike. However, the male can mate while he is being aggressive, but not while he is fleeing; equally, the female can mate when she is submissive but not while she is being aggressive. Male and female fish presumably therefore recognize one another by behaviour, and settle down to mate when the male has established dominance over a female.

Here again, sexual displays can be carried too far. The pea-hen recognizes the peacock by his gorgeous tail, which, however, is so large and heavy as to make it hard for him to fly (and hence to get food and escape predators).

(4) This leads again to the establishment of hierarchies, or 'pecking orders' as they were called when the original research was done on domestic fowls. These are found among many animals, including some of man's nearest relatives, such as the chimpanzees. In such an order, A pecks B; B does not retaliate but pecks C with impunity; C pecks D, and so on. It might seem as though this would mean that everybody would peck the unfortunate animal Z at the end of the line; but this does not happen. On the contrary, if (say) M or N pecks Z, then A will interfere. The result is that not much pecking actually takes place – only just enough to maintain rank order.

Rank orders of this sort have important functions, for example in a flock of gregarious birds such as jackdaws where status is related to age and experience. If an immature young male gives the alarm call, other birds tend to ignore it; if, however, the senior male is alarmed, then all take flight. Similarly, Yerkes found that chimpanzees learned new ways of getting food from older males; young males' discoveries, however, were ignored.

As we have said, aggression in wild animals hardly ever leads to death or serious injury, even among predatory species like hawks or wolves which are armed with dangerous weapons in beaks, claws, or teeth. (Predation, the killing of animals of another species for food, is a totally different kind of behaviour.) Among the natural defences against aggression, three are important.

The first is, quite simply, flight. The outcome of a fight between two cock robins can be predicted if one knows how far from the two nests the fight occurs. Near home a bird fights fiercely; farther away he becomes more timorous, and flees if attacked. Thus birds on two adjacent sites establish a kind of frontier where their aggressions balance, and no fight is pressed to a deadly conclusion. (We have already seen the significance of this for territory formation.)

Secondly, some species have what are called *specific inhibitors*. For example, turkey hens attack all moving objects near the nest unless they make the 'cheep! cheep' sound of turkey chicks. Thus a deaf hen will peck her own chicks. Similarly, rats attack all other rats unless they have the right smell, that of the same clan.*

In some cases, the specific inhibitor consists of behaviour by other animals which has the effect of turning aggression into ritualized play-fighting. Such inhibiting behaviour may also take the form of submission; for example, when two wolves fight, after a while one submits to the other by lying down and exposing his neck. The victor could then kill him with one bite – but, strangely enough, he refrains from doing so. The submissive behaviour of the loser seems to excite a powerful inhibition in the winner, which checks the aggressive drive and prevents a fatal outcome. We have seen how this kind of behaviour leads to the formation of hierarchies or 'pecking orders' of dominance and submission in such species.

*For an account of clan organization in rats, see Lorenz, *On aggression*, ch. X.

Behaviour of this sort may further lead to the formation of a 'bond' (as Lorenz calls it) very much like friendship or love in man, in which pairs or groups of individuals engage in ritual behaviour towards one another, and reserve aggressive behaviour for outsiders; with much affectionate detail, Lorenz cites the grey-lag goose as a particularly striking example. The significance of 'bonding' of this sort is very great. Clearly it can only occur when individuals of a species are capable of recognizing other individuals; in such behaviour, therefore, we have the dawn of individuality or personality. Further, though clearly there is more to love than non-aggression, a species which is incapable of aggression is incapable of love. From this point of view, *love involves redirected or protective aggression, against outsiders, on behalf of those individuals with whom there is a personal bond.* This has very great significance for social control in our own species, as will appear below.

Turning to man, Lorenz suggests that in the enormously rapid, recent development of culture (rapid, that is, by comparison with the millions of years involved in biological evolution), man has suddenly been equipped with deadly weapons, but lacks the instinctive controls on aggression which characterize natural predators like wolves. It is, he says, as if doves had suddenly acquired the beaks of ravens.[2] The resulting situation for the human species is, to say the least, extremely dangerous. Lorenz's own suggestions for dealing with this situation do not seem particularly adequate. His analysis, however, is of importance to sociologists as a challenge. How, in fact, is violent aggression controlled in human societies? Granted the ever present danger of deadly outbreaks of war, how is it that even some measure of control is achieved? What is the place of conflict in human life, and how is it prevented, even some of the time, from taking violent forms?

CONFLICT AND CONSENSUS

In attempting to answer these questions, we have to consider a long-standing and fundamental debate in sociology — that between the functionalist view which stresses the importance of consensus, and the rival view which attaches more importance to conflict and coercion. We saw in chapter 6 how this affected the two views of social class: we must now deal with it directly.

The view that human society possesses order through consensus (that is, a state of affairs in which people are agreed on important questions of value, right and wrong) is an ancient and well-established one. It can be traced back as far as Plato, it was expressed in the idea of 'the general will' by Rousseau, and 'the moral law' by Kant. Among earlier sociologists perhaps the greatest exponent of this view was Durkheim, who clearly thought that it was the sentiments which they had in common that made men into a society. More recently, as we saw in chapter 1, Parsons has elaborated an analytical theory which suggests that a social system, viewed as a system of roles, exists just in so far as there is agreement about the behaviour expected of each role. There is accordingly a strong emphasis on the *normative* elements in social action – that is, on conformity to rules, values and the expectations of others; and this emphasis is related again to the *functionalist* view that each system of action contributes positively to the maintenance of the social system as a whole.

Sociologists who take this general position accordingly tend to see conflict as a negative force. Its occurrence is not denied; but it is seen as a disruption of the normal functioning of the social system. It is, that is, abnormal; also, it is usually transitory, since there are (as it were) built-in forces in a social system that tend to restore equilibrium, that is, bring the system back into a state of balance and stability. Thus for every type of conflict there tend to be institutions for containing and resolving conflict – for example, courts of law, recognized procedures for settling industrial disputes, legislatures where party political conflicts are resolved in a war of words, i.e. in debate and discussion, markets where competitive conflicts between buyers and sellers are settled through the bargaining process, and so on.

The other grand tradition in sociology is that which sees conflict, not as abnormal and transitory, but as permanent and even necessary. Its pedigree too is an ancient one; it can be traced back, perhaps to Aristotle, certainly to Thomas Hobbes, Hegel and Marx; and its more recent exponents include the German sociologist Ralf Dahrendorf and the English David Lockwood. According to this view, the fact of scarcity in itself is enough to ensure conflict, as people in any group try by one means or another to increase their share of scarce resources, if necessary at the expense of others. If among the scarce resources we include leadership, power, and prestige, then the occasions for conflict are sharpened. Unlike material goods, these are not things that we can make more of and ensure that everybody's share is increased. Power, for example, is called a 'zero-sum' concept; if A has power over B, C, and D, then A can be thought of as having a positive amount of power, while B, C, and D possess negative amounts – so far from having power, they are the objects of power. The sum of the power of all members of a group, therefore, is zero. In any society that relies on co-operative effort for survival, there is bound to be leadership – someone directs operations; and this leads to people being divided into those with power and those whose power is negative, with conflict between them. Nor is this the only possible source of conflict. Groups, each with its own leadership, may compete for the control of resources. Thus there are analogies between the process of territory-formation among some other animals, and institutions like property and international frontiers in human societies.

Conflicts may take many forms. The word as used by sociologists is a wide one, and includes debate, bargaining, competition, and controlled institutionalized fighting (e.g. duelling) as well as out-right violence. Nevertheless, behind all lesser means of settling disputes there lies the possibility of aggression in the form of physical violence – or the threat of violence; that is, coercion. Sociologists who take this view, therefore, see in coercion rather than consensus the ultimate source of social order.

Further, conflict is closely associated with change. If society represents a balance of forces, that balance may change. 'The more strongly people are involved in given conflicts, the more far-reaching their demands are likely to be, and the more radical will be the changes resulting from this conflict.'[3] When two people, or two groups, are in conflict, one possible outcome is that one wins and the other loses; and the winner then proceeds to have his way, exercise his will despite the other's objections, and change the state of affairs in his own favour. An obvious example is when a nation which has won a war takes some of the loser's territory. However, another possible outcome of conflict is that both sides may be better off. Thus an industrial dispute may end in the workers getting higher wages; but this may in turn lead to the management devising better ways of working, or installing better machinery, so as to use expensive labour to better advantage; and in the end the employer, too, may make bigger profits as a result of increased efficiency and productivity. Needless to say, this by no means always happens; but it happens often enough to be a realistic example. Thirdly, by contrast, a conflict may result in both parties being worse off. Thus a strike that forces a firm into bankruptcy benefits neither employers nor workers. Equally, the two major wars in Europe in 1914–18 and 1939–45 were undoubtedly harmful to both victor and vanquished alike.

There remains the fourth possibility that conflict may result in deadlock or stalemate – that is, in no change; in which case we usually speak of tension rather than conflict. In general, however, it is clear that most conflicts result in change of some kind or another; and the two are very closely linked in the coercion view of society.

Dahrendorf accordingly sets out the two views thus:[4]

Structural-functionalist, consensus or integration view	Coercion view
(1) Every society is a relatively persistent, stable structure of elements.	(1) Every society is at every point subject to processes of change; social change is ubiquitous.
(2) Every society is a well-integrated system of elements.	(2) Every society displays at every point dissensus and conflict; social conflict is ubiquitous.
(3) Every element in a society has a function, i.e. renders a contribution to its maintenance as a system.	(3) Every element in a society renders a contribution to its disintegration and change.
(4) Every functioning social system is based on a consensus of values among its members.	(4) Every society is based on the coercion of some of its members by others.

It should be added that neither Dahrendorf nor Lockwood says that the coercion view is wholly right and the consensus view wholly wrong. They say that there is some truth in both, contradictory though they may seem to be; and that in looking at any sociological problem we should keep both approaches in mind.

An attempt at the difficult task of reconciling the two views of society is that by Lewis Coser, significantly titled *The functions of social conflict.*[5] Coser's treatment of conflict in man, which is based on the earlier work in German of Georg Simmel, is indeed remarkably parallel to that by Lorenz on aggression. Like Lorenz, he asks, in effect, 'What is conflict good for? What does it do – for individuals, for groups, for societies? What are its positive or integrative functions?' Among the answers he gives are the following. Conflict delimits groups and makes their boundaries clear; it makes clear, that is, who is on which side. It unites groups by giving their members a common interest in the group's survival and victory. (Indeed, we may remark that to end internal dissensions by stirring up a quarrel with an outside enemy is one of the oldest tricks in the trade of government.) Conflict gives groups coherence, organization, and leadership. Moreover, it gives each conflicting party an interest in the other's coherence, organization, and leadership, since it is much easier to negotiate with a group that has a leader who can be relied on to keep his group in order and honour any agreements that are eventually reached. Military leaders, for example, prefer to fight a regular army with a commander, whose surrender will be binding on his troops, than unorganized guerillas; similarly, in industrial disputes it may be easier for a trade union to negotiate with a single large employer, or a well-organized employers' federation, than with thousands of small traders. Conflict may (though it does not always) remove what Coser calls 'dissociating elements' (such as pent-up grievances) in a relationship, and re-establish unity. The outcome of conflict may accordingly be a resolution of tension which might otherwise threaten basic consensus. And if this looks like an argument on the 'consensus' side of the great debate, Coser follows with one from the other side; conflict 'prevents the ossification of the social system by exerting pressure for innovation and creativity'.

Coser makes the further point that conflicts are less disruptive when there are many of them in any one social system, and when the lines of cleavage or opposition do not coincide – that is, when there are many cross-cutting conflicts. In such a society, A and B may be in conflict over one issue; but A is careful not to damage B more than is necessary, because A and B are allies on a second issue against C. Cross-cutting conflicts like this 'sew the social system together', Coser says. From this point of view, the state of affairs most likely to lead to the disintegration of the social system occurs when all the lines of cleavage coincide. Such a case would be the classical class-conflict model of Marxian theory, where the lines that separate employers from workers are also those that separate rich from poor, and rulers from subjects. A contemporary African example would presumably be the racialist societies of southern Africa.

In criticism of Coser, it may be suggested that he rather exaggerates the 'positive' or 'functional' aspects of conflict. True, conflict produces internal unity in the conflicting groups; but it usually does so at the expense of unity over a wider social system. Thus Germany may have been united in conflict with France and Britain in the two world wars, but from another point of view those conflicts look like tragic disunities within Europe. In the same way, hostility to Israel may produce internal unity in countries like Egypt, and even lead the different Arab states to patch up their quarrels with one another, but it can hardly be said to make for the peace and unity of the Middle Eastern region. To say that conflict unites groups leaves unanswered the vital question – which groups, and against whom?

More seriously, Coser does not adequately deal with the all-important problem of the *modes* of conflict. Angry words and thumped tables may do no harm, and conflicts conducted in this way may have all the positive functions Coser lists whether in the course of a family argument, an industrial dispute, or an international conference. At the other end of the scale, war between nation-states with modern weapons is so hideously destructive of life and property (and hence indirectly of life too, when the property includes stocks of food or the means of producing food and shelter) that it is hard not to think of it as *dysfunctional* (that is, the opposite of positively functional) as well as highly undesirable from anybody's point of view.

The heart of the problem, then, is the question: How are conflicts to be kept to the non-violent modes? And the answer: Through the existence of an over-arching system of social control. But before we can fully comprehend this, we must go back to the concept of culture, the nature of law and custom, the ideas of legitimacy and authority, and the nature of the state.

CULTURE AND CONFLICT

As we saw in chapter 1, precisely the difference between man and other animals lies in speech, language, and the ability to perform operations upon symbols. Through symbolic cultures, man is equipped with distinctive ways of controlling conflict, which are different from those of other animals. Disputes between humans can be dealt with by manipulating symbols – by 'talks', as journalists say; by discussion and debate; by reference to abstract rules and principles, such as laws, customs, conventions, and moral ideas of right and wrong.

It is important to note that we say 'can be'; as a fact of everyday experience, disputes are not always settled in this way. Behind the symbol lies the reality; behind the abstract words like 'right' and 'justice' lie the sanctions, which range from physical violence at one extreme to the mildest social disapproval at the other. Nevertheless, again in complete contrast to all other animals, there is in every known human society some set of rules or principles for the settling of disputes, capable of symbolic expression in words, which we are justified in calling law or custom. Law or custom, that is, forms a part of every known human culture.

In sociology, following Weber, we speak of the rules as *laws* if there is an institution or system of institutions – courts, police, and so on – whose function is to compel conformity or to punish disobedience of them. It is obvious that this definition applies to many of the laws of a modern state. It applied also to many traditional African societies, some of which had systems of courts to try cases and messengers, askaris, etc., to execute their judgements. Some such societies were kingdoms, like the Kgatla (court) among the Lovedu; in others, such as the Kikuyu, the courts functioned without the existence of chiefs.

According to the usual English usage, we call *custom* a body of rules comparable with law, but upheld otherwise than by specialized institutions. Traditional African societies which lacked chiefs or courts nevertheless had rules to cover such serious, major matters of life as marriage and inheritance, land tenure, theft and homicide. The difference lay in the method of enforcement and the recourse of an injured person. For example, among the Nuer – who, since Evans-Pritchard's famous account was published, have become a classical instance of a stateless society – an aggrieved person could not take a case to court for there was no court for him to take it to. Instead, he had to get the support of his kinsmen in a feud:[6]

In the strict sense of the word, the Nuer have no law. There is no one with legislative or juridical functions. There are conventional payments considered due to a man who has suffered certain injuries . . . but these do not make a legal system, for there is no constituted and impartial authority who decides on the rights and wrongs of a dispute and there is no external power to enforce such a decision if it were given. If a man has right on his side and, in virtue of that, obtains the support of his kinsmen and they are prepared to use force, he has a good chance of getting what is due to him, if the parties live near to one another.

In stateless societies where custom takes the place of law, sanctions notably include those of reciprocity, publicity, and magic. The intricate systems of exchange of goods and services which characterize primitive societies leave a wrongdoer, a defaulter, or a person who makes himself unpopular in any way, vulnerable to the sanction of reciprocity. For example, people do not come to his beer party when he wants to build a house, or will not help him out at a peak period such as harvest time. Publicity can also be effective in small-scale societies where everybody knows everybody. The abusive screams of an aggrieved wife are meant to come to the ears of everybody in the village. In some societies, indeed, the sanction of publicity may be formalized in the composition of satirical songs or the acting of satirical plays to shame a wrongdoer. Magical sanctions for custom notably include the curse, and in many primitive societies there exist beliefs designating persons whose curse is believed to be specially effective; for example, a man may go in fear of his uncle's curse, and his uncle may thus have considerable power to control his actions.

In English usage, again, we use the term *convention* for rules, which are rather like custom in being upheld by the informal sanctions appropriate to a small group, but are usually concerned with less important aspects of life. Where custom deals with inheritance or theft, convention governs styles of dress or manners. Convention may coexist with law in a society which has a state organization. In a modern state, for example, the law will usually be called in to deal with a case of theft, but a case of unconventional dress may be dealt with by a raised eyebrow.

If conventions constitute relatively unchanging rules, *fashions* are rules that are expected constantly to change, but which, like conventions, deal with the more trivial aspects of life – like women's dress. It is conventional for women to wear skirts; their length frequently changes in response to fashion.

The terms *custom* and *convention* are used the other way about by some American sociologists. Parsons, in translating Weber, defines convention as 'that part of the custom followed within a given social group which is recognized as binding and protected by sanctions';[7] and Gerth and Mills in their textbook *Character and social structure* write:[8]

Conventions are more exacting than customs . . . In the case of the customary you may 'take it or leave it' – part your hair on the right or left side, eat your soup with or without salt – but this is not true of 'conventions', or as W. G. Sumner termed them 'the mores'.

Finally, *morals* constitute a system of ideas about right and wrong behaviour about which there is, if not unanimity, at least wide agreement in a given society. The discussion of moral ideas, and the basis for their existence, is a matter for philosophy rather than sociology. However, morals have sociological significance. The ideas which any group of people have about what is right and what is wrong (whether we agree with them or not) are obviously liable to influence their behaviour. Generally speaking, people will tend to express their moral ideas in the form of social rules binding upon all who participate in their society. There are, however, a number of important limitations to the process by which morals tend to be realized as laws or customs. In the first place, people's moral ideas are frequently confused and inconsistent; to take a trivial example, people may think it a moral duty to care for animals, yet may also think meat an essential part of the diet. There is clearly a difficulty in a case like that of framing a guide to conduct. Secondly, it is rather rare for what is termed moral consensus to prevail throughout society – that is, for everybody's moral ideas to be identical. Where, as is more usual, there is moral dissensus, the laws or customs reflect the moral ideas of those who have the powers to put them into effect. How closely they correspond to the morals of the majority depends on how democratic the society is. Since few societies are really ruled by the will of the majority, the laws tend to reflect the moral ideas of the ruling elite; and the more the difference between their ideas and those of the majority, the more detached or even alienated will the majority feel from the operation of the law. (Colonial Africa clearly represented an extreme case where the law was made and administered by a tiny minority, and the mass of the people felt quite uninvolved.) Thirdly, moral ideas change. Change in moral ideas is, indeed, closely related to the notion of dissensus, for it is most commonly a minority among whom the change begins, so that there is a dissensus, accompanied by anything from a peaceful debate to a revolution. When moral ideas change, there is usually a time-lag between the acceptance of the new ideas and the consequent institutional changes in law or custom. In democratic societies, therefore, one of the chief functions of the legislature is continually to amend laws following changes in the moral ideas of the people, or of important sections of opinion. In a later section I shall look again at the possible outcomes of movements of protest or reform whose aim is to change the existing rules of society.

SANCTIONS, EXTERNAL AND INTERNAL

Any system of social control depends on sanctions, which may be positive or negative. Positive sanctions are rewards for actions that are approved, and they tend to reinforce the motivation to act in an approved way. Sometimes the rewards are material and tangible, but very often they are not. In a family, for example, children may be rewarded for good behaviour (that is, behaviour their parents regard as good) with gifts, specially tasty food, or other longed-for treats. But in many cases material inducements are not necessary, and the mere expression of approval is enough. For many adults as well as children, approving words or gestures from 'significant others' – kinsfolk, close friends, persons of prestige and authority – may serve as powerfully positive sanctions. Thus symbolic honours like medals and orders cost a state little, but may be much prized as rewards indicating the recognition of specially distinguished service.

Negative sanctions, on the other hand, may be defined as the deprivations which accompany or follow behaviour which is disapproved. Punishments or retribution which follow a disapproved act are negative sanctions. So also are counter-actions like the suspension of rights or facilities, which are imposed while a disapproved action is persisted in, with the understanding that they will come to an end when the wrong actions stop; this is the meaning of the term as applied, for instance, to sanctions against the former regime in Rhodesia. Sanctions may vary in severity from death or violence against the person, loss of liberty or civil privileges, through fines to expressions of social disapproval like ostracism, jeering, even the singing of satirical songs or the use of unfriendly nicknames. As we shall see, too, there is considerable variation in different societies in who is supposed to apply the sanctions.

Another way of classifying sanctions is to divide them into external and internal. External sanctions are the actions of others in relation to acts of which they approve or disapprove. Internal sanctions are those applied by the actor to himself. Like external sanctions, these can be either positive or negative. On the negative side, it is often the case that a person who has done wrong in others' eyes has also done wrong in his own, and experiences accordingly unpleasant feelings of guilt, shame, uneasiness, remorse, or self-accusation. On the other hand, however, a person may persist in actions of which everybody around him clearly disapproves, because of an inner conviction that he is right and they are wrong. In extreme cases, religious or political convictions, patriotism or personal loyalties may provide the positive internal sanctions which enable people to persist in their actions in defiance of hostility, ill-treatment, and even the threat of death from people immediately around them.

I suggest, indeed, that the greater the extent to which a system of social control relies on internal sanctions, the more effective it is. To rely entirely on external sanctions would be so wasteful of time and effort it would be literally impossible. One imaginary example which has been given is that of the schoolmaster going round to the homes of each of his pupils one by one and physically constraining them to come to school. It would take him so long that by the time school was assembled he would have little time or energy left to teach them. In reality, schools are not assembled by pure coercion. Some children like school and come eagerly, some come because of hoped-for later rewards – examinations passed, jobs secured – some through habit, some resignedly because they know they will get into trouble if they don't, and many no doubt with a mixture of all these motives. Much the same could be said of the mixed motives which keep most citizens most of the time obeying the law. A particular law (for example, cutting out swollen shoot in cocoa) may commend itself to us as good and worthy of observance; or, even though it is irksome, we regard ourselves as law-abiding and so rather grudgingly observe it. We should feel fools if we were caught, and to be summoned to court would be a tedious nuisance, even apart from the possibility of being fined or worse.

From the psychological point of view, this raises the important question of the different kinds of motivation that are involved in social behaviour in man. A defect of many sociological treatments of this question is, I suggest, to overlook the importance of what psychologists call 'affiliative' behaviour and particularly the need or desire for affiliative responses in others.[9] We seem to seek, that is, responses which are favourable or approving, including smiles or tender gestures, as well as verbal approval. In socializing children, as we saw in chapter 4, what Bowlby called 'a warm, intimate, and continuous relation', a source of 'satisfaction and enjoyment', is believed to be essential; without it, socialization is so imperfect as to result in serious behaviour disorders. We may perhaps extend this, and see in the relations and responses of approval among kinsmen, age-mates, school-mates, fellow-workers, friends, comrades in arms, good neighbours, something closely analogous to Lorenz's 'The Bond', and a part of the very nature of human society itself which tends to be overlooked both in the consensus and the conflict views.

For, as a matter of everyday observation, human aggression is more a group than an individual matter. When men are aggressive, it is not usually on behalf of their own private self-interests; more commonly, as I suggested earlier (p. 166), it is a matter of *protective aggression*. Men may indeed fight fiercely enough in one way or another for their individual self-interests, but they seem to fight far more fiercely on behalf of others with whom they have an affiliative bond. Aggression, that is, tends to be directed against outsiders who are regarded as threatening a group within which affiliative bonds prevail – an 'in-group', as it was called by some earlier sociologists. I go further and suggest that the problem of the size and composition of human groups is very largely a question of a balance between affiliation (within the group) and aggression (directed against outsiders).

LEGITIMACY AND AUTHORITY

From the sociological point of view, the idea of internalized sanctions leads us to the very important concept of legitimacy. If we accept that a particular person or group of people has the right to give orders, issue instructions, settle disputes and so on, we may do so because we fear the negative sanctions which they have the power to bring to bear against us; equally; however, we may do so because we wish for positive, affiliative responses from them. If, in addition, there is a moral component in our acceptance – if, that is, it is accepted that the person or group in question has a *right* to make decisions – then we recognize in the full sense the legitimacy of authority.

In so far as an authority can appeal to something other than naked coercion, that is, it is said to have legitimacy. Legitimacy may be defined as a consensus (that is, a widespread agreement within a society) that the authority possesses its power rightfully. To acknowledge legitimacy and authority is not necessarily the same as to support its every action and every decision. On the contrary, its actions and decisions may be deplored or questioned; there may be opposition, or there may be attempts to get particular decisions altered. What is fundamental to legitimacy is an acknowledgement that in the last resort the decision rightfully belongs to the people who have the power to enforce it. Thus, as Hobhouse wrote, even in the case of a state established by military conquest, 'the conqueror cannot bear to rest his title permanently on force alone. He seeks to transmute force into authority.'[10]

Legitimate authority, according to Max Weber, may be of three types: traditional, rational-legal or bureaucratic, and charismatic.[11]

The term traditional authority is presumably self-explanatory; this is the authority whose legitimacy is based on some such justification as 'since time immemorial', or 'since the memory of man runneth not to the contrary'. It is the type, obviously, to which traditional African chiefs and councils of elders belong, together with the traditional German princes who were no doubt the example uppermost in Weber's own mind.

Rational-legal authority is, in Weber's work, the occasion for an analysis of bureaucracy, which had been greatly growing in strength in the Prussian-dominated Germany of his day, and pervaded not only the organization of the state but also to some extent that of private business enterprise. It is the authority of an official – that is, one who holds an office. The office is separable from the person; it was there before he occupied it, and it will be there after he has gone. In a rational organization, whether of government or private business, offices are limited in scope and are arranged in a hierarchy, each official being responsible to the one above him.

There is division of labour on rational lines, so that each official knows exactly what is expected of him and which work belongs to his colleagues; and he also knows how far he may go in making decisions, and at what point he should refer questions upward to his more responsible superior. Selection for office is according to rationally defined criteria of suitability, and quite characteristically by examination. Personal likes and dislikes, that is, do not enter into selection, promotion, or dismissal procedures. This is in contrast to the personal way in which a traditional chief chooses his courtiers and confidants; it is intended to ensure that the one most fitted for the job gets and keeps it, and to avoid nepotism and patronage, that is, systems of selection which favour the kinsfolk or the personal favourites of those in power. The civil service of a modern state, of course, affords a good example of what Weber had in mind; as we have suggested, bureaucracy operates also to some extent in large private business enterprises; and, as Weber himself pointed out, the concept of 'office' may sometimes extend into the posts which, in contrast to a permanent civil service, we call 'political'. For example, in the United States it is common to speak of the office of president. In such a case, the presidential election may be regarded as the equivalent of the examination for executive civil servants – a rational procedure, designed to ensure that the best person gets the job. The legitimacy of the president's authority accordingly derives in part from his or her having emerged victorious from a rational selection procedure to fill an enduring office, which Weber characterized as bureaucratic.

Charismatic authority is, in Weber's words,* 'a certain quality of an individual personality by virtue of which he is set apart from ordinary men and treated as endowed with supernatural, super-human, or at least specifically exceptional powers and qualities'. It is charismatic authority that binds together the followers of a leader in a movement such as a religious sect or a revolutionary party. There is no career, promotion, or dismissal; there is only a call. In its pure form 'there is no such thing as a salary or benefice', and the material needs of the leader and his disciples or lieutenants are met by sporadic gifts of the faithful, by the acceptance of hospitality, by a 'God will provide' attitude. There are, Weber continues, 'no established administrative organs; no system of

*To be exact, Weber's words as translated by Parsons and Henderson.

formal rules; no legal wisdom related to judicial precedent. The charismatic leader says "It is written . . . but I say unto you".'

In its pure form, that is, charismatic authority is outside the established structure of society, and its appeal is to something different from the regular routine of existing expectations. A charismatic movement is therefore essentially unstable. Either it 'fails', the leader loses his following, and the movement ceases to be active; or it 'succeeds' in establishing itself as a new social structure. If this happens, the forces of routine are bound to impose themselves upon it, so that Weber writes of 'the routinization of charisma'. The material resources of the movement have to be organized in a more regular way than the sporadic gifts and hospitality of the faithful, and arrangements have to be made for the remuneration of the leader and his chief disciples. Routine supervenes, too, in the regular activities of the movement; for example, if it is of a religious character, meetings or services may at first be conducted spontaneously, 'as the spirit directs', but later something like a ritual grows up as the form of proceedings tend to follow a regular pattern. Questions of membership arise; it may become necessary to distinguish between members and non-members, the regular payment of subscriptions or dues may become a rule, and defaulters' membership may lapse; or there may have to be doctrinal tests requiring acceptance of the explicit beliefs of the movement. Members get married, and the manner of their wedding has to be considered; they have children, and the question arises whether those children are born into the movement or have to enter it an age when they can decide for themselves. Members die, and forms of mourning are devised. And above all, the death of the original leader himself cannot be delayed for ever, so that provision has to be made for the designation of a successor. At this point procedure is adopted that tends to become binding on the movement for ever afterwards – whether the procedure is that of succession by a son or other relative, by election, by the nomination of the original leader before he dies, or by some magical means. In all these matters, precedent comes to have increasing importance. Any charismatic movement that continues to exist, then, becomes 'routinized'; which is to say that it ceases to be purely charismatic, and the nature of authority within it becomes partly traditional, or partly bureaucratic, or both. (Weber even writes, for example, of 'the charisma of office' in a well-established religious denomination.) What we have in the real world, then, are mostly mixed types of authority, though in many cases one or another type predominates.

In colonial Africa, Weber's three types of authority might neatly be exemplified by the chief representing traditional authority, the District Commissioner as the agent of a bureaucratic system, and the nationalist politician as the charismatic leader. Modern Africa abounds with examples of charismatic movements. We have a particularly valuable detailed history of one, both in Apter's account of its rise and in its subsequent routinization, in the C.P.P. in Ghana.[12] A particularly striking charismatic figure was that of Patrice Lumumba; indeed, his charisma was in one sense his undoing, for it was precisely the extraordinary power of his oratory over large masses of the people of Zaïre that led his political opponents to fear and hate him.[13] Among religious movements, there is a rich field among the separatist sects in South Africa, as described by Sundkler.[14]

Before leaving the subject of legitimacy, I must make one important final point. An authority may be more or less legitimate; the moral consensus on which it rests may be more or less complete; it is a matter of degree. It would seem, too, that the lower the level of legitimacy, the more reliance has to be placed on coercion. Thus we could imagine at one extreme a state of affairs in which legitimacy is virtually complete, so that everyone willingly accepts the authority of a person or group (such as the chief, king, elders, legislature) as the final arbiter of all important matters concerning the society in question. Such a model would clearly appeal to those who prefer the consensus view of society. Equally, one could imagine a state of affairs – in a country recently conquered, and under the military rule of a foreign state, for example – in which the legitimacy of the regime was virtually zero, and in which indeed it was thought of as a patriotic duty to disobey, subvert the rules laid down from above, kill policemen, destroy government buildings, etc. Clearly in such a case government would be a matter of almost pure coercion and terror. In between, many modern societies have governments with a high but not complete legitimacy; though most people accept authority, there are those who question it and try by various means to subvert it. The concept of legitimacy, therefore, is important as bridging the two apparently contradictory views of society which we outlined earlier in this chapter. If we view legitimacy as an empirical variable (that is, if we set out to enquire in a particular case just how complete or incomplete it is) we may find that the conflict view and the consensus view both have some bearing on the society we are studying; it becomes a matter of ascertaining *how far* conflict prevails and *how far* there is consensus.

I have tried to express this analysis in the form of a diagram (Fig. 11).

At the centre of the figure, I put consensus – that is, general agreement – giving rise to conformity. It is well to remember that so-called breakdowns of law and order, seriously disruptive though these are, are never complete. Even in the most disturbed periods of wars, revolutions, army mutinies and the like, most people most of the time observe most of the rules. They go on working, getting married, bringing up children, and getting on with the business of life according to the ordinary rules of society in question, to as great an extent as circumstances permit.

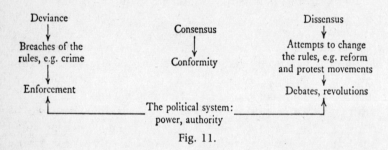

Fig. 11.

On one side of this central tendency, I put deviance, that is, breaches of the rules of the general nature of crime or delinquency. On the other, I put dissensus – that is, any tendency on the part of some people to disagree with the rules and try to get them changed. It is of the utmost importance to distinguish between dissensus and deviance, not only as a matter of sociological theory, but also in practice, for there is a very common tendency to confuse them on the part of people in positions of authority. Crime is not a critique of the social order, and conversely, criticism of the social order is not, or ought not to be regarded as, a crime.

To a differing extent in different societies there are people who protest against what they regard as unjust laws, or who object to various aspects of the existing order of society; and they adopt various methods to try to bring about change. Their methods may be peaceful, as for example forming associations, writing pamphlets or newspaper articles, holding meetings and making speeches, in the hope of persuading others to be of their way of thinking; or they may involve offences against the ordinary law, for example if property is stolen or damaged or acts of violence committed. The activities of dissident groups may accordingly lead either to public debate on the one hand, or revolution on the other, or something in between. Where the balance is struck depends on the nature and ideology of the movement itself, and the reaction to it of the people who hold power in the society in question.

Much depends on the protest movement itself. Some movements have remained determinedly non-violent despite the use of violence against them by intransigent and repressive authorities. In the United States, for example, the movement for Black civil rights in the southern states has on the whole refrained from violence, despite the ill-treatment of its supporters, and despite the sporadic and unorganized rioting of Blacks in states unaffected by segregation. Perhaps the classic example of a non-violent freedom movement was that in India under British rule, where indeed many techniques originated which have since been followed and developed by later movements.

Much also depends on the prevailing practices of the country concerned. It is probably true to suggest that nowhere in the world is freedom of speech quite absolute; in every country there are criticisms that are disallowed and suppressed because they are felt to strike at the very foundations of ordered society itself.

Conversely, it is probably true that in every society there is at least some area of public life in which free debate is permitted. This said, it must be added that in some countries the area of free debate is very much wider than in others. Publicly to advocate communism in the United States, publicly to criticize the Crown or to urge soldiers to leave the army in Britain, would be to invite trouble. But, with comparatively few exceptions, in both these countries the whole field of public policy is open to debate by anyone who cares to make his voice heard. Much the same could be said of India and most of the states of northern and western Europe. In communist countries, as is well known, the area within which criticism is permitted is not so wide, though it exists. In the Soviet Union, for example, to query the principles of Marxist-Leninist thought would be hazardous, and to organize a second political party impossible; but to write a letter to the local newspaper saying that the manager of your factory was incompetent would be perfectly proper. In South Africa, to criticize apartheid is regarded as striking at the foundation of society; the two main African political parties are banned, and the use of the Suppression of Communism Act, the '180-day clause', and similar laws to suppress movements of criticism and protest is well known. In some newly independent African states, too, sensitivity to criticism and a tendency to mistake it for subversion have led to the imprisonment, exile, or flight of many well-known political leaders. In such circumstances, opposition movements of protest or reform are (in the usual metaphor) 'driven underground', and may in desperation resort to methods that are violent or criminal in the ordinary sense. Recent African history affords ample illustrations of the saying that 'one person's "terrorist" is another's "freedom fighter"'.

STATE, NATION, AND NATIONALISM

Weber's analysis of authority applies rather widely. He himself used the German word *Herrschaftsverband*, which according to Dahrendorf is best translated in English as 'imperatively co-ordinated association', to cover the sort of social unit in which authority might be exerted, and this would include business firms, churches and so on, as well as political organizations. But clearly political life is what we chiefly have in mind, and a type of social organization of particular importance in this connection is accordingly the state, to which we now turn.

The state is not a universal institution; some societies, including some African traditional societies, are stateless, and I have already cited one classic case – the Nuer. All known stateless societies are small in scale, and it is hard to imagine how a large-scale society could lack this particular institution. Many large-scale societies, indeed, have become so because of the widening of the geographical area over which a state has exerted control, thus forcing people into the unity of subjection to one state; this process is, of course, thoroughly familiar in modern Africa, where most of the recently independent states are made up of tribes whose original unity was that of subjection to a colonial power.

A state may be defined as an institution that successfully claims for itself a monopoly of legitimate violence with a defined geographical area. It reserves for itself the right to compel. Within its boundaries, force or the threat of force is legitimately used only by the state itself, on its behalf (as for example by soldiers, policemen or prison officers), or under its licence (for example, in English common law a father has the right to chastise his children within limits). Any other use or threat of force – for example, by criminal gangs or mutinous soldiers – is illegitimate, and will be suppressed if possible by the state. If the state fails to suppress illegitimate violence it ceases to be a state. This is what happens when a state fails to suppress a revolution or rising: the revolutionary army wins a civil war, and turns its leaders into a government in charge of the state; and it may be a nice point of timing to decide when a revolutionary party has won and is to be recognized as the government.

It will be clear that a state is a quite different kind of thing from a nation. A nation is a community; a state is an institution, or as Max Weber called it a 'compulsory association'. As we have seen, many states in the past have included within their boundaries more than one nation or tribe. Obvious examples are the great empires of the past – Roman, British, Austro-Hungarian – which have resulted in whole peoples being subjected to the rule of foreigners. A very common reaction to this state of affairs is known as nationalism, which may be defined as the sentiment or proposition that each nation ought to have its own state. Although a very widespread sentiment in the modern world, this should not be allowed to go entirely without question, and two important objections may be raised against it. One is the difficulty of deciding, in particular cases, who or what is a nation. No one would deny that the French, for example, are a nation; even so, there are French-speaking people in Belgium, in Switzerland, and in the Channel Islands which form part of the United Kingdom. Is Britain a nation? One is inclined to say yes at first sight – and then remember the Scots and the Welsh, and the anomalous province of Northern Ireland. When we come to multi-lingual and multi-cultural states like Belgium, Switzerland, or India, things become more difficult still.

Turning to Africa, we have the statement – no less true for being oft repeated – that the new states are in many ways the artificial legacy of colonial rule, whose boundaries part like from like as often as they join unlikes in an uneasy unity – Hausa, Ibo, and Yoruba; Buganda, the other southern Bantu, and the north; the Muslim Arab north and the pagan or Christian black south – and so on round the map of Africa. Nationalism so ill-defined seems as likely to disrupt states as to unify them.

Secondly, it may be argued that for each nation to have its own state is wasteful, inconvenient, and even dangerous. Wasteful, because of the sheer financial cost of maintaining a central government, a legislature, foreign embassies, a United Nations representative, and so on. Inconvenient, because the natural areas for trade and economic planning may not be the same as the ethnic areas of common culture; thus the break-up of the Austro-Hungarian empire after the First World War was the break-up also of a common market within which goods moved freely paying no customs dues, and the economies of large-scale production and marketing could be gained. And dangerous, because most states have armies and possess accordingly the means to make war; and war is, it may be argued, the greatest social evil of the twentieth century. From this point of view, the institution of the nation state is the chief obstacle to the setting up of a world state, which offers certainly the best and probably the only hope of abolishing war.

It is really a very simple problem – as simple as the following quite realistic example. Two tribes who used to fight each other with spears can now be kept at peace by a small body of police armed with rifles. The inclusion of any two conflicting groups in the boundaries of a state means, precisely, that there is a power which can overawe them both because it possesses the means of quite overwhelming violence against either or both of them. If there were a world state, likewise, it would by definition have the power to suppress any violent aggression anywhere by the threat of overwhelming violence. It would, that is, disarm all lesser states. War would become impossible, and the level of world armaments could be lowered to that necessary for mere police work. It is this which I had in mind when I said earlier (p. 171) that conflict can be limited to non-violent modes only by the existence of an over-arching system of social control.

Nevertheless, simple and attractive though the idea of a world state may be, there are two very great difficulties about it.

The first is obvious. Before it could come about, there would be fierce argument about its constitution and who should control it. It is obvious that the two major world powers would not agree easily or quickly about this. Yet if the world state does not come about by agreement, there seems no escape from the conclusion that the only other way it could come about would be by a war between the two nuclear-armed super-powers, as a result of which one of them would dominate the world – or what was left of it.

The second is less obvious. It has been suggested by the sociologist Ernest Gellner that, if there were a world state, it would be rather like present-day South Africa in denying to the poor non-white two-thirds of mankind the political rights and economic privileges of the rich white industrial peoples. Though this suggestion may be a surprising one, Gellner's argument has some force. If a world state were to be fully democratic, with one man one vote and equal civic rights for all, there would be nothing to stop the majority of mankind from voting themselves social services, 'welfare state' benefits, and the like, to an extent that would prevent the accumulation of capital upon which industrial growth – and hence in the longer run a rising standard of life for the world as a whole – vitally depends. Faced with this prospect, Gellner thinks, it is unrealistic to assume that the rich industrialized societies would consent to the setting up of a world state on those terms. And since it is inconceivable that a world state should come about without their consent, the most probable outcome would be that economic inequalities would be sustained by a system of race discrimination – apartheid on a world scale, in fact, and a curious acknowledgement that after all South Africa's problems may be those of the world in miniature. From this point of view, Gellner implies, it is political independence in the developing countries that makes economic inequality bearable.[15]

MILITARY ORGANIZATION AND 'THE POLICE IDEA'

We can return now to another aspect of the topic with which we began this chapter on the control of violent aggression, namely the actual social institutions – army and police – for the organization of violence.

In some societies, the control of violence is diffuse. All men bear arms and can legitimately use them to counter aggression or get their rights. In some societies indeed, such as the Masai, Nkole, and other pastoral peoples of Africa, men habitually carry lethal weapons to defend their herds against wild beasts as well as human raiders. In stateless societies such as the Nuer, too, the carrying of arms may be usual because there is no authority to control it. In such societies, any quarrel may lead to bloodshed and any fight may end in a killing.

In some other societies, the use of weapons is restricted to particular men who alone have the right to carry them. This has the very great advantage of lowering the general level of violence, but with the corresponding disadvantage of putting great power into the hands of the men with arms, who may use it to oppress and extort. The extent to which they can do so successfully, however, is more limited than might appear at first sight. It depends partly on the nature of military technology in the society in question.[16] For example, the carrying of simple arms like spears and swords can hardly be restricted to a few, since they are relatively easily and quickly manufactured and can even be made in secret by people resentful of the power of the armed minority. To be the basis for oppression, arms must be more complex and costly. In feudal Europe, common peasants could afford neither the armour and horses of the knights nor the fortified castles in which they were safe from surprise attack with small arms; those who commanded these things were accordingly able to oppress the peasantry. Their power was first threatened by the longbow, able to pierce some armour, and finally overthrown by the introduction of firearms, muskets whose bullets could pierce armour with ease, and cannon which could batter down castles. Somewhat similarly, as was shown at Sharpeville, white power in South Africa rests on exclusive control of firearms and armoured vehicles, against which clandestinely manufactured weapons are ineffective. Secondly, the power of an armed minority is greatly reduced when the society they control is attacked from outside. They must then allow more people to have arms to fight the attackers; once armed, the people have a better chance of gaining political or economic concessions. Thus it is only when a country is safe from outside attack that the bearing of arms can become the privilege of a small, oppressive minority; a good example were the

Samurai of traditional, isolated Japan. Thirdly, although as we have seen the prevailing weapons must not be so simple and cheap that anyone can get hold of them, they must not on the other hand be so large and clumsy as to be ineffective against internal opposition – for dispersing hostile crowds or quelling riots – if they are to be useful for oppression. In early nineteenth-century England, where the dominant armaments were warships, the ruling class had no effective weapons at their disposal for dispersing unruly political meetings. Attempts to use cavalry led to the notorious incident on St Peter's Field, Manchester, which was named 'the Peterloo massacre', and it was this as much as anything which stimulated the development of a civil police force, while it also meant that the ruling class were unable to resist popular demands for reform. A more modern example would be the nuclear weapons on which the great powers rely for retaliating against attack, but which are so undiscriminating as to be quite useless for suppressing a rioting crowd.

In modern states – since, indeed, the experience of early nineteenth-century England – it has become usual to separate the internal and external control of violence into two institutions, police and army (including in this term navy and air force). This is a logical development from modern military technology, for though a state tries to maximize its potential for external violence (subject to what it can afford to spend on soldiers and weapons), it has an interest in keeping the level of violence internally as low as possible. Police, unarmed or armed only lightly with minimum weapons of self-defence, are a much more flexible and discriminating means of maintaining law and order among the citizens of the state, and can include among their functions that of enforcing the laws relating to the sale and possession of arms, or indeed of any objects capable of violent use – even down to lengths of bicycle chain!

In conjunction with this development there has grown up what has been termed 'the police idea', that it is right to use only just sufficient violence to overcome illegitimate violence and apprehend offenders.[17] This is in such complete contrast to the tendency of states to offer the maximum of violence externally through their armies that the question is now being asked whether police principles can be applied to international relations also. This question is closely bound up with that of the possibility of a world

state, which we discussed above, since a world state would undoubtedly control a world police force. Even without the establishment of a world state, however, this idea seems to underlie some
recent developments. One example was the United Nations forces
in the Congo (now Zaïre), who though composed of military
units were said with some truth to be engaged in an essentially
police operation. Many military operations in recent times,
indeed, have been carried out in circumstances in which the
deployment of the really big weapons has been for one reason or
another impracticable. The British in Malaya, for example, learned
to minimize rather than maximize brutality, and to co-ordinate
the army's actions with police and political action, in what was
termed 'the struggle for the hearts and minds of the people'; while
the suppression of the East African army mutinies in 1964 called
for similar skills in overcoming and disarming rather than killing,
and the operation was carried out with a minimum of bloodshed.

We turn finally to another problem arising from the existence of
a specialized institution, the army, for controlling violence –
namely, who controls the army? As Professor S. E. Finer has
pointed out, it might seem at first sight as if there would be an
overwhelming tendency in all societies towards military government.[18] Armies are generally well disciplined, closely organized, and popular; and above all they control the weapons. What
is really surprising indeed, is not that there are so many military
governments in the world, but that there are so few. What factors
inhibit military rule, and favour civilian control of the army? In the
most highly developed industrial states, there seem to be three
such factors. First, the administration and the economy of such
states are so complex that the army can hardly hope to maintain
control, unless at the cost of 'civilianizing' itself – deputing its
officers to man the boards of industrial concerns, the ministries,
the banks, the universities, etc., in which case they would become
almost like civilians themselves. Secondly, there is in such
societies a rich complex of associations, such as churches, political
parties, trade unions, all of which the army could hardly hope to
penetrate, and some of which might prove very resistant to such
penetration. And thirdly, there tends to be in such countries a
strong feeling that the army cannot properly or legally overrule
the civil power; in other words, it lacks legitimacy. This idea may
be shared not only by civil politicians, but also by senior army

officers, who may themselves be identified with the idea of civil control and very reluctant to overthrow those to whom their loyalty is legitimately owed.

In many of the new nations, however, not all these conditions hold. In what Finer has called states at the middle level of political development, there may be a well-organized and well-equipped army officered by able men. At the same time, however, the administration of the country may not be unduly complex, associational life may not be particularly highly developed, and, even though the army lack a legitimate claim to rule, so also may the new government of a state recently emerged from colonial rule in which many sentiments of legitimacy may cling to tribal authorities. Indeed, there may be circumstances in which there is widespread dissatisfaction with politicians, so that the army come to be regarded as the saviours of the state against mismanagement and corruption. In such a case the obstacles to military rule will be few and weak. It need hardly be stressed how well Finer's analysis has been borne out by events in Africa since 1960.

SUGGESTIONS FOR FURTHER READING

K. Z. Lorenz, *On aggression* (London, Methuen, 1966). See also his earlier work, *King Solomon's ring* (London, Methuen, 1952), ch. XII.

E. F. M. Durbin and J. Bowlby, *Personal aggressiveness and war* (London, Kegan Paul, 1939).

R. Dahrendorf, *Class and class conflict in an industrial society* (London, Routledge and Kegan Paul, 1959), esp. chs V and VI.

David Lockwood, 'Some remarks on "The Social System"', *British Journal of Sociology*, 7 (1956), 134–46.

L. A. Coser, *The functions of social conflict* (London, Routledge and Kegan Paul, 1956).

Max Weber, *The theory of social and economic organisation* (translated from the German by A. R. Henderson and T. Parsons, Edinburgh, William Hodge and Co., 1947).

No section has been included on social control in traditional African societies, since there are two books which deal with this subject systematically:

M. Fortes and E. E. Evans-Pritchard, *African political systems* (Oxford University Press, 1940).

L. P. Mair, *Primitive government* (London, Penguin, 1962).

On this subject also, a subtle and perceptive approach is that of M. Gluckman, *Custom and conflict in Africa* (Oxford, Blackwell, 1959).

On military organization, a highly original and suggestive though very technical book is S. Andrzejewski (or Andreski), *Military organization and society* (London, Routledge, 1954).

The trend towards military rule in many modern states is analysed in S. E. Finer, *The man on horseback* (London, Pall Mall Press, 1962).

CHAPTER 8

Magic, religion and society

If a being from another planet were to visit Earth, he would find one thing puzzling. He would (as more than one writer has suggested)[1] be able to understand most of the human activity he observed – getting food and shelter, bringing up the young, caring for the unable, settling disputes – activities like these would be clearly and simply related to the needs of an intelligent, gregarious mammal. But there would be other and somewhat inexplicable things. Buildings not used to live or work in, but the scene from time to time of stranger activities – singing, intoning, speech addressed apparently to no one present – and even at other times the place for curiously inhibited behaviour such as speaking in hushed tones or removing shoes. Groves of trees which no one approaches, until one day a group of boys climb them and tear down branches, amid scenes of excitement. A small knot of men giving poison to a fowl and asking it questions as it dies. Or a strange contraption of shells, sticks, feathers, and bits of string, which its owner and others feed with fowl's blood in the belief – contrary to all reason – that it has the power to fly at night and kill an enemy, or set a hut on fire. Such activities would appear quite useless – a waste of time and resources to no benefit. Yet if such a suggestion were made to the people concerned, they would invariably resist it most emphatically. On the contrary, they would say, not only are these actions important, they are of supreme importance. What can be the explanation for so strange a delusion?

Moreover, man is the only living species which engages in magical and religious activities of the sort just mentioned. (It seems probable that at least one extinct human species, namely Neanderthal man, did so too; there is definite evidence of ritual burial of the dead by Neanderthalers and probably of magical cults also.)[2] Magic and religion, then, which are integral to practically all human cultures, must be seen in relation to what is distinctively human.

Human cultures, as I have already suggested, consist of a system of tools linked with a system of symbols. The really distinctive feature of human cultures is their symbolic nature, and it is his ability to perform symbolic operations, learned through culture, that distinguishes man from other animals. Viewed in this light, magic and religion take their place among the ways in which human beings try to control their world by performing symbolic operations.

Further, although as has been shown tool-making is not quite confined to man, it has been carried to a far higher pitch of development in the rise of human cultures than with any other animal. As an important consequence of this, human cultures make for foresight and hence for anxiety. Unlike the simple tools made by some other animals most human tools are made for needs which are foreseen in the future rather than immediately experienced in the present. Men make arrows because they foresee a hunting party tomorrow; women plant crops because they foresee next year's hunger. Moreover, through language, tomorrow's needs can be discussed in symbolic terms. Human beings intelligently anticipate future events. But intelligent anticipation of future events implies intelligent anticipation of all the things that can go wrong before future needs are met. If human beings can see hunger a year ahead, and so plant crops to meet it, they can also foresee the droughts or floods, the locusts or enemy raids that may spoil the crop. Above all, alone among animals, man can foresee his own death. And so he is, as an American anthropologist has said, 'nature's great and only worrier; he can worry alone and he can worry in unison, always with justice'.[3] Foresight leads to anxiety; anxiety finds expression in action. Where something sensible and effective can be done, human beings – within the limits of the available technology – will do it; till the ground as well as they know how, make the most seaworthy vessel possible. All that they can control they will. But there are always uncontrollable hazards: the weather, disease, other people's malice. Yet to do nothing about such hazards seems to be insupportable. There must be *something* we can do. Magic and religion can be seen as symbolic activities whose function is to allay the anxiety that results from the gap between foresight and control.

These might at first sight be termed irrational activities, since it is clear that they cannot in general have the desired result through any direct process of causation. No rain-maker can in any literal sense make it rain, for example. Nevertheless, beliefs in the efficacy of magical or religious rituals may help humans to perform tasks or face hazards they would otherwise shirk. Ritual raises morale, and for this reason alone it may 'work' as long as people believe in it. For example, the ritual that fortified the young Bemba men for the hazardous task of cutting the high branches of trees,[4] or the way in which traditional healers would raise the morale of a sick person even though their medicines might, in pharmacological terms, be useless. Moreover, the latent function of ritual may be real, even though its manifest function may be imaginary. For example, the rain-queen of the Ba-Lovedu of the Transvaal was believed to be unable to make rain properly if she were dissatisfied, angry, or sad – as she was when her daughter was having an affair with a commoner and on another occasion because of her people's evil works and witchcraft.[5] Even erroneous beliefs, then, can have positive social functions.

DISTINCTION BETWEEN MAGIC AND RELIGION

It is usual to draw a distinction between magic and religion. We normally think of magic as an attempt by individuals to attain particular private ends – the success of a crop, good hunting, the death of an enemy, a favourable decision in a law case – by invoking supernatural means. In the case of 'black' or anti-social magic, such as that aimed at harming an enemy, this is of course done in secret; 'white' or beneficent magic may not necessarily be secret, but it is a matter of private, not public, concern. The aim is to manipulate or control occult forces in one's own favour and a person who wishes to do this may either do it for him- or herself, or call in a professional magician who will do it for a fee or reward. Whether called witch-doctors, diviners, mediums, or by any other name, magicians are indeed often the nearest equivalent in a primitive society to the professional practitioners of a modern society. They are regarded as experts to whom, for a fee, ordinary people entrust part of their affairs which they do not feel capable of managing themselves.

By contrast we think of religion as a public matter, devoted to public, general ends – not just the fertility of one particular garden, for example, but the fertility of all the land. Religious rituals are thought of as being performed on behalf of a group, and – typically though not invariably – as involving the participation of a congregation. The priest is accordingly a publicly designated leader, not a privately rewarded professional. The priest leads a congregation, a magician has a clientele. And, so far from manipulation or control, religious acts aim (in Frazer's classic definition) at 'the propitiation or conciliation of powers superior to man which are believed to direct and control the course of nature and of human life'.[6] The characteristic utterance of magic is the spell, of religion the prayer.

Such a distinction is not without its value or validity; yet it leaves a wide category of borderline and ambiguous cases. Ceremonies for the blessing of particular pieces of equipment – from fishing nets to power stations – are one such group of cases. Ambiguous also is the fact that in many rituals which we would, on the face of it, class as religious, there may, nevertheless, be an element of attempted control or compulsion rather than prayer and submission. One such example is afforded by the totemic rituals of Australian aborigines. Although these are public and involve the participation of the whole totemic group, their aim is quite explicitly to *make* the totem multiply.[7] Another excellent example is the ritual procession in a small Chinese town afflicted by cholera, when an effigy of the Wen god was taken outside the town and burnt, together with a sacrifice of food and an amulet collected from each house in the town. By an obvious symbolism, this represented an attempt to make the disease leave the town.[8] Thirdly, there may be ambiguity in particular cases between being the leader of a worshipping congregation, and acting as a professional man carrying out a service for his clients – as, for example, when a Christian priest conducts weddings and funerals for a fee. Particular persons may be believed to possess supernatural authority, which makes it natural that they should act in both the roles of magician and priest, exercising authority in the one case on behalf of an individual, in the other on behalf of the group. Among the Kikuyu, for example, elders believed to be supernaturally powerful would, on some occasions, lead public prayers (e.g. for rain) at the sacred grove, as well as performing the purifying rite for removing *thahu* (ritual uncleanness) for individuals.[9] And I have been told by an Anglican clergyman how much he enjoyed performing, on behalf of English countrymen, the purely magical rite of laying a ghost.

MAGIC AND SOCIETY

Although, then, the same person may appear from time to time in different roles, in considering magic it is important to distinguish these roles, at least in principle. Healers or herbalists who traditionally possessed a mixture of medical and magical skills have sometimes been called (in English) 'witch-doctors'; in Luganda, the same word *musawo* is used for them and nowadays for western-trained medical practitioners. Another beneficent role (which might be played by the same person) was that of diviner, who would magically diagnose the cause of misfortune. On the side of 'black' magic, it is important to distinguish between a sorcerer and a witch. A sorcerer is a real person who 'wittingly directs injurious magic on others'.[10] Such acts are (from the standpoint of science) quite ineffectual, but they are real and observable actions like making a concoction of a person's faeces and drawing a line with it across a path. By contrast, a witch is a person to whom imaginary powers are attributed, like that of making oneself invisible. In European folklore, for example, witches were traditionally depicted as flying through the air at night on broomsticks; in traditional African beliefs they became invisible or turned themselves into animals. Witchcraft is of importance largely in the context of a witchcraft accusation. A person accused of witchcraft may, indeed, have been guilty of sorcery; but the important thing about a witchcraft accusation is that it can never be disproved. From a scientific point of view, it is of course an empty accusation; but in a society in which witchcraft beliefs prevail it may be a serious one, and because of the impossibility of disproof a highly convenient means of discrediting a person who has become unpopular.

Where witchcraft beliefs prevail, their logical corollary is a belief in witch-finding techniques. Among the functions of a diviner, therefore, is usually that of detecting witchcraft and designating who is responsible. It was beliefs of this sort that led to the sharpest collision between traditional African beliefs and those of European administrators and missionaries in the colonial period. From their point of view, any accusation of witchcraft was by definition an empty one; it could, however, lead to harmful consequences such as assault against the person accused, and for that reason it was usual for the Witchcraft Ordinances to make it an offence to name a person a witch or to impute witchcraft. This contrasted sharply with the traditional African view of a witch-finder as essentially a friend, performing a valuable service on behalf of the whole community.

We have already mentioned some of the social functions of magic. In the case of 'white' or beneficent magic they are plain enough – it allays anxiety, raises morale, nerves us for difficult or dangerous tasks, gives the sick a new hope of recovery, and generally affords everyone the satisfaction of knowing that everything which it is possible to do to control the uncontrollable has been done. It may be less obvious what the positive social functions of 'black' magic are; yet if we reflect that no real harm can possibly occur as a result of any act of sorcery, it can be seen as a harmless outlet for feelings of aggression or frustration against other people.

Thus, as Marwick has shown in his study of sorcery among the Cewa of Zambia and Malawi, injurious magic is commonly practised against people from whom one cannot get redress by other means, whether by force or through a court case. Among the Cewa it is matrilineal relatives who '"practise sorcery against each other" because they are unable to settle their quarrels by the ordinary judicial procedures available to unrelated persons who quarrel. Litigation is generally between one person supported by his matrikin and another supported by his.'[11] Both sorcery and witchcraft accusations can, it seems, serve as indices of strained relations.

A classic study of a people dominated by witchcraft beliefs is that by Evans-Pritchard of the Azande of the southern Sudan. Here all major misfortunes are attributed to witchcraft, and many minor ones too. Witchcraft, indeed, is regarded as so commonplace that Azande do not fear it; they merely find it annoying. So many everyday occurrences are attributed to it – if crops do not grow, if a wife is barren, if a boy stubs his toe on a root in the path – that most of the time they do nothing about it. Evans-Pritchard goes on to show how witchcraft beliefs involve a need for two explanations of every event. For example, when termites gnawed the posts of a granary so that it collapsed and injured some people who were sitting in its shade, the Azande were perfectly able to understand the natural process of causation that brought about the effect. A scientifically minded westerner would look for no further explanation; people who sit under granaries are (as statisticians say) 'at risk' of being hurt if the granary collapses; the event is seen as the more or less random intersection of two sequences – the gnawing termites, and the hot afternoon that induced people to seek shade. Azande, however, characteristically demanded to know why the collapse should have taken place at that particular moment, injuring those particular people. In addition to the naturalistic explanation, that is, they demanded an explanation which, in their culture, could only be in terms of witchcraft.

The search for a dual explanation, however, led them into a logical fallacy in the case of death. Death, like all other misfortunes, was attributed to witchcraft (as well as to whatever naturalistic explanation – such as old age, disease, accident – was appropriate in each particular case). Unlike other misfortunes, however, it was always a matter for vengeance against the witch, and it was accordingly the duty of the surviving relatives to do vengeance magic. Thus if a man A died, A's relatives would do vengeance magic. After a while, in the course of nature, someone else, B, in the locality would die. The question was then whether B's death was the result of the vengeance-magic for A, or not; and this was ascertained by divination, subject to confirmation by the chief's oracle. If the answer was no, vengeance-magic continued; if it was yes, then A's death was considered avenged. But B's relatives did not know this, and would initiate vengeance magic until it was considered to have caused the death of a third person C . . . and so on without end. Evans-Pritchard says he pointed this out to Azande, who took the point, but 'were not incommoded by it'. He continues:

So long as they are able to conform to custom and maintain family honour, they are not interested in the broader aspects of vengeance in general . . . Princes must be aware of the contradiction because they know the outcome of every death in their provinces . . . Some princes said that they did not allow a man to be avenged if they knew he had died from vengeance-magic, but I think they were lying.[12]

Magical beliefs, then, are against logic and inconsistent with a scientific attitude. They are moreover deplored by the great world religions, including Christianity and Islam, even though some Christians and some Muslims may sometimes engage in magical practices. Under the double attack of science and Christian faith, indeed, magic has become very much less important in western societies than it was in traditional conditions. It has not entirely disappeared. Some people continue to believe in astrology, for example, and there are minor residual beliefs in good and bad luck and signs or actions that cause them. But its importance is small; it certainly cannot be said to dominate life as it evidently does among the Azande or the Cewa. It might seem at first sight as if the importance of magic would dwindle in Africa as modern education brings a scientific attitude and as the influence of Christianity and Islam weigh against it. But, while it may decline in the long run, at present it shows no sign of doing so. On the contrary, all observers agree that as new conditions bring new anxieties, so these are met by new forms of magic. In addition to the old anxieties about the failure of the food supply and so on, which as yet modern developments have done little to lessen (though they may well do so in the long run), there are new ones – getting and keeping employment, passing examinations, making a profit in trade. And so to quote Marwick again,

Cewa believe sorcery to be on the increase . . . They believe that people who have become rich – and becoming rich is largely a modern phenomenon – are in constant danger of being attacked by sorcerers . . . When a labour migrant returns from his place of work, he enters his home village under cover of darkness. This practice is attributed to his fearing the sorcery of his matrikin. According to African mores, he should be sharing his newly acquired wealth with them, and thus reinforcing matrilineage bonds; but his newly acquired attitudes impel him rather to the more universal norm of raising his own standard of living. The same applies to people who have become rich locally, e.g. from selling maize or vegetables or from running a village shop. Their preoccupation with fears of sorcery is, according to informants, reflected in their keen interest in acquiring strong protective medicines.[13]

Somewhat similarly in Mulago, a suburb of Kampala, Gutkind reported that many shopkeepers consulted a magician who charged substantial sums for 'medicines' to bring customers into their shops and keep them away from rivals' shops. When one day this magician was brought to court on a charge of witchcraft, the trial was attended by a large crowd. One of them called out that this was 'a very bad trial' because if he were convicted then a lot of cooked banana sellers and shopkeepers would lose money.[14] Yet another example is that of divination in Langa, a suburb of Cape Town, as described by Wilson and Mafeje.[15]

THE SOCIOLOGICAL ASPECTS OF RELIGION

We must now consider in more detail the sociological aspects of religion – its functions, or what it does to and for individuals and society, ways in which the religious activities are organized, and the relation of religion to other aspects of the social structure and to social change.

Religion is, in Durkheim's famous definition, a system of beliefs and practices. The beliefs, indeed, are logically prior to the practices: people act in particular ways because they believe particular things, not the other way about.[16] We cannot therefore avoid considering religious beliefs in any sociological treatment of the subject, and I must first set out, therefore, what is the sociological approach to matters of religious faith. It is important to bear in mind in all that follows that the truth or otherwise of religious beliefs is not a matter for sociological consideration. Individual sociologists may assent to particular religious beliefs, they may dissent from them, or they may find them inconclusive, meaningless, or incapable of demonstration. Many sociologists are agnostic in matters of religion, and the sociological temper is to be sceptical and anti-dogmatic; there are also, however, many competent sociologists who are committed to religious faith of one sort or another. But the state of individual sociologists' beliefs is not the point. What is sociologically relevant is not the truth or otherwise of particular beliefs, but their social consequences. Thus, to take just one example, the statement 'There is one god' may be true or false, or incapable of demonstration. Christians and Muslims would doubtless assent, ancient Greeks and traditional Baganda would dissent, Hindus would add 'But god takes many forms.' For a sociologist, however (that is, when he is acting in his role as a sociologist), the relevance of that statement lies not in its truth or otherwise, but in any connections that can be traced between the belief and the actions of those who believe it. Does it, for example, make them want to engage in controversies with polytheists? Does it sometimes lead them to destroy objects (idols, fetishes) which are regarded as embodying wrongful beliefs in false gods? How does it affect the relations between Christians and Muslims on the one hand, and the followers of pagan African religions with many gods and spirits on the other? Beliefs, whether true or false, are social facts. They are facts about the people who believe them, and from a sociological point of view they require to be treated with the same objectivity as other social facts, like kinship systems or laws.

We have already seen how religious ritual, like magical ritual, can allay anxiety and raise morale. We may now perhaps enlarge upon this and, following Nadel, consider religion in terms of four functions, or as he prefers to call them 'capacities' or 'competences' – the things that religion can do, the effects it may have, the desires, needs, or purposes that it may serve. These are first, the cosmological aspects – 'the capacity of religion to furnish certain supplements to the view of the world of experience'; secondly, its capacity to announce and maintain moral values; thirdly, its competence to hold together societies and sustain their structure; and fourthly its competence to furnish individuals with specific experiences and stimulations.[17]

Religion tends to be linked with cosmology (that is, a view or conception of the nature of the universe and man's place in it) because of the need which people experience to 'relativize' (as Yinger phrases it) the risks and disasters to which human life is subject from the action of natural forces.[18] Among the deeper anxieties which we feel are those about the whole nature of the world and our place in it. Is the rest of the universe hostile to us, or friendly, or indifferently neutral? Can particular disasters like floods, droughts, locust swarms, be 'relativized' by being seen as part of some larger good? Is there more to the universe than the evidence our senses conveys to us – some deeper design, some cosmic purpose? We seem to experience a need for reassurance about such large, vague problems as these, and religion's 'capacity to furnish certain supplements to the world of experience' goes at any rate some way towards meeting it.

It is a need which arises most poignantly at death – at the death of a person's close kin or friends, and in contemplation of his own inevitable end. Here the desire for reassurance – or if not reassurance at least for some view which makes the process tolerable – is overwhelming. It is no accident that all religions are very largely concerned with death. All have rituals for the disposal of the dead, affording a means of marking in a socially and psychologically acceptable way the transition of a human body from a living person to a piece of decaying flesh, to be disposed of in some effectively hygienic manner. All have a set of beliefs about the continuation of the personality in some form after death, since the shock of absolute bereavement and the prospect of absolute extinction seem to be unbearable to most human beings.* Hence arise beliefs in ghosts, in other worlds to which the souls of the dead migrate – worlds which have to be fitted in to whatever view is taken of the nature of the universe. Hence also is a relation to the nature of time – for example, beliefs in the circulation of souls through their rebirth in new bodies or, by contrast, beliefs in an eternity to which souls go when they have left their earthly bodies.

Religion, then, is quite largely concerned with furnishing the individual with a view of the universe that provides some kind of an answer to questions like the origin of the personality and the nature of death. Not, it must be added, an answer with an intellectual emphasis. Religion is not science. What is sought is not the kind of cosmology which satisfies us in our scientific mood – a view of the universe based on facts, observations, and logical deductions from them – but one which is emotionally helpful to people at times of stress. To ask so specific a question as, Where is heaven? Is it above or below the ground?, still more to object that the answers conventionally given are hard to reconcile with the known facts about the solar system, is irrelevant and even unsympathetic when one is consoling a bereaved friend who desperately wants to be told that the dead person has gone somewhere good.

Secondly, religion may be concerned with morals, though not all religions are and the connection may not be a simple one. Christianity and Islam – both heirs to the Judaic tradition – stand at one extreme in linking faith and morality very strongly. The ten commandments, which are the basis of morality and can be elaborated into secular law, are regarded as having been divinely handed down, and there are beliefs about punishment for bad deeds and rewards for good ones in the life after death. Buddhism too is a very strongly ethical religion. Indeed, in its pure, original form it was nothing else; the saintly prince Gotama's prescriptions for right conduct were accompanied by no more than a promise that those who followed them would find inner peace and a

---

*One exception to this exists, namely Buddhism in its pure, original form.

withdrawal from the stresses of the world. There were no beliefs in gods or spirits, nor were any rituals or sacrifices prescribed.

In traditional African religions, at the other extreme, there seems characteristically to have been little or no connection between religion and morals. Right actions consisted of what a man owed to his kinsmen; they were grounded in the kinship system, rather than being thought of as sanctioned or rewarded by the gods or spirits. Nadel indeed concludes that, so far as this second 'capacity' goes, Nupe religion was amoral, and somewhat similar conclusions were reached about the traditional religions of the Ba-Lovedu by Krige, Rwanda by Maquet, and Ashanti by Fortes.[19]

In other religions, the connection between faith and morals may be more complex. The gods of religions like those of ancient Greece and Rome, or those of the traditional beliefs of north-west European peoples, included bad gods as well as good, and gods among these pantheons committed acts such as incest, murder, and treachery in a manner that would have been highly immoral among mortals; but possibly the social function of such myths was to emphasize that what is permitted to gods may be forbidden to mortals. In Hinduism, the relation between belief and morality is intricate. The gods (or forms or manifestations of god) include the destroyer as well as the creator; every aspect of the universe and of human life, indeed, is so personified. There are beliefs about rewards and punishments in the form of rebirth into a higher or lower caste, but the morality which is prescribed is not a set of rules applicable to all. First, people should follow the rules of the caste into which they were born, so that for instance Rajput men should be fierce and warlike whereas Brahmins should be pious and studious; and further, the religious adviser may prescribe for each person a set of rules especially applicable to him or her. Thus one devotee may find it right to fast three days a week, another may find it a pious duty to walk barefoot to the source of the Ganges river; this does not mean that it is necessarily desirable for all Hindus to do so.

We may conclude, then, that though religion *may* have a moral function, not all religions do, and the relation between religion and morals is not a simple or straightforward one.

Thirdly, Nadel listed the competence of religion 'to hold together societies and sustain their structure'. It was upon this aspect of the sociology of religion that the greatest emphasis was laid by Durkheim in his profoundly important study *Elementary forms of the religious life*. It is not possible here adequately to summarize Durkheim's analysis. I can only baldly state his main conclusion, that *the* social function of religion is to engender and sustain social solidarity. Durkheim, indeed, goes so far as to suggest that the god is the group; when an assembled group are worshipping a god, whom they think of as being beyond themselves, they are really strengthening the bonds that link them to one another in a social group. Ritual employs all the resources of art and drama, the dance, and the feast to symbolize and uphold the values that the participants have in common, and hence to re-affirm their solidary membership of the group.

It goes without saying that Durkheim's theory reflects the consensus, integration, or functionalist view of society which we discussed in the last chapter, and of which Durkheim was perhaps the greatest exponent. When it is used to analyse the rituals of the people whom Durkheim took as his example – Australian aboriginal tribes as described in the works of Spencer and Gillen, and other sources – the analysis is certainly extremely persuasive. Here it is a whole community, a totemic group, which participates in a common ritual and, as Durkheim says, 'revivifies the sentiment it has of itself by assembling'. I could, indeed, go a little further than Durkheim does at this point and say that his analysis seems also to apply to some forms of secular ritual like a University graduation ceremony. The group congregates; its values are symbolically expressed in the award of academic distinction to those who have earned it by study and research; the unity, coherence, and continuity of the Academe are impressively revivified. Such an analysis, then, seems to work in the case where the participating group forms a community characterized by consensus or among whom at least consensus can be presumed.

It even continues to hold, up to a point, when we are considering a society riven by denominational strife; for the rituals of the different denominations continue to assert the unity *of each group* and to uphold its distinctive values. But when Anglicans or Catholics, Muslims or Seventh-Day Adventists assemble, what is asserted is the unity of each group in contradistinction to the others. In such a case, religion can scarcely be said to unite the community as a whole, and we clearly need to move over towards an interpretation in terms of dissensus, conflict and change.

Characteristically, Durkheim's theory is incomplete in giving no indication of how dissenting groups can arise. Based as it is on the assumption that moral consensus is what makes a group a group, it leaves no place for the dissenting individual who may get a following which can turn into a group expressing its unity in a distinctive ritual. Without, therefore, controverting Durkheim's analysis so far as it goes, I may say that it is insufficient by itself and needs to be supplemented; and as we saw in the last chapter, Weber's theory of charismatic leadership and its routinization affords the kinds of supplement we need.

Another way of putting it would be to say that Durkheim's is essentially a conservative view of religion; that is, it views religion as a conservative force, upholding and sustaining the existing social structure. To a large extent and in a great many cases this is undoubtedly justified, but we must also take account of the fact that religion is sometimes and in some circumstances an innovating force, tending to make for social change. The dissenting individual is one case in point; another, perhaps more familiar in the recent history of Africa, is the introduction of new religious ideas from outside a society. Both Christianity and Islam, well-established and on the whole conservative parts of the social structure in the countries from which they spread to Africa, appear here as revolutionary forces, drastically changing people's ideas and associated with other changes, such as literacy, modern education, and modern medical methods, which have also been revolutionary in their impact on traditional African societies. We shall try in the next section to say a little more about the very large subject of religion and social change.

Nadel's fourth heading, religion's 'competence to furnish individuals with specific attitudes and stimulations', amounts to looking at the social 'competences', which he has already listed, from a different viewpoint – that of individual psychology. Nadel's analysis is well borne out here by the evidence assembled by the psychologist Michael Argyle and drawn mainly from British and American studies.[20] Many of these studies show that those who undergo a definite religious experience of conversion do so mostly in adolescence. Equally, however, adolescence in western countries is the age at which religious doubts grow, and church attendance – encouraged by the institutionalized religious teaching which children receive in school – tends to fall off. This apparent paradox is resolved if we view adolescence as a time of decision – a period in the individual's life when a definite standpoint is taken up, either of faith or doubt, which is more often than not maintained throughout life. Religious activity (whether church attendance or the saying of private prayers) declines steadily with age into young adulthood, but recovers after the age of 30. American studies in particular show that certainty of an after-life increases sharply in old age. More women than men go to church, say private prayers, and avow belief in God – commonly about twenty-five per cent more. Finally, some American studies show a consistently negative relation between intelligence and faith.

Such evidence fits in well with the view that we arrived at earlier, of religion as the institution that enables men to allay the anxieties natural at the crises of life such as adolescence (with all the phenomena of sex, love, and choice of marriage partner) and old age (with the regular toll of death among one's friends, and one's own approaching end). The greater religious activity of women can perhaps be related to their particular anxieties about childbirth and the rearing of children, and the roles conventionally assigned to them on the 'expressive' side of family life.[21] In the light of evidence such as this it perhaps seems reasonable to postulate, arising from the anxiety which is distinctive to man, a *need for ritual*, especially at the crises of life – ritual which is derived from, and intelligible in the light of, belief or faith. This need is presumably common to all, but possibly it is experienced more strongly by those who are less likely to be satisfied by a rational or naturalistic view of the hazards of life. Hence, perhaps, the significance of the American finding of a negative relation between intelligence and faith.

FORMS OF RELIGIOUS ORGANIZATION

It would follow from this analysis that any religion that is a viable social institution affords a framework of regular and occasional rituals within which people's needs for ritual can find fulfilment. Any institutionalized religion, that is, must prescribe definite things to be done both regularly (for example, every day, every seventh day, at the seasons of the agricultural year) and on particular occasions (birth, marriage, death, sickness, disaster, or rejoicing) which are related to the lives and needs of the people.

At this point we must draw a broad distinction between ethnic or folk religion on the one hand and the great world religions on the other. It is characteristic of ethnic or folk religions that their relation to the way of life – the culture, the economy, and hence the prevailing anxieties – of the people is relatively simple and direct. Sometimes it seems as if one could almost predict the religion from the rest of the culture; for example, among many African peoples, anxiety about a fickle but crucial rainfall leads to religious systems like the rain-dance of the Lango[22] or the rain-queen of the Lovedu.[23] Further, folk religions are associated with particular tribes or groups, all of whom share in the main rituals; and mark off those groups from others. In Parsons' terms they are particularistic.

By contrast, the great world religions are universalistic. Beginning as 'revealed' or 'prophetic' (i.e. charismatic) movements, their membership extends across the boundaries of particular groups, cultures, languages, or nations. Muslims of northern Nigeria, for example, share their Islamic beliefs with Muslims in Buganda, with Arabs, with people in Pakistan, Indonesia, and in many other parts of the world. People of widely different languages, cultures, and standards of living all congregate in Mecca and Medina. The appeal is to all believers, and ultimately to all men since all men can become believers if they choose. It follows that a world religion cannot be so directly or simply related to any particular culture as a folk religion; on the contrary, the world religions have a certain independence of time, place, or particular circumstance. This is associated with the fact that, whereas most folk religions are essentially traditional in the strict sense of being handed on by word of mouth from one generation to the next, the world religions are associated with writing. Religions of the book, they have scriptures, commentaries, exegesis, which accumulate over the centuries, in a body of theological knowledge which exceeds the capacity of any one believer to know. Hence accordingly the world religions tend (though not all to the same extent) to have a specialized body of priestly scholars whose function is to know the scriptures and expound them to the ordinary laity.

From this point of view, Christianity, Islam and Buddhism are clearly to be included among the world religions, while at the other extreme come the pagan folk religions. In between we can perhaps put such religions as Hinduism and Judaism; they have many of the attributes of the world religions – books, theology, a high intellectual level, a specialized class of priestly scholars – but they remain also the traditional religions of particular peoples rather than having originated as charismatic movements; and they embody a whole way of life rather than a set of definite beliefs to which a person can assent or be converted.

Where a system of belief and practice unites a whole community, it is normal in sociology to use the term church. This usage follows Durkheim who defined religion as 'a system of beliefs and practices . . . which unite into one single moral community called a church, all those who adhere to them'. Following Weber, it has become accepted sociological usage to distinguish a church from a sect, by which is commonly meant a dissident minority group, often with charismatic leadership, as we saw in chapter 7. A simple distinction between these two forms of religious organization, however, seems inadequate, and we need other categories.

First, as we have seen, the pure or charismatic phase of a religious (or for that matter political) movement is an unstable phenomenon. Such movements tend to settle down and become routinized, and to be accepted as a more or less stable part of the local social structure. Instead of a two-fold distinction between sect and church, therefore, we need to recognize a third intermediate category, that of the denomination. Such a three-fold distinction is now generally accepted in the sociology of religion, and has been elegantly set out by David Martin.[24] Where a church recruits its members by birth, and a sect primarily by conversion, a denomination does so in both ways. Family tradition usually plays an important part, but many denominations require their young members to reaffirm their faith by means of an act of positive choice. Generally speaking, a church is largely identified with the local political order. As an example we may contrast the attitudes of different Christian bodies to war. Since a church ministers to all members of a community, including soldiers, it can hardly reject war absolutely, though it may qualify its acceptance of the necessity of war in certain circumstances by defining 'just war' doctrines. A sect usually unites a small minority who are persecuted or at least dispossessed by the wider society, and are at odds with the local political system. Many sects accordingly reject secular wars outright and try to dissuade their young male members from joining the army, urging them to refuse compulsory military service.

Denominations characteristically take up a middle position on this issue. They do not withdraw their ministrations from those of their members who join the army, but they may well stand up for the rights of those who as a matter of conscience refuse to fight. Again, a church generally upholds the laws of the state and the authority of those whose duty it is to enforce them. Denominations generally accept the necessity of state laws and enjoin their members to obey them so long as conscience and morality are not outraged. In the political arena they accordingly act as pressure groups urging the reform of the law or campaigning against administrative practices that they find objectionable. Though not in general hostile to the state, they emphasize their independence from it and their right to criticize its actions. Sects tend to reject the laws and institutions of the state altogether, and are often found in direct conflict with it, for example by refusing to pay taxes or by defying health regulations. In matters of doctrine, a church usually stresses the essential and central nature of the sacraments. Many sects reject the sacraments outright. Denominations tend to find a place for the sacraments, but to regard them as secondary to more important aspects of the religious life such as preaching and fellowship. Finally, for a church the world and its place in it have been validated by events which took place in the past – for example, among Christian churches, the incarnation of God in human form. Characteristically a sect looks to some dramatic event in the future – a Second Coming or Day of Judgement, when the existing social order will be overturned. For a denomination, the important events are those which take place in the present, such as the repeated conversion of sinners and the fellowship of believers.

The term denomination, then, is applied to groups which were originally sects and have settled down and become rather church-like, though their members form only a minority of the community. It also enables us to deal with a situation like that in the United States, where there is no one established form of religion but where a number of religious organizations are regarded as more or less equally acceptable alternatives, and all form more or less stable parts of the social structure. To be nothing – agnostic, atheist – is associated with being socialist or communist, and is accordingly disapproved as potentially un-American. As Morris Cohen has put it, 'The number of our outspoken atheists is negligible and even to call oneself a free-thinker is considered "bad form".'[25] To belong to any of the accepted denominations is better than nothing, though they are not quite exact equivalents for one another. They differ in social status, some Protestant denominations being respected more than others, and more than Catholics and Jews.

Secondly, we need to consider those large international religious organizations that have the character of a sect in one place, a church in another, a denomination in a third. For example, the Roman Catholic church is (sociologically regarded) a church in Italy, a denomination in the United States; yet it is one body, owing spiritual allegiance to one head. Much the same could be said of the Anglican church, or of Judaism – a church in Israel, elsewhere a denomination. In the case of Islam, again, it has the characteristics of a church in the Arab countries; a division like the Shia Ismailia Khoja is a denomination in a country like Kenya or Sudan; while the Black Muslims in America are clearly a sect, or at any rate they certainly were while Malcolm X was alive.[26] Yet all Muslims revere the Koran and if possible make the pilgrimage to Mecca and Medina.

Thirdly, we must distinguish a class of movements that have been variously called nativistic, messianic, or millenarian. In movements of this type the discontents of the underprivileged find expression in beliefs that a millennium is at hand and practices related to these beliefs, usually including states of possession, frenzy or dancing. In many cases such movements are charismatic in the sense that there is a leader who is regarded as inspired and who initiates the movement; but equally in many cases they unite, for the time being, whole communities, and so can hardly be called sects. For such movements the term cult is possibly the most appropriate. They have arisen in every part of the world at times of crisis or social strain, and there is a very large literature about them. During the middle ages in Europe, for example, there were many outbreaks of what was called 'enthusiasm' in which people rushed through the streets, danced, inflicted injuries upon themselves, saw visions, and cried out such messages as 'Repent and be baptized!' Not uncommonly these phases followed periods of distress from plague or famine. The Ghost Dance among some North American Indian peoples in 1870 and 1890, the Hau Hau movement among the New Zealand Maori, and the cargo cults in Melanesia take their places along with African examples of cults of this general type which have arisen among peoples whose traditional way of life has been disturbed during the expansion, within the last century, of modern industrial society.[27]

The beliefs of such movements may stem from widely different sources. In the medieval European cases, the main references were to the Christian beliefs which the church had succeeded in implanting, thought there were also echoes of earlier witch beliefs. Islam, too, has provided the beliefs which have inspired frenzied cults like that of the Mahdiya. In the colonial cases, there might be a desire to revive or perpetuate traditional pagan beliefs, the white man's god being regarded as having failed; or there might be a synthesis of traditional, modern, and Christian ideas. For example, in the well-documented cargo cults of New Guinea and other parts of Melanesia, people believe – or at any rate act as if they believe – that 'cargo' (European goods), together with the ships and aircraft that bring it, can be summoned from a non-human or divine source. People accordingly stop their normal routines of cultivation and other work, and build jetties or airstrips, make wooden radio sets and erect aerials, like those they have seen Australians and Americans use. They carry out rituals to the Christian God and ancestor spirits – or a confused mixture of both – to 'open the road of the cargo', and then settle down to wait for it to arrive. In other cases, religious movements may shade over into political. As Worsley has pointed out, in some of the medieval European 'enthusiasms' there were strong elements of political radicalism, for example the communist millenarianism that arose in the town of Tabor in Bohemia in the fifteenth century.[28] Similarly, there is a link between millenarianism and nationalist reaction to the activities of Europeans in nineteenth-century China in the Taiping rebellion of 1850–65. Two African examples of a similar nature spring to mind: the Mahdiya movement in the Sudan, which held Khartoum against the British from 1885 to 1898, and the Maji-Maji rebellion against German rule in parts of Tanzania in 1905–6.

To sum up this discussion, we need to distinguish religious organizations at several points on a scale, extending from 'universal churches' like Islam or the Roman Catholic church, through national churches, denominations, and sects, to cults.[29]

RELIGION AND SOCIAL CHANGE

Equipped with these ideas, we may perhaps begin to approach

the very large and complex subject of religion and social change.

Sometimes religious movements may be seen as the results or consequences of social changes not themselves specifically religious in character. The cargo cults which I have just discussed seem to be a clear example of this, for they are interpreted as a reaction to the vicissitudes of the modern world which have impinged on the people of Melanesia. Labour recruiting, Christian missionary activity, the presence in their territory of white settlers, colonial rule, and the episode of the 1940–5 war when they experienced Japanese invasion and American counter-operations, all produced new strains, deprivations, indignities, and sources of anxiety. These were interpreted in the light of traditional beliefs in a world in which gods and ancestors, never very distant, could be called on to join and work together with men securing desired ends. When the desired ends were the white man's power and wealth, the actions which followed were from this point of view perfectly logical.[30]

The separatist sects of which there is such a rich growth in South Africa may be seen in a somewhat similar light as a reaction – virtually the only permitted reaction – to the well-known tensions and anxieties of Africans' life there. Political activity being for all practical purposes impossible, and with severe restrictions on trade unionism, journalism, and other collective activities to redress grievances and better their lot, adherence to a sect offering an emotional outlet in this world and a promise of better things in the next offers a release from tensions and anxieties that is permitted (tolerated, indeed with a kind of amused contempt) by the white authorities. The many separatist sects described by Sundkler, then, may be regarded as a consequence of the stresses produced by social change.[31]

Secondly, religious movements may on the other hand initiate social changes. Modern Africa affords ample illustrations of this process; I have already described as revolutionary the social changes that have been brought about by the spread of Islam and the activity of Christian missions in Africa, and that will presumably be too familiar to readers to need enumerating in detail. Yet another example, to which I referred in chapter 5, was the part played by religious ideas in initiating the industrial revolution in Europe.

Thirdly, religious organizations themselves are subject to

change. I may perhaps schematize in figure 12 the processes to which, rather frequently, they are subject.

New religious movements commonly start, as we have seen, as charismatic sects in revolt against an established order. A sect which begins in this way may, of course, 'fail' and die out. If it does not fail, however, and succeeds in establishing itself, it tends by the process of routinization to become either a church (embracing a whole community) or a denomination (one of many tolerated, established religious organizations).

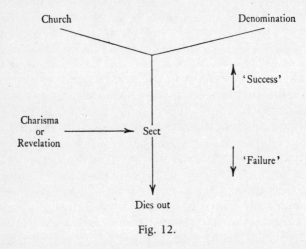

Fig. 12.

In this process, however, it generally has to dilute or compromise the pure, simple ideas with which its founder set out to dissent from the existing order. Because it is subject to the condition we suggested above, that to be a viable social organization a religion must offer a ritual to meet the felt needs and anxieties of the people who adhere to it, it may have to compromise with or incorporate many alien elements. Local beliefs and customs may be tolerated or incorporated, and a converted people may continue many of their old rituals in new guises. Buddhism, for example, has everywhere incorporated local beliefs and practices for the placation of spirits, and allowed old gods to re-appear as incarnations of the Buddha in a manner completely contrary to the ideas of its founder. In a somewhat similar way, pagan pre-Christian festivals like those of midwinter (with fire, feasting, and bringing greenery into houses) and the spring rites (with eggs and other fertility symbols), have been incorporated into or amalgamated with the Christian festivals celebrating the birth and resurrection of Jesus, in the actual ritual life of the people of northwestern Europe.[32]

At this point, the church or denomination is open to the process of revival. The compromises that have been struck may appear as corruptions, departures from the pure doctrines of the founder; a charismatic leader may arise, saying so urgently and eloquently; and either a new sect may be founded in schism from the old church, or a sect-like movement be accommodated within the church by some process of tolerant compromise. In time the new sect settles down into a church or denomination, and the whole process is then repeated.

At any one time, therefore, each of the major faiths tends to present a various and divided front. In the case of Islam, there are the major Suni schools with a long tradition, virtually unbroken since the time of the Prophet; there are denominations like the Shia Ismailia and Ithna'asheri Khojas regarded as heretical in their time, but now established; and there are eager new sects like the Ahmadiyyas, established only in the last century. In the same way, in the case of Christianity there are the historic Roman and Orthodox churches with a long continuity from the early church, denominations such as the Methodists who began as a sect about 200 years ago, and newer and more radical sects such as Jehovah's Witnesses and Seventh-Day Adventists.

SUGGESTIONS FOR FURTHER READING

E. K. Nottingham, *Religion and society* (New York, Random House, 1954). A short yet comprehensive introduction.

J. M. Yinger, *Religion, society and the individual* (New York, Macmillan, 1957). A larger textbook on the same general lines.

E. E. Evans-Pritchard, *Witchcraft, oracles and magic among the Azande* (Oxford, Clarendon Press, 1937). A classic field study of magic among an African people.

E. Durkheim, *Elementary forms of the religious life* (translated by J. W. Swain, London, Allen and Unwin, 1915).

Notes

CHAPTER 1

1 Jane van Lawick-Goodall, *In the shadow of man* (1971).
2 See note 4 below.
3 Ralph Piddington, 'A study of French-Canadian kinship', *International Journal of Comparative Sociology*, XII (1965); reprinted in C. C. Harris (ed.), *Readings in kinship in urban society* (1970); see especially footnote 2.
4 A. Myrdal, *Nation and Family* (1945); J. A. Banks, *Prosperity and Parenthood* (1954); Irene B. Taeuber, *The population of Japan* (1958).
5 For a full discussion and illustrations of this process, see C. G. Hempel, *Fundamentals of Concept Formation in Empirical Science* (1952).
6 M. Argyle, *The Psychology of Interpersonal Behaviour* (1967), ch. VI. The quotation is from p. 108.
7 Max Gluckman. 'Malinowski's "functional" analysis of social change', *Africa*, XVII (1947), 103–21. Reprinted in his *An analysis of the sociological theories of Bronislaw Malinowski* (1949) (Rhodes-Livingstone paper no. 16); also in his *Order and rebellion in tribal Africa* (1963), ch. VIII. See also his contribution in A. W. Southall (ed.), *Social change in modern Africa* (1961), pp. 69–70.
8 P. H. Gulliver, *Land tenure and social change among the Nyakyusa* (1958). See also Monica Wilson, *Good company* (1951); *Communal rituals of the Nyakyusa* (1959), ch. XIII.
9 R. S. Lynd and H. M. Lynd, *Middletown* (1929), p. 506.
10 Gunnar Myrdal, *Asian drama* (1968), pp. 707–8.
11 Polly Hill, *The migrant cocoa-farmers of southern Ghana* (1963).
12 A. I. Richards (ed.), *Economic development and tribal change* (1954).
13 See note 8 above.
14 G. Jahoda, 'The social background of a West African student population', *British Journal of Sociology*, V (1954), 355–65 and VI (1955), 71–9.
   K. A. Busia, 'The present position and aspirations of elites in the Gold Coast', *International Social Science Bulletin*, VIII (1956), 424–40.
15 H. H. Smythe and M. M. Smythe, *The new Nigerian elite* (1960).
16 Leo Kuper, *An African bourgeoisie* (1965).
17 J. E. Goldthorpe, *An African elite* (1965); Pierre L. van den Berghe, 'An African elite revisited', *Mawazo*, I, 4 (1968), 57–71.

216

18 R. Clignet and P. Foster, *The fortunate few* (1966).
19 H. S. Morris, *The Indians in Uganda* (1968).
20 P. H. Gulliver, *Tradition and transition in East Africa* (1969).
21 See for example E. Jacques, *The changing culture of a factory* (1951), ch. I.
22 M. Kirk, *The Seminar*; paper circulated in the University of Leeds, 1965.

CHAPTER 2

1 Auguste Comte, *Positive politics*, vol. IV, appendix, pp. 149–50 (quoted by N. S. Timasheff, *Sociological theory, its Nature and Growth*, 1955).
2 W. S. and K. Routledge, *With a prehistoric people: the Akikuyu* (1910).
3 Lewis H. Morgan, *The League of the Ho-de-no-sau-nee, or Iroquois* (1851); *Systems of consanguinity and affinity of the human family* (1871); *Ancient society* (1877). See also Introduction by Leslie H. White to the 1964 reprint of *Ancient society*.
4 Bishop Codrington, *The Melanesians* (1891).
5 The Rev. John Roscoe, *The Baganda* (1911).
6 Sir Baldwin Spencer and F. J. Gillen, *The native tribes of Central Australia* (1899), and other subsequent works.
7 Franz Boas, *The central Eskimo* (1888).
8 F. le Play, *Les ouvriers Européens* (1855).
9 C. Booth and others, *The life and labour of the people in London* (17 vols. 1903). The quotation is from the final volume, p. 32.
10 E. Durkheim, *Les formes élémentaires de la vie religieuse* (1912; English translation by J. W. Swain, 1915); *De la division du travail social* (1893; English translation by G. Simpson, 1947).
11 See especially L. T. Hobhouse, *Morals in evolution* (2 vols. 1906).
12 L. T. Hobhouse, G. C. Wheeler and M. Ginsberg, *The material cultures and social institutions of the simpler peoples* (1915).
13 A. R. Radcliffe-Brown, *The Andaman islanders* (1922); *Structure and function in primitive society* (1952).
14 B. Malinowski's field studies were embodied in: *Argonauts of the western Pacific* (1922); *Crime and custom in savage society* (1926); *Sex and repression in savage society* (1927); *The sexual life of savages* (1928); *Coral gardens and their magic* (2 vols. 1935). His later general writings embody his considered view of functionalism, especially *A scientific theory of culture* (1944).
15 Margaret Mead, *Growing up in New Guinea*, ch. I.
16 B. Malinowski, *A scientific theory of culture* (1944), pp. 218–19.
17 Robert S. and Helen M. Lynd, *Middletown* (1929).
18 W. Lloyd Warner. *A black civilization* (1937); 'Yankee City' series, with various collaborators: *The social life of a modern community* (1941); *The status system of a modern community* (1942); *The social systems of American ethnic groups* (1945); *The social system of a modern factory* (1947); *The living and the dead* (1959).

19 C. Madge and T. H. Harrisson, *Britain, by mass-observation* (1939). See also M. Abrams, *Social surveys and social action* (1951), pp. 105–13.

20 R. Redfield, *Peasant society and culture* (1956); *The primitive world and its transformations* (1953); *The folk culture of Yucatan* (1941).

21 C. M. Arensberg and S. T. Kimball, *Family and community in Ireland* (1940).

22 H. Miner, *St Denis: a French-Canadian parish* (1939).

23 H. Miner, *The primitive city of Timbuctoo* (1953).

24 R. W. Firth, *We the Tikopia* (1936).

25 A. I. Richards, *Land, labour and diet in Northern Rhodesia* (1939); *Bemba marriage and present economic conditions* (1939) (Rhodes-Livingstone paper no. 4).

26 See note 7 to chapter 1 above.

27 J. Clyde Mitchell, *The Yao village* (1956); *The Kalela dance* (1956) (Rhodes-Livingstone paper no. 27).

28 G. and M. Wilson, *The analysis of social change* (1945).

29 L. P. Mair, *An African people in the twentieth century* (1934).

30 Sir Apolo Kagwa, *Ekitabo kye Bika bya Baganda* (1949); *Ekitabo kye Mpisa za Baganda* (1952); *Basekabaka be Buganda* (1953).

31 A. I. Richards (ed.), *Economic development and tribal change* (1954).

32 D. A. Low and R. C. Pratt, *Buganda and British overrule* (1960).

33 David E. Apter, *The political kingdom in Uganda* (1961).

34 L. A. Fallers (ed.), *The king's men* (1964).

35 J. H. M. Beattie, *Other cultures* (1964), pp. 5, 30–2.

36 Gunnar Myrdal, *An American dilemma* (1944); see also Arnold M. Rose, *The Negro in America* (1948).

37 For example, M. N. Srinivas, *Religion and society among the Coorgs of South India* (1952); D. N. Majumdar, *Himalayan polyandry* (1962).

38 S. Collins, *Coloured minorities in Britain* (1957).

39 E. U. Essien-Udom, *Black Nationalism: the rise of the Black Muslims in the U.S.A.* (1962).

CHAPTER 3

1 C. Booth, *Life and labour of the people in London* (1903), final volume, p. 32.

2 B. Seebohm Rowntree, *Poverty; a study of town life* (1901); *Poverty and progress* (1941); *Poverty and the welfare state* (1951); A. R. Bowley and A. R. B. Hurst, *Livelihood and poverty* (1915).

3 M. Parten, *Surveys, polls, and samples* (1950), pp. 23–4.

4 W. Albig, *Modern Public Opinion* (1956), ch. XI.

5 D. V. Glass (ed.), *Social mobility in Britain* (1954).

6 For a good summary account of the Chicago school, see: J. H. Madge, *The origins of scientific sociology* (1963), ch. IV.

7 P. Townsend, *The family life of old people* (1957).

8 J. Carlebach, *Juvenile prostitutes in Nairobi* (East African Studies series, no. 16, 1962).

9 R. W. Firth, *We the Tikopia* (1936).

10 J. H. M. Beattie, *Understanding an African kingdom: Bunyoro* (1965), p. 47.

11 J. E. Goldthorpe, 'Need publication take so long?' *New Society*, 13 May 1965.

12 E. Colson, *Social organization of the Gwembe Tonga* (1960); T. Scudder, *The ecology of the Gwembe Tonga* (1962).

13 *International Social Science Bulletin*, vol. IX, no. 3 (1957).

14 A. I. Richards (ed.), *East African chiefs* (1960).

15 R. M. Marsh, *The Mandarins* (1961); W. Eberhard, *Social mobility in traditional China* (1962).

16 Lorraine Lancaster, 'Kinship in Anglo-Saxon society', *British Journal of Sociology*, IX (1958), 230–50, 359–77.

17 P. Laslett, *The world we have lost* (1965).

18 J. A. Banks, *Prosperity and parenthood* (1954).

19 D. C. Marsh, *The changing social structure of England and Wales, 1871–1961* (1965), pp. 118, 125–7.

20 D. A. Levitsky and R. H. Barnes, 'Nutritional and environmental interactions in the behavioural development of the rat: long-term effects', *Science*, 7 April 1972, pp. 68–71.

21 E. Mayo, *The human problems of an industrial civilization* (1933), chs. III and IV.

22 R. F. Bales, *Interaction process analysis* (1951).

23 H. T. Himmelweit, A. N. Oppenheimer and P. Vince, *Television and the child* (1958).

24 See *Murder, 1957 to 1968*, Home Office Research Studies no. 3 (London, H.M.S.O., 1969); Walter C. Reckless, *The crime problem* (1967), pp. 532–4, 542–3; Hugh Klare, 'Capital punishment', *New Society*, 19 June 1969, p. 958.

25 Robert K. Merton, *Social theory and social structure* (1957), chs. I and IV.

26 D. Lockwood and J. H. Goldthorpe, 'Affluence and the British class structure', *Sociological Review*, XI (1963), 133–63.

27 J. H. Goldthorpe, D. Lockwood, F. Bechhofer and J. Platt, 'The affluent worker and the thesis of embourgeoisement: some preliminary research findings'. *Sociology*, I (1967), 11–31.

28 T. Parsons, *The structure of social action* (1937).

29 G. C. Homans, *The nature of social science* (1967), pp. 15–18.

30 D. H. Wrong. 'The over-socialized conception of man in modern sociology', *American Sociological Review*, XXVI (1961), 183–93.

31 R. Dahrendorf, *Class and class conflict in an industrial society* (1959), esp. chs. V and VI.

32 D. Lockwood, 'Some remarks on "The social system"', *British Journal of Sociology*, VII (1956), 134–46.

33 N. Gross *et al.*, *Explorations in role analysis* (1958).

34 E. Goffman, *Asylums* (1961).

35 For a useful summary of these concepts, see Sheila Patterson, *Dark strangers* (1963), pp. 9–16.

36 S. Collins, *Coloured minorities in Britain* (1957).

37 K. Wittfogel, *Oriental despotism* (1957).

38 *Encyclopaedia of the social sciences* (1968), art. 'Sociology: the field', p. 17.
39 Cyril S. Smith, 'The employment of sociologists in research occupations in Britain in 1973', *Sociology*, IX (1975), 309–16.
40 *U.N. statistical yearbook for 1978*, table 207.

CHAPTER 4

1 J. Bowlby, *Child care and the growth of love* (1953), p. 11.
2 M. L. Rutter, *Maternal deprivation reassessed* (1972); A. M. Clarke and A. D. B. Clarke, *Early experience* (1976).
3 A. I. Richards, *Land, labour and diet in Northern Rhodesia* (1939), ch. VIII.
4 P. Laslett, *The world we have lost* (1965); *Household and family in past time* (1972); *Family life and illicit love in earlier generations* (1977).
5 L. A. Fallers (ed.), *The king's men* (1964), pp. 71–2.
6 C. Daryll Forde, 'Double descent among the Yakö', in A. R. Radcliffe-Brown and Daryll Forde (eds.), *African systems of kinship and marriage* (1950).
7 W. A. Shack, *The Gurage: a people of the Ensete culture* (1966); see also R. Needham, 'Gurage social classification', *Africa*, XXXIX (1969), 153–66.
8 W. A. Shack, *The Gurage* (1966), p. 89.
9 *Oxford English Dictionary*, art. 'Cousin', 3.
10 D. N. Majumdar, *Himalayan Polyandry* (1962).
11 Sexual Offences Act, 1956; Marriage Act, 1949, and Marriage (Enabling) Act, 1960. P. M. Bromley, *Family law* (1971), p. 527.
12 *Report of Committee on the Marriage Law of Scotland*, Cmnd. 4011 (1969); David M. Walker, *Principles of Scottish private law* (1970), pp. 203–5; T. B. Smith, *Short commentary on the law of Scotland* (1962), p. 316.
13 Robin Fox, *Kinship and marriage* (1967), p. 55.
14 Including, regrettably, earlier editions of this book. The confusion is found in sources as authoritative as the *Oxford English Dictionary* and the 1966 edition of the *International Encyclopaedia of the Social Sciences*. The 1970 edition of the *Encyclopaedia Britannica*, however, makes the distinction clear and has a useful summary of the law in England, Scotland, and the United States.
15 T. Parsons, 'The incest taboo in relation to social structure and the socialization of the child', *British Journal of Sociology*, V (1954), 101–7.
16 For references to the Kikuyu age-system, see chapter 6, note 2.
17 Monica Wilson, *Good company* (1951).
18 R. W. Firth, *We the Tikopia* (1936), pp. 329–36.
19 R. F. Winch, *Mate selection* (1958).
20 A. I. Richards, 'Authority patterns in traditional Buganda', in L. A. Fallers (ed.), *The king's men* (1964), pp. 267–70.
21 E. E. Evans-Pritchard, *The Nuer* (1941). See also his summary description in M. Fortes and E. E. Evans-Pritchard (eds.), *African political systems* (1940), pp. 286–7.

22 T. Parsons, *Family, socialization and interaction process* (1956), p. 20.
23 W. J. Goode, *World revolution and family patterns* (1963), ch. II; P. Laslett, *The world we have lost*; Lorraine Lancaster, 'Kinship in Anglo-Saxon society', *British Journal of Sociology*, IX (1958), 230–50, 359–77.
24 P. Townsend, *The family life of old people* (1957).
25 P. Willmott and M. Young, *Family and kinship in East London* (1957). ('East London' here means the eastern part of London, England – not the town of East London in the Republic of South Africa.)
26 P. Willmott and M. Young, *Family and class in a London suburb* (1960).
27 P. C. Glick, *American families* (1957), table 33.
28 Alva Myrdal and Viola Klein, *Women's two roles, home and work* (1956 and 1968); S. Yudkin and Anthea Holme, *Working mothers and their children* (1963); Audrey Hunt, *A survey of women's employment* (1968); M. P. Fogarty, Rhona Rapoport and Robert Rapoport, *Sex, career and family* (1971).
29 Lyndon Harries. 'Christian marriage in African society', in A. Phillips (ed.), *Survey of African marriage and family life* (1953), pp. 335–6.
30 L. P. Mair, *Native marriage in Buganda* (1940), p. 5.
31 For such a discussion, see O. R. Macgregor, *Divorce in England – a centenary study* (1957).
32 Chie Nakane, *Kinship and economic organization in rural Japan* (1967); Fujiko Isono, 'The family and women in Japan', *Sociological Review*, XII (1964), 39–54; Ezra F. Vogel, *Japan's new middle class* (1967).
33 W. J. Goode, *World revolution and family patterns* (1963 and 1970).

CHAPTER 5

1 Marshall Sahlins, *Stone age economics* (1974), ch. I; United Nations, *Determinants and consequences of population trends* (1953), ch. II.
2 L. T. Hobhouse, G. C. Wheeler and M. Ginsberg, *The material cultures and social institutions of the simpler peoples: an essay in correlation* (1915).
3 Adam Smith, *The wealth of nations*, ch. III.
4 A. I. Richards, *Land, labour and diet in Northern Rhodesia: an economic study of the Bemba tribe* (1939), pp. 244–66. See also H. Kuper, *An African aristocracy* (1947), ch. IX.
5 R. W. Firth, *Primitive Polynesian economy* (1939), pp. 275–7.
6 N. Dennis, F. Henriques, and C. Slaughter, *Coal is our life* (1956).
7 J. R. Goody (ed.), *Literacy in traditional societies* (1968).
8 Margaret Mead, *Coming of age in Samoa* (1928); *Growing up in New Guinea*; *Sex and temperament in three primitive societies*. Also published together in one volume. *From the South Seas* (1947).
9 David E. Apter, *The politics of modernization* (1965), p. 10.
10 C. M. Arensberg and S. T. Kimball, *Family and community in Ireland* (1940); H. Miner, *St Denis: a French-Canadian parish* (1939).
11 Fei, H. T., *Peasant life in China* (1939); Hsu, F. L.-K., *Under the ancestors' shadow* (1949); Yang, M. C., *A Chinese village* (1945).
12 T. Shanin (ed.), *Peasants and peasant societies* (1971); E. R. Wolf, *Peasants* (1966).

13 K. Marx, *The poverty of philosophy* (1847) (English edition, 1935).
14 K. Oberg, 'Banyankole kinship organization', *Africa*, XI (1938), 129–59; 'The kingdom of Ankole in Uganda', in M. Fortes and E. E. Evans-Pritchard (eds.), *African political systems* (1940).
15 J. E. Goldthorpe, *An African elite: Makerere College students, 1922–60* (East African Studies No. 17, 1965), pp. 22–3, 86.
16 D. Lerner, *The passing of traditional society* (1958), esp. chs. I–III; A. Inkeles and D. H. Smith, *Becoming modern* (1974).
17 Everett M. Rogers, *The diffusion of innovations* (1962).
18 Paul F. Lazarsfeld *et al.*, *The people's choice* (1948).
19 J. Trenaman and D. McQuail, *Television and the political image* (1961).
20 L. W. Doob, *Becoming more civilized: a psychological exploration* (1960).
21 W. W. Ogionwo, 'The adoption of technological innovations in Nigeria', Ph.D. Thesis, University of Leeds (1969).
22 Adam Smith, *The wealth of nations*, ch. III.
23 Kingsley Davis, 'The urbanization of the human population', *Scientific American*, (September 1965), 40–53; reprinted in Gerald Breese (ed.), *The city in newly developing countries: readings on urbanism and urbanization* (1969).
24 B. F. Hoselitz, *Sociological aspects of economic growth* (1960), esp. essays 7, 8 and 9.
25 Z. Bauman, *Between class and elite* (1972).

CHAPTER 6

1 A. R. Radcliffe-Brown, *The Andaman islanders* (1922).
2 A summary and bibliography of the literature on the Kikuyu is given in: J. Middleton and G. Kershaw, *The Kikuyu and Kamba of Kenya* (International African Institute, Ethnographic Survey of Africa series, 1965).
    Of the original literature, the following may be selected: W. S. Routledge and K. Routledge, *With a prehistoric people: the Akikuyu* (1910); C. W. Hobley, *Bantu beliefs and magic* (1922); J. Kenyatta, *Facing Mount Kenya* (1938); L. S. B. Leakey, *Mau Mau and the Kikuyu* (1952); H. E. Lambert, *Kikuyu social and political institutions* (1956).
3 A comprehensive and thorough book on Buganda is: L. A. Fallers (ed.), *The king's men* (1964). The literature is summarized in: M. C. Fallers, *The Eastern Lacustrine Bantu* (International African Institute, Ethnographic Survey of Africa series, 1960). Other sources still of value include: J. Roscoe, *The Baganda* (1911); L. P. Mair, *An African people in the twentieth century* (1934).
4 G. S. Ghurye, *Caste and class in India* (1957); E. Senart, *Caste in India* (1930); J. H. Hutton, *Caste in India* (1946); E. Leach (ed.), *Aspects of Caste* (1960); M. Singer (ed.), *Traditional India* (1959); Louis Dumont, *Homo hierarchicus* (1970).
5 J. E. Goldthorpe, *Outlines of East African society* (1958), ch. III.
6 A. I. Richards, *Land, labour and diet in Northern Rhodesia* (1939), pp. 147–50.

7 Kingsley Davis and Wilbert E. Moore, 'Some principles of stratification', *American Sociological Review*, X (1945), 242–9; reprinted in R. Bendix and S. M. Lipset (eds.), *Class, status and power* (1960), pp. 47–53.

8 G. Lenski, 'Status crystallization', *American Sociological Review*, XIX (1954), 405–13. W. S. Landecker, 'Class boundaries', *American Sociological Review*, XXV (1960), 868–77; 'Class crystallization and class consciousness', *American Sociological Review*, XXVIII (1963), 219–29.

9 D. V. Glass (ed.), *Social mobility in Britain* (1954).

10 S. M. Lipset and R. Bendix, *Social mobility in industrial society* (1959). See also B. Barber, *Social stratification* (1957), ch. XVI.

11 J. H. Goldthorpe *et al.*, *Social mobility and class structure in modern Britain* (1980).

12 *World Bank development report, 1979*, table 24.

13 J. P. Nettl, *The Soviet achievement* (1967), p. 254.

14 H. Chenery *et al.*, *Redistribution with growth* (1974).

15 J. Newson and E. Newson, *Infant care in an urban community* (1965); J. W. B. Douglas, *The home and the school* (1964); J. E. Floud, A. H. Halsey and F. M. Martin, *Social class and educational opportunity* (1956); B. Bernstein, 'Some sociological determinants of perception', *British Journal of Sociology*, IX (1958), 159–74.

16 David Lane, *The end of inequality?* (1971); *Politics and society in the USSR* (1970); *The socialist industrial state* (1976); J. S. Berliner, *Factory and manager in the USSR* (1957); A. Nove, *The Soviet economy* (1968); Z. Bauman, 'The second generation socialism', in L. Schapiro (ed.), *Political opposition in one-party states* (1972); 'Officialdom and class; bases of inequality in socialist society', in F. Parkin (ed.), *The social analysis of class structure* (1974).

17 R. N. Berki, *Socialism* (1975).

18 P. Worsley, *The third world* (1964), p. 201.

19 W. H. Friedland and C. G. Rosberg (eds.), *African socialism* (1964), pp. 3–4.

20 M. Dia, *The African nations and world solidarity* (1962).

21 L. S. Senghor, *On African socialism* (English edition, 1964), p. 10.

22 J. E. Goldthorpe, *An African elite* (1965).

23 L. S. Senghor, *On African socialism*, p. 5.

24 Kenya Government Sessional White Paper, *African socialism and its application to planning in Kenya* (1965).

25 C. Morse, in Friedland and Rosberg, *African socialism* (1964), pp. 47–8.

CHAPTER 7

1 K. Z. Lorenz, *On aggression* (1966).

2 *Ibid.* p. 208.

3 R. Dahrendorf, *Class and class conflict*, p. 235.

4 *Ibid.* pp. 161–2.

5 L. A. Coser, *The functions of social conflict* (1956).

6 E. E. Evans-Pritchard, in M. Fortes and E. E. Evans-Pritchard (eds.), *African political systems* (1940), pp. 293–4.

7 *Theory of social and economic organisation*, p. 116. See also the discussion by Parsons in footnotes 7 and 8, pp. 110–11.

8 H. Gerth and C. W. Mills, *Character and social structure* (1954), p. 258.

9 See for instance M. Argyle. *The psychology of interpersonal behaviour* (1967), ch. I, sect.3.

10 L. T. Hobhouse, *Morals in evolution* (1915), p. 57.

11 Max Weber, *The theory of social and economic organization* (translated by A. R. Henderson and T. Parsons, 1947), ch. III.

12 D. E. Apter, *Ghana in transition* (revised edition, 1963).

13 Patrice Lumumba, *Congo My Country* (1962); see especially the Foreword by Colin Legum.

14 B. G. M. Sundkler, *Bantu prophets in South Africa* (1948).

15 E. Gellner, *Thought and change* (1965), pp. 175–8.

16 S. Andrzejewski, *Military organization and society* (1954), ch. II. See also M. Bloch, *Feudal society* (1961), pp. 289–92.

17 C. Reith, *The police idea* (1938); *Police principles and the problem of war* (1940), esp. chs. VI and XI–XIII. See also M. Janowitz, *The professional soldier* (1960), ch. XX on 'The constabulary concept'.

18 S. E. Finer, *The man on horseback* (1962), esp. chs. I–III.

CHAPTER 8

1 Including A. C. Bouquet, *Comparative religion* (1942), p. 13; Joy Davidman, *Smoke on the mountain* (1955), pp. 47–9.

2 R. Linton, *The tree of culture* (1961), pp. 137–8.

3 W. W. Howells, *The heathens* (1948), p. 17 (p. 22 in the English edition, Gollancz, 1949).

4 A. I. Richards, *Land, labour and diet in Northern Rhodesia* (1939), pp. 352–3.

5 E. J. and J. D. Krige. *The realm of a rain queen* (1943), ch. XV.

6 Sir J. G. Frazer, *The golden bough* (1920), I, ch. IV, p. 222.

7 See for example B. Spencer and F. J. Gillen, *The Arunta* (1927), p. 146.

8 F. L. K. Hsu, *Religion, science, and human crises* (1952), pp. 20–5.

9 C. W. Hobley, *Bantu beliefs and magic* (1938), pp. 40–1, 104–5.

10 *Notes and queries in anthropology* (1954 edition), p. 189.

11 M. G. Marwick, *Sorcery in its social setting; a study of the Northern Rhodesia Cewa* (1965), p. 95.

12 E. E. Evans-Pritchard, *Witchcraft, oracles and magic among the Azande* (1937), pp. 28–9.

13 Marwick, *op. cit.* p. 97; see also his ch. IX on 'Sorcery and social change'.

14 A. W. Southall and P. C. W. Gutkind, *Townsmen in the making* (1956), pp. 164–5 (in the original edition).

15 Monica Wilson and A. Mafeje, *Langa: a study of social groups in an African township* (1963), pp. 110–12.

16 E. Durkheim, *Elementary forms of the religious life* (1915).

17 S. F. Nadel, *Nupe religion* (1954), ch. IX.
18 J. M. Yinger, *Religion, society and the individual* (1957), pp. 15–16.
19 C. D. Forde (ed.), *African worlds* (1954), pp. 78–82, 182–5, 207–9.
20 M. Argyle, *Religious behaviour* (1958), esp. chs. VI–VIII.
21 T. Parsons, 'The incest taboo, etc.' *British Journal of Sociology*, V (1954), 101–7.
22 J. H. Driberg, *The Lango* (1923); T. T. S. Hayley, *The anatomy of Lango religion and groups* (1947).
23 E. J. and J. D. Krige, *The realm of a rain queen* (1943), ch. XV.
24 David Martin, *A sociology of English religion* (1967), pp. 79–80.
25 Morris Cohen, *American thought* (1954), p. 181.
26 C. E. Lincoln, *The Black Muslims in America* (1961); E. U. Essien-Udom, *Black nationalism* (1962).
27 P. Worsley, *The trumpet shall sound* (1957); Vittorio Lanternari, *Religions of the oppressed* (1963).
28 See also Norman Cohn, *The pursuit of the millennium* (1957).
29 J. M. Yinger, *Religion, society and the individual* (1957), pp. 142–55.
30 P. Lawrence, *Road Belong Cargo* (1964), pp. 30–3.
31 B. G. M. Sundkler, *Bantu prophets in South Africa* (1948).
32 See W. M. Williams, *Sociology of an English village* (1956), ch. X.

Index